THE ROMANCE OF COIN COLLECTING

Bowers and Merena Galleries, Inc.

BY THE SAME AUTHOR

MEDALLIC PORTRAITS OF JOHN F. KENNEDY
COINS QUESTIONS AND ANSWERS (co-author, first edition)
THE OTHER SIDE OF THE COIN

Published by:

BOWERS AND MERENA GALLERIES, INC.
Box 1224, Wolfeboro, NH 03894

While several of the stories published in this book appear for the first time, many are selected from columns by the author that have been published in *COINage* magazine, *COINS* magazine, *The Numismatist, Numismatic News,* or have appeared in his weekly column distributed by the *Los Angeles Times Syndicate*. All are reprinted with permission.

Copyright © 1991 by Edward C. Rochette. Printed in the United States of America. All rights reserved. This book, or any part thereof, may not be reproduced in any manner without written permission except in the case of brief quotations embodied in critical articles and reviews.

ISBN No. 0-943161-28-2

INTRODUCTION

Here, in *The Romance of Coin Collecting,* I have attempted to retell some of the unusual stories found in the annals of the country's second most popular hobby. Here are a few of the tales recorded, from the earliest days of coined money, down through the ages, pausing briefly at the era of the development many called "The Wild West," before proceeding to the present.

Nosing into records and files, archives, letters, and yellowed old newspaper clippings, is as much a part of the hobby as keeping abreast of the latest trends, grades and prices—and far more fun. For too many, the mere acquisition of a coin for their collection is the little pleasure they derive from the hobby. I have attempted to make the lore of the legends, the romance of money, and the history recorded, a part of the reward numismatics offers the advocate.

The stories selected for presentation here are not, by any means, intended to be definitive studies, let alone the last word on any subject. It was never my intention to produce a compendium of essential information. For that, I refer you to such scholarly treatises as produced by more noted authors, serious numismatists like Q. David Bowers, Walter Breen, Eric P. Newman and Gene Hessler, to name but a few. This book is intended, instead, to be a selection of stories picked from the many that I have written for my regular column distributed by the Los Angeles Times Syndicate, and from articles that I have prepared for *The Banknote Reporter, COINage, Coins Magazine, Hobbies, Numismatic News, The Numismatist, World Coin News,* and other hobby publications.

The stories collected here were picked, for the most part, more in reponse to reader comments than for any other reason. It is my wish to entertain more than educate, to show that the hobby can be fun, and that the stories told by coins and currency can be as varied as they are limitless.

Some of the tales are long, others brief. This arrangement is intentional, for it is my hope that this book becomes something that you will pick up and put down at odd times when you have a minute, or several, to spare, or when you are in need of a numismatic or historical anecdote to share with collectors of kindred interests.

While the person who first said, "If wishes were horses, beggars might ride," certainly did not have the hobbyhorse of coin collecting in mind, I do have a similar wish for you. That you, the reader, will enjoy the ride over the wide range that we collectors call numismatics.

E.C.R.
Colorado Springs
February 1991

ACKNOWLEDGEMENTS

There are 30,000 members of the American Numismatic Association and to each individually I owe a note of thanks. They are the ones who made it possible for me to enjoy this lifetime of numismatic endeavors. Without them I doubt that the enjoyable hours of research that went into this book would have ever been attempted.

I also wish to thank Grant Carey, Hall of Presidents, Colorado Springs, Colorado, for arranging the interview with President Millard Fillmore; Cornelius W. Heine, U.S. Capitol Historical Society, Washington, DC, for the behind-the-scenes tour of the Capitol Building; and Bekele Endeshaw, Ministry of Commerce and Industry, Addis Ababa, Ethiopia, for archival research assistance.

I would be remiss not to mention the invaluable assistance received from these numismatic professionals: Q. David Bowers and Michael Hodder, Bowers and Merena Galleries, Wolfeboro, New Hampshire; Andre de Clermont, Spink & Son Ltd., London; Grover C. Criswell, Ft. McCoy, Florida; Bill Fivaz, Dunwoody, Georgia; and Robert Hoge, ANA Museum, Colorado Springs, Colorado.

CONTENTS

Introduction iii
Acknowledgements iv

ON AMERICAN COINS 1

New Jefferson Portrait A Way of Saying, We're Sorry 2
Bare Breasted Coin Not the Nudest Thing On Money 3
Was Miss Liberty a Bag Lady? 5
A Flip Over a Flapper 7
A Story Seldom Told About the Freedom Statue 9
Just a Minute, He's Our Man 10
Why South Carolinians Love the Palmetto Tree 13
The Lafayette Dollar 14
America's Irish Rose 16

NOTES ON PAPER 19

The Man Who Would Have Been The Hero 20
A Legend of the West Comes Alive on a $10 Note 22
The Story Not Told On U.S. Currency 24
The Dog Notes of Virginia 24
A Man Who Sees What Others Miss 26
The Secret of the Number in the Shadow 27
After "Total" Destruction Gas Ration Coupons Begin To Surface ... 28
After the Model-T Came the Henry Ford Dollar 30
Canada Saves the Whales By Changing the Scene 33
The Last of the Big Bucks 34

TOKENS AND MEDALS HAVE TALES, TOO! 37

"Coins" of the Alaska Commune—A Token Reminder of the
   American Communist Experiment........................38
The Ghost of Peck House 40
First the Coins, Now the Sticks 42
Lucky Cents Gave Birth to a Major Industry 43
In Search For the Truth (About Some "Old" Tokens)..........44
A Ha'Penny's Worth of Protest 46
Advertising Goes to the Dogs 48
The Token Issues of the Radio Priest 49
When Baked Beans Were in Bad Taste 51

FROM OUT WEST 53

The Last Word on Millions for Defense 54
The Two Horse Race & the Clark, Gruber Purse 56
When Women Won the Right to Vote in Colorado Collectors
   Lost the Chance For an Unusual Coin....................58
Tokens of the Last War Between the States 60
The Bimetallic Coins of the Hermit of Arbor Villa 62
History Fibbed About the Golden Spike Ceremony 64
Deaf Smith—A Gourmet Brand of Note 66
A Tale of Ostrich Feathers 67
The Third Little Trianon 69

FROM THE LIGHTER SIDE OF THE COIN 73

"Come Up and See Me Sometime!"..........................74
Real Collectors Don't Eat Nuts 76
God Took Caruso Away, But Left His Coin Collection For Others........77
A Penchant for the Pachyderm 80
In Defense of Anthony Comstock 80
Smile, Susy B., There May Still Be a Need for You Yet 82
When He Failed to Counterfeit Gold, He Created a Man 83
Things Could Be Verse 85
Why Cheshire Cats Grin....................................86

IN OTHER WORDS..89

The Origin of the Sign of the Dollar 90
The Use of Coins Has Led to Countless Innovations and Contributed to
   Our Language..91
Carpetbagger, Another of Our Words Appropriated..........92
The Lost and Gentle Art of Lobbying 94

The Art of Speaking Emphatically Numismatically 95
At Odds With the English Language................................96
Don't Bet Your Bottom Dollar 97
One Should Start at the Very Beginning 98
So What's A Plugged Nickel? 100

IN OTHER WORLDS 103

Goodbye, Columbus—Coin Says It Wasn't So 104
When the Shadow of New Coins Shut Out the Sun 105
Coins Tell the Sad Tale of the Little Princess of Baltimore 106
A Token Remembrance of a Great Famine 108
He Coined a New Way to Advertise 109
Marcus Garvey 111
Canada's Misplaced Bronco Buck 113
Angels of a Lesser God...114
The Last Wampum Mill in America................................117

ON TRAVEL AND OTHER ADVENTURES 121

Coins—Passports to Adventure 122
Diving For Treasure and A Story 123
Where First This Onion Flourished and Its Coin Was Spent 124
Putting Your Fate in the Hands of the Kitchen Help
    In the Name of the Hobby 125
Tangier, City of Intrigue—Past 127
Coins For "The Rock" 129
Treasure at Devil's Head 130
West Point—America's Secret Mint 131
Beware the Coins of Chinatown 133

ON PRESIDENTS AND HOPEFULS............................135

What This Country Needs is a Good Five-Cent Nickel 136
The General the Army Wanted to Forget...........................137
The Unusual Sides of the Kennedy Half Dollar 140
The Candidate From Lake Nebagamon............................141
The Perfect Gift For the President 142
Hart's Name Short Changed 144
Presidential Candidate Promised Coin Design Change
    And Much More 145
Quayle Episode Recalls Civil War Draft Money 146
A Few Words With Millard Fillmore 147

ON THE STATE OF THE HOBBY 151

Is This Any Way To Buy Coins? 152
Eliminating the Penny Will Not Make Cents 154
The Industry With Friends in High Places 155
Mottoes On Money May Face New Challenges 156
In the New Hobby, Grading Is a Way of Life 158
To Have and to Hold—Forever 159
The Spring Rite of Whimsy 160
The Numismatic Age of the Computer Has Arrived 161
Cherrypickers' Top 25 162

REFLECTIONS 165

Going Straight to the Source Often Contradicted the Coin Books 166
Growing Up Numismatic 167
All For the Sake of a Story 168
The Strawberry Money of Missouri 170
On Meeting Indians in Colorado 171
Iola: A World Capital 172
The First Coin Show on Ice 173
It Wasn't In the Book 175
A Yen for the Supernatural 177

Index 179
About the Author 184

ON AMERICAN COINS

NEW JEFFERSON PORTRAIT A WAY OF SAYING "WE'RE SORRY!"

Should the members of the present Congress of the United States see fit to pass legislation calling for modernizing the designs of coins currently in circulation, they will have an opportunity to correct an ignominious deed of 150 years past.

Toward the end of the 1980's, legislation pending before the House Subcommittee on Consumer Affairs and Coinage called for the designs of the present half dollar, quarter dollar, 10-cent, five-cent and one-cent coins to be revised. Presidential likenesses were to be changed, but the presidents currently represented would be the same men.

The current five-cent piece portrays a profile of Thomas Jefferson adapted by the designer, Felix Schlag, after Houdon's marble bust in the Museum of Fine Arts in Boston. While it is true that Jefferson sat for Houdon, in Paris in 1789, for the model that gave us the profile for the five-cent piece, there is another period statue of Jefferson in the nation's capital that deserves to be examined when designs for the next Jefferson nickel are prepared, if for no other reason than to apologize for an unconscionable slight.

In 1834 a heroically proportioned bronze statue of Jefferson, with the Declaration of Independence in his hand, was placed in the Capitol Rotunda. French sculptor David d'Angers had received a private commission from a navy lieutenant to create this magnificent statue. After it was unveiled, however, no one in Congress officially moved to accept the statue on behalf of the people of the United States. The quality of the art was not in question, the religious beliefs of the donor, Uriah P. Levy, a Jew, were.

Within months of the unveiling, the statue was quietly hauled from the Capitol, trucked down Pennsylvania Avenue, and placed out-of-sight on the tree-shaded grounds of the White House.

Four decades later, during the Administration of Ulysses S. Grant, descendants of Lt. Levy petitioned Congress that his gift be formally accepted or be returned to the heirs. Shamefaced, Congress acquiesced. The statue was brought back to the rotunda. Today, it is viewed by thousands of visitors unaware of the Congress' unfortunate display of prejudice.

What better amends could be made than to consider the handsome visage of Jefferson, as seen on this statue, for the new portrait on the next Jefferson nickel?

Bronze statue of Thomas Jefferson by David d'Angers

BARE-BREASTED COIN NOT THE NUDEST THING IN MONEY!

Nudity in art has been with us since the time of the ancient Greeks. We admire the beauty of the human body in the carved marble of the temples and in the halls of the great museums of the world. But, bare so much as a breast on a coin, and the public is in an uproar or so latter-day numismatists would have you believe. The story of the scandalous pose of the Standing Liberty quarter of 1916 is one of the great tales of the hobby but, alas, only a legend.

The year 1916 premiered a new age in American coin design. It was the first time in history that all subsidiary silver coins were of different designs. Adolph A. Weinman's Mercury dime and Liberty Walking half dollar, introduced along with Hermon A. MacNeil's quarter-dollar design, replaced the staid, unimaginative Liberty Head series designed late in the 19th century. Current numismatic researchers like to tell that Weinman's designs were readily acceptable, but that MacNeil's, choosing to portray Miss Liberty with one breast exposed, evoked shock and led to redesign. It was not that the offending body part was easily discernible. A full length Liberty, standing forward on so small a coin, displays far more to the imagination than to actual view. Nonetheless, we are told that Americans flooded the papers with letters of outrage to their editors.

A careful search of the editorial pages of the day fails to confirm any such outcry, although the editors of the *New York Times* did have some unkind words about MacNeil's masterpiece. The writers described Miss Liberty as one of the Mint's "silvern beauties," adding, "the newly designed quarter on one side has the full figure of a woman coming through a gate in a wall, the reverse side shows an eagle in flight."

"This must be," they opined, "some too darkly veiled allegory of the Woman's Party and the suffrage movement." But, other than saying that Miss Liberty was "full figured," no comment was found about over-exposure.

Although usually identified by collectors as the "Standing Liberty" quarter, Miss Liberty is not standing. She is descending a flight of stairs, symbolic of her being "welcomed to the world." In one hand she holds a laurel branch of peace, while a shield indicative of her will to defend her rights and honor, if necessary, is held in the other hand. MacNeil described his Miss Liberty as "stepping forward in civilization and the defense of peace as her ultimate goal."

On the reverse, continuing the symbolism, MacNeil placed an eagle in flight. Here critics had their say panning the bird as having "the head of a hawk, the wings of an eagle and the body of a dove." There was sharp criticism about the overall design, but not from outside the Mint. The quarter, along with the companion dime and half dollar, were designed by artists of other than Mint employ. Chief engraver Charles E. Barber, whose design series these coins were replacing, unsuccessfully fought the use of outside help in redesigning coinage. Barber exerted whatever muscle he could raise, with anyone who would listen, to prove his point that outside artists were incapable of coin work. At the same time Barber ignored such biting press comment about the new work replacing his "unhandsome, masculine lady's face" now on the coins. And "the uncomfortable eagle, suspended in space, with arrows in one claw, a twig in the other, and a motto in its beak, will be given an eternal rest." Said the *New York Times*, "Neither the lady nor the bird will be missed."

For Barber and his staff, it was a losing battle. With the introduction of the three new designs in 1916, no current U.S. coin design, save the silver dollar, was the work of a Mint employee. Victor D. Brenner had given the public the Lincoln cent; James Earle Fraser, the Buffalo nickel; Weinman, the dime and half dollar; MacNeil, the quarter; Bela Lyon Pratt, the $2½ and $5 gold pieces; and Augustus Saint-Gaudens, the $10 gold and the $20 double eagle. Chief engravers were facing the threat of being reduced to die mechanics.

In 1916 there was little mention of bared breasts. Still, MacNeil did modify his designs. The immodest Miss Liberty donned a coat of mail and pinned her hair back. Then, on the reverse, to insure a better flow of metal, MacNeil raised the eagle and moved three of the thirteen stars to lower center. Even this failed to achieve the desired results of saving the date on the opposite side from excessive wear. In 1925 another modification left the date more deeply recessed to insure its preservation in circulation. But the changes were made more for the purpose of better striking than for reasons of prudery.

Perhaps it was MacNeil's adding a cloak of mail to the immodest Miss Liberty's torso or the carping of prudish Mint employees that gave rise to the tale of the bared breast. But it was not a story born from the outcry of a shocked public that gave rise to the legend. Furthermore, why should coins of the realm be less daring in appearance than National Currency?

National Currency left little to the imagination, while Standing Liberty quarters left it up to the viewer's fancy.

Original series $10 National Bank Notes, introduced in 1863, and similar appearing National Gold Bank Notes of 1870 are just two examples why the Liberty Standing quarters of 1916 were far from the nudest thing in money!

WAS MISS LIBERTY A BAG LADY?

Binghamton, New York, can lay claim to the first liberal arts college in a state university system, but in the world of numismatics its claims to fame are few. A notable exception, perhaps, is its latter-day boast of being the home of Empire Coin Company, Inc., predecessor of today's giant Bowers & Merena Galleries. However, in 1908, as the political seat of Broome County, it was a brief bit of notoriety that first brought Binghamton into the national numismatic spotlight.

Ordinarily the remanding of an indigent to the Broome County Almshouse would not be considered newsworthy, let alone make the headlines of the national papers. But when Mrs. Caroline Williams was institutionalized, the 80-year-old, poverty stricken woman protested the indignity. She was, after all, Miss Liberty! It was her portrait that appeared on all silver dollars in circulation at the time, or so she said. This latest circumstance in the unkind hands that fate had dealt her through life was frontpaged in the Friday, April 24, 1908, edition of *The New York Times*.

"DOLLAR MODEL DESTITUTE," topped the special to the *Times* news item. And Mrs. Williams went on to say that she never received a cent for her portrait on the dollar; she had been robbed of the honors due her.

The circumstances of her profile being selected for the silver dollar are meagre, but plausible. In an interview, Mrs. Willams told a reporter that at the time the selection was made she was living in Philadelphia earning a most meagre income.

At the age of 18, as Caroline Scott, she had been the bride of George Snyder of Albany, New York. He was one of the 349,944 men of the Union who lost their lives in the Civil War. Widowed, she made her own way by peddling notions on the streets of the City of Brotherly Love, Philadelphia. There, she said, she once had a daguerreotype taken but could not afford to pay for it. One day a man from the Mint found her picture in the artist's studio and obtained it to use as his model for the new silver dollars. The year was 1876.

Although the story of Mrs. Williams did not resurface for almost 80 years after its first publication, it is worth investigating. The first editorial clue as to the true identity of the model for the coin, that has since become known as the Morgan dollar, appeared in the Philadelphia *Sunday Republic* early in 1878. There she was identified only as, "a young lady who is a teacher in one of the public schools in the Fifteenth Section, and who naturally objects to having her name published." A brief quote from that article appeared in the April 1878 issue of the *American Journal of Numismatics*.

The first editorial mention of the model's name appeared two decades later in the New York *Mail and Express*. It was reprinted in the May 1896 issue of *The Numismatist* under the title, "To Marry A Goddess."

The coin was called the "Bland Dollar" in the days of its manufacture, so named after Congressman Richard Parks Bland, author of the legislation that brought the coin into being, and not so called for the lack of artistic detail.

Said the forerunner of the American Numismatic Association's official journal in its reprint of the story:

> The announcement that the goddess of Liberty is about to be married has aroused new interest in the woman whose face is known to more people than that of any other woman on the American continent. Every man, woman or child who has a silver dollar carries the handsome profile of the Philadelphia schoolteacher, Miss Anna W. Williams. Her classic features have been stamped upon millions of the silver disks.
>
> It is 20 years since the pretty blonde girl became world-famous.

It was then stated that Miss Williams' profile was the original goddess of Liberty on that much abused, much admired and equally disliked Bland silver dollar. The friends of the young woman placed every obstacle in the way of possible identification, but failed in their object. The story of how Miss Williams came to be the goddess of Liberty may be retold, now that it is said she is soon to become a bride.

In the early part of 1876 the Treasury Department secured through communication with the Royal Mint of England, the services of a clever young designer and engraver named George Morgan. Upon his arrival in this country Mr. Morgan was installed at the Philadelphia Mint and was assigned the task of making a design for a new silver dollar. After many months of labor the young engraver completed the design for the reverse side of the coin upon which he represented the American eagle. His attention then turned to the other side, and his original inclination was to place on it a fanciful head representing the goddess of Liberty. But the ambitious designer was too much of a realist to be satisfied with a mere product of fancy. Finally he determined the head should be the representation of some American girl and forthwith searched for his beauteous maid.

It was a long search, although pleasant. He told his friends of his desires, and one of them spoke highly of the really classic beauty of Miss Anna Williams. The English designer was introduced to the girl. Mr. Morgan was at once impressed by her beautiful face and studied it carefully. Then he told her what he desired, and she promptly refused to permit herself to be the subject of the design. Her friends, however, induced her to pose before the artist. After five sittings the design was completed.

Mr. Morgan was so enthusiastic that he declared Miss Williams' profile the most nearly perfect he had seen in England or America. His design for the Bland silver dollar was accepted by Congress, and so the silver coins have been pouring from the mints all these years adorned with the stately face of a Quaker City maiden.

Miss Williams is a decidedly modest young woman. She resides on Spring Garden Street, not far from the school in which for years she has been employed as an instructor in philosophy and methods in the kindergarten department. She is slightly below the average height, is rather plump, and is fair. She carries her figure with a stateliness rarely seen and the pose of the head is exactly as seen on the silver dollar. The features of Miss Williams are reproduced as faithfully as in a good photograph.

Not all contemporary comment about the new dollar was favorable. The *American Journal of Numismatics* editorialized, "The long line of monstrosities issued from the United States Mint, certainly receives its crown in the new dollar." Most adverse criticism, and there was a great deal of it, was reserved for the reverse. "We have noticed no commendation of the eagle," said the

George T. Morgan's goddess of Liberty.

Philadelphia *Sunday Republic*. The paper's cross-town competitor, the Philadelphia *Record*, was far more critical by reporting, "(the) eagle looks as if it was just recovering from a severe spell of sickness." The paper went to say that it believed that the director of the Mint feared that the eagle "might get loose and fly off, so he ordered its wings clipped."

But there was apparent unanimity of credit for Miss Liberty. "The head is chaste and beautiful, and, in an artistic sense, is considered the best executed head that has ever appeared upon a United States coin," said one paper. Another, from Boston, reported, "It has been well remarked that the great prominence of the cheek and the chin of the goddess of Liberty is truly emblematic." The American press had fallen for Miss Liberty, but was she Miss or Mrs. Williams?

Cornelius Vermuele, in his *Numismatic Art in America*, calls the story of Miss Williams an apocryphal, romantic legend and that the artist himself credits a Greco-Roman statuary head as the model. Was George T. Morgan respecting the wishes of a Philadelphia schoolteacher in not revealing her name or hiding the fact of his unauthorized use of another lady's photograph?

Is it just mere coincidence that the surnames of both claimants to the title of Miss Liberty are the same? If we are to believe the long ago published tale from the pages of *The Numismatist*, we have a story with an apparently happy ending.

If we are to believe the headlined feature from the front pages of *The New York Times* of April 24, 1908, we have the tale of a despondent, destitute old woman committed to an institution without so much as one of the dollars for which she claimed to have been the model.

A FLIP OVER A FLAPPER!

She made her debut late in 1921 and she could have been described as the classic beauty of the post-World War I era. She was the darling of sculptor Anthony de Francisci and the protege of numismatic entrepreneur Farran Zerbe. Known as Miss Liberty to most, as Teresa Cafarelli to intimates, she should have captured the hearts of everyone. But, her admirers were few, her critics many. Time would vindicate those who supported her, for today she is the vision of an era and now her suitors are many, the quest of thousands of collectors—for Teresa Cafarelli is the Peace dollar personified.

Cafarelli was born in Italy and came to the United States as a child. Famed sculptor de Francisci met young Teresa and could not keep his eyes off of her. In Teresa, de Francisci saw the embodiment of Liberty as portrayed by the Statue of Liberty. To a columnist de Francisci once wrote, "I opened the window of my studio and let the wind blow through her hair while she was posing for me." De Francisci was describing his creation of the Liberty head for the Peace dollar, "the nose, the fullness of the eye, and the mouth are much like my wife's."

The young lady was not only the sculptor's model, he had married her, too. "You will see that the Liberty is not a photograph of Mrs. de Francisci," he explained. "It is a composite face and in that way typifies something of America. I did not try to execute an 'American' type. I wanted Liberty to express something of the spirit of the country—the intellectual speed and vigor and virility America has, as well as its youth." But those who knew Teresa knew that it was her face on the face of the coin.

At the 1920 annual convention of the American Numismatic Association, former president Farran Zerbe proposed that the Association support legislation calling for the issuance of a coin to commemorate the end of the World War and the signing of a peace treaty with Germany. Zerbe, once editor of *The Nu-*

mismatist, the official journal of the ANA, had been the prime mover of earlier commemorative coins and had acted as the "numismatic agent" for the Panama-Pacific Exposition in San Francisco in 1915.

His idea for a peace commemorative caught on. A committee was formed and the proposal forwarded to the chairman of the House committee concerned with the coinage of the U.S. A bill was introduced in Congress (but never acted upon) and a number of sculptors were invited to submit proposed designs. Those of Anthony de Francisci were selected and approved by President Warren Harding. Collectors waited for Miss Liberty's debut.

Silver dollars in the early twenties enjoyed wide circulation. They were used extensively in the West—Montana, Nevada, Colorado, and they were used in the day-to-day transactions in East Coast cities with large immigrant populations. Recently arrived Europeans distrusted paper currency and many textile mills of the East paid their wages in hard coin.

But Liberty's debut was greeted with acidic press reviews. The *Wall Street Journal* asked editorially why Miss Liberty's hair had not been bobbed in the style of the day and suggested that a sculptor with talent would have produced something better. Of the reverse side of the coin the journal described the eagle as "stuffed," and noted that the bird appeared to be basking in the rays of a street lamp or motorcar headlight. Other newspapers were no less friendly.

All editorialists took exception to the artist's liberty in using a classic "V" in place of the standard "U" in "In God We Trust." Had de Francisci been more consistent with his lettering, the difference might not have been noticed; but in all other instances he used a regular "U" for his legends.

Production of the 1921-dated Peace dollars was limited to just over one million coins, leading speculators to ask premium prices for this introductory year of issue. The issue continued until 1935. Then, decades later, several thousand Peace dollars were struck at the Denver Mint in 1964 as the government's answer to the Franklin Mint's production of "gambling tokens" for use in Nevada's casinos. Before any 1964-dated dollars were released into circulation, however, the increasing price of silver bullion made the Treasury realize that the intrinsic value of the coins would soon exceed their face value and the project was discontinued. All 1964 silver dollars were reported to

Anthony de Francisci's spirit of Liberty.

have been melted, but rumors persist that some specimens escaped the melting pots. None has surfaced, at least not publicly, perhaps out of fear of confiscation by the Secret Service.

Teresa Cafarelli de Francisci is gone now. She lived to be a very old woman, but America remembers her only as their eyes saw her—a very young, very beautiful Miss Liberty.

A STORY SELDOM TOLD ABOUT THE FREEDOM STATUE

Two very handsome American coins were recently released, not into circulation but to the collections of numismatists and patriotic citizens who ordered directly from the U.S. Mint. The two are part of a three-coin, legal tender commemorative set authorized by the Congress of the United States on the occasion of its 200th anniversary.

Both coins feature the Statue of Freedom as it appears at the top of the Capitol dome in Washington. The silver dollar depicts a full length rendition, the half dollar details the head only. The third coin of the series, the $5 gold piece, is too small do to justice to the statue. Proceeds from the sale of these coins, available singly or in sets, are destined to go directly to the Capitol Preservation Fund, an official fund set up to restore the historic public areas of the Capitol Building.

The statue that served as the model for these coins is destined for restoration, as well. The elements have been unkind to the lady who represents freedom. She has stood steadfast atop the dome since 1863. Her bronze skin is badly pitted and corrosion has taken its toll of the iron supports that hold her

Closeup views of the headdress on the Statue of Freedom, seen on the commemorative coins of the bicentennial of the Congress, help still rumors that the statue is of an Indian princess.

7½ ton figure in place.

Ironically, while the coin issue is expected to earn up to $22 million for the preservation fund, the estimated $250,000 cost to restore the statue itself must come, according to a Washington report, from "other sources." The statue, it appears, is not in a "public area."

But there is another story about the statue, refected in the designs of the coins, that is seldom repeated. For years it had been a widely held belief that the statue represented an American Indian princess. More than one congressman identified her to visiting constituents as Pocahontas! The error was understandable. Freedom, after all, had donned a warrior's helmet bearing an eagle's head and feathers.

Freedom had not always been so fashioned. When the sculptor, Thomas Crawford, submitted his original designs in the late 1850s, she wore a softly folded liberty cap. The man in charge of the construction of the Capitol dome, saw not an emblem of freedom, but a Yankee abolitionist plot. The cap had been copied from ones worn by freed slaves in ancient Rome and the man in charge was—Jefferson Davis! The future president of the Confederate States of America would have nothing to do with anything remotely suggesting freedom for slaves.

While Davis' objection to the headdress caused the change, it had little effect on the desire of some secessionist states to use illustrations of the statue on their own currency. The state of Mississippi's $100 bill, for example, went so far as keeping the letters "U.S." that appear on Freedom's brooch.

Jefferson Davis' objection resulted in a more imposing statue and, consequently, a better design for two handsome American coins of the 20th century.

JUST A MINUTE HE'S OUR MAN!

Listen my children and you shall hear Of the midnight ride of Paul Revere, On the eighteenth of April, in Seventy-five:

Had Henry Wadsworth Longfellow been a little less poetic with his tale of American history and a little more accurate, the midnight ride might have immortalized Major John Pedrick; Patriot's Day would have been on the 26th of February; the saga of Lexington and Concord would have been replaced by that of Salem and Marblehead; and collectors would have had one less commemorative half dollar to collect!

While the actions of April 19, 1775, are generally accepted as marking the beginning of the War of American Independence, they were but a repetition of similar events occuring two months earlier, when first blood was drawn.

The British marched on Concord to destroy military supplies gathered by the colonists. Paul Revere and William Dawes rode to warn the patriots that "the British are coming." But, two months prior, the British marched on Salem to seize colonial munitions, and it was there, at the North River Bridge, that first blood flowed. Granted, no shot was fired to be "heard 'round the world." No patriots died, but one was bayoneted. It was an event overlooked by the poets.

Rumors that the Americans were establishing an ordinance depot at Salem had reached the British command at Boston. The 64th Infantry Regiment, under the command of Col. Alexander Leslie, was dispatched by General Gage to seize these arms. The regiment sailed from Boston port to Marblehead. Their orders: proceed to Salem, confiscate the cannon being mounted by the colonial militia. The British expected some resistance, but not the insurmountable obstacle found in their path, a drawbridge across the North River. The patriots simply raised the bridge, the draw was on their side. Stopped, the British threatened and cursed, but the bridge stayed raised. On spying two flat barges in the river below, Col. Leslie ordered them commandeered, but the patriots raced the soldiers to the boats and scuttled them. It was here that Joseph Whicher was stabbed with a bayonet, his blood being the only blood drawn that day. His wound was slight and he lived to proudly display, at little urging, the "first wound received in the War of Independence." The British retreated that day in February without achieving their goal and without losing a man.

Two months later they were not so fortunate. On April 19, at Lexington and Concord, and on the retreat to Boston, the British suffered 273 casualties— killed, wounded or missing. The Americans lost 93 men. A century later, in 1875, Daniel Chester French was called upon to create a memorial to honor the brave men of Concord. French was 23 at the time, it was his first commission. He chose to make a statue, entitling it "The Grand Concord Man." To everyone else it became known as, "The Minute Man." President Ulysses S. Grant presided at the unveiling. A half century later commemorative coins were in vogue and Congress authorized the striking of an issue to mark the 150th anniversary, the sesquicentennial of the Battle of Lexington and Concord.

It would seem that since the claims of these two towns as sites for the start of the war were accepted over those of Salem and Marblehead, the least that Lexington and Concord could do was to work hand-in-hand to mark the anniversary. While they fought side by side, as one, during the war, their observance of the anniversary was to be singular. Each town had its own independent committee. When Congress first considered legislation for the commemorative coin, it was in answer to the Lexington town committee's petition for a "Battle of Lexington" half dollar. The two committees soon compromised—each would have their side of the coin and neither would have any say on what was placed on the other's side, much to the chagrin of Chester Beach, the artist commissioned to prepare the models.

Beach found that he had to correspond with each of the committees individually, each equally opinionated about what they wanted to have appear on their side of the coin. The committee from Concord insisted that French's statue be identified as "The Concord Minute Man," even if the lettering had to be so small as to be unreadable. Lexington, on the other had, was equally adamant that the Old Belfry, used to summon Lexington's men to action, be identified by the words, "Old Belfry, Lexington." Congress required the words, "In God We Trust," so to balance the crowded verbiage, all agreed

The 1925 Lexington-Concord commemorative half dollar.

that the date of issue, "1925," be dispensed with. After all, it already appeared as part of the terminal dates of the sesquicentennial. On completion of the models, the Commission of Fine Arts and the director of the Mint swore never to let two committees design one coin again.

Of the total 300,000 coins authorized, only 162,013 were made. The coins were packaged in an unusual wooden case and sold at $1 each through the Concord National Bank and the Lexington Trust Company. Perhaps it was best that Longfellow's view of history prevailed. It is hard to imagine a commemorative half dollar with a scuttled scow on one side and a raised drawbridge on the other being attractive enough to sell.

While Marblehead and Salem claim first blood of the Revolution, Lexington the firing of "the shot heard 'round the world," and Concord the site of Daniel Chester French's famed statue of a Revolutionary patriot, it is to Worcester that the term Minute Man must be credited.

This story is not a suggestion to remove the statue from the green of Concord Common, but to reconcile hometown pride and, at the least, let the collecting world know that whenever they handle a Lexington-Concord commemorative half dollar, that had it not been for the patriots of Worcester, a name, other than Minute Man might have been applied to the coin.

Worcester, too, had prepared for a march by the British stationed in Boston, 35 miles to the east. Its citizens had been busily engaged in the purchase and production of arms, the casting of musket balls and the processing of gunpowder. When a messenger, on the day of the battles at Lexington and Concord, galloped through Worcester shouting, "To arms. To arms. The war is begun," 110 volunteers mustered on Worcester Common and marched toward Concord. When word reached them that the British were in retreat, they turned toward Boston in pursuit. Later, in the year that followed, the Declaration of Independence was read from the porch of Worcester's Old South Meeting House. It was July 14, 1776, and that day marked the first reading of the Declaration on Massachusetts soil. More germane to this story, we need turn to a volume entitled, *The Journals of Each Provincial Congress,* reporting on the proceedings of a meeting held in the court house at Worcester on September 21, 1774. On page 664 is to be found the following passage:

> The Worcester County Convention asked the militia officers to resign and soon thought a new force desirable. The new officers were to be chosen by the respective towns, and the militia, organized under purely American or "constitutional" authority, was to be ready "to act at a minute's notice."

This new force was immediately called Minute Men!

P.S.—I first filed this story a few years ago. Its appearance in a non-numismatic publication was scheduled to coincide with Patriot's Day. April 19 is a Massachusetts holiday set aside to honor her brave sons of Liberty and to run a marathon marking the day on which the War of the Revolution began in 1775. The story was in no way an attempt to belittle the ride of Paul Revere nor detract from the poetic words of Emerson or Longfellow. The intent was to give credit where credit was due. However, pangs of editorial conscience have bothered me ever since the story first appeared. True recognition, ignored by all but a few historians, was overlooked. Hometown pride requires that a postscript be added to the original story: hometown being—Worcester, Massachusetts.

WHY SOUTH CAROLINIANS LOVE THE PALMETTO TREE

One balmy spring afternoon, not too long ago, a formal ceremony was conducted at the South Carolina Statehouse in Columbia. Governor Carroll Campbell was the principal speaker.

Although the capital city is more than 100 miles inland, the subject of gentle sea breezes and palmetto trees was as much the featured topic of discussion as was the purpose of the gathering, the unveiling of the first commemorative stamp issued with the new first-class postage rate. The timing of the ceremonies had been set to mark the bicentennial anniversary of South Carolina's ratification of the Constitution. It was the eighth state to do so.

Johnny Thomas, Eastern Regional Postmaster General, waxed poetic in describing the design of the new stamp: "Coastal breezes gently bend sea oats/while palmetto trees stand erect against a gray sky."

To understand the South Carolinian fancy to the palmetto is to appreciate the history of the state. In 1778 General Clinton and the British fleet found the tree to be their curse. In attempting to seize Fort Moultrie in Charleston Harbor, the British discovered that after 12 hours of continuous bombardment they had succeeded in killing 12 colonials and burying a few cannon balls harmlessly into the palmetto logs that made up the fort. However, they lost hundreds of personnel and their oaken ships had sustained major damage from American shelling. The palmetto became recognized as the symbol of South Carolina's fight for independence. Three years after the British defeat at Fort Moultrie, the palmetto appeared on the state's paper currency notes.

While philatelists find the appearance of the state tree on this newest postage issue most appropriate, coin collectors recall the palmetto's appearance on a most valuable 50-cent piece minted during the era when commemorative coins marked such observances, along with the little, rectangular pieces of gummed stock that stamp collectors continue to seek.

The year 1936 saw the approval of no less than 16 commemorative coin issues, the first marking the sesquicentennial of the founding of Columbia, South Carolina. Congressional legislation authorized the striking of 25,000 silver half dollars of a design to be selected by the state and approved by the Commission of Fine Arts.

A. Wolfe Davidson, then a sculptor student at Clemson, was given the as-

The 1936 Columbia Sesquicentennial half dollar.

signment of preparing the models for the half dollar. One side was to portray a figure of Justice, flanked by renditions of the old statehouse on one side and the new one on the other. The reverse was to feature, of course, a palmetto tree. The first models confirmed the student's lack of training and the Fine Arts Commission rejected them. However, the commission asked that one of its own members, Lee Lawrie, be allowed to work with Davidson. The tutoring helped and the new models were accepted.

The sesquicentennial commission judiciously restricted early sales to Columbia residents first, then to collectors, disallowing any bulk sales to dealers. Of the 25,000 authorized, 8,000 were to be produced at each of the three mints—Denver, Philadelphia and San Francisco—for placement into sets priced at $6.45. The remaining 1,000 coins authorized were made at the Philadelphia Mint and sold singly at $2.15 per coin. The entire mintage quickly sold out.

Today, those who bought the coin with the palmetto design for such modest investment find that the sets, in average Uncirculated condition, sell for at least $1,000. The individual type coin is now valued at almost $300.

THE LAFAYETTE DOLLAR

Few motorists driving Connecticut's capital city streets realize as they pass through Lafayette Circle, at Capital Avenue and Washington Street, in downtown Hartford, that they can look up and see the model for the reverse design of America's first commemorative silver dollar.

Local historians admit that Paul Wayland Bartlett's equestrian statue of the Marquis de Lafayette is a copy of an older piece now at the Louvre in Paris. Few seem to realize that the Hartford statue helped earn the funds to "base" the original in France.

The Lafayette dollar has an unusual tale to tell, not only in numismatic studies, but with American relations with France. While few are unaware of the fact that the Statue of Liberty was a gift of the citizens of France to the people of the United States, it is not such common knowledge that fourteen years after "Liberty Enlightening the World" was unveiled in New York harbor, a reciprocal ceremony took place in the city of Paris.

If one is fortunate enough to visit the Louvre, one will find the granite base of the statue of the Marquis de Lafayette inscribed, "Erected By The Youth of the United States in Honor of Gen. Lafayette." American school children contributed five million pennies to fund the project. However, before the statue was unveiled at the Paris Exposition of 1900, the promoters discovered that the $50,000 raised by the youngsters represented just one half the costs. A similar sum needed to be raised to pay for a base. The Lafayette Memorial Commission petitioned the Congress of the United States to authorize the striking of 100,000 commemorative half dollars and, from the profits derived, build a monumental base. Before Congress finished with the authorizing legislation, however, the coin doubled in face value—to one dollar—and the quantity requested halved to 50,000 coins.

United States commemorative coin issues had been extremely limited up to that time. Only a quarter and two differently dated half dollars had been struck, all for the Columbian Exposition of a few years earlier.

The Lafayette coin represented a number of "firsts." The piece was the first commemorative silver dollar, the first legal tender coin to bear the portrait of a president (Washington), and to this day remains the only United States coin struck without a date of issue!

The responsibility for designing the Lafayette dollar was assigned to Charles Barber, chief engraver of the Mint. In a letter to the director, George E. Roberts, Barber proposed to use Houdon's bust for the head of Washington and a medal designed by Caunois and struck by the Paris Mint for Lafayette's portrait. Astute numismatists were quick to catch the striking similarity of the obverse to a medal designed by P. L. Krider, for the centennial of the Battle of Yorktown observed almost two decades earlier.

Charles Barber can be forgiven for the discrepancies noted on the reverse side of the dollar. The chief engraver worked from an early model of sculptor Paul Wayland Bartlett's statue, different from the ones that appear in the Louvre and oversee the traffic around Hartford's Lafayette Circle. On the coin, Lafayette is shown astride his horse—offering his sword, still unsheathed and hilt first, to

The 1900 Lafayette commemorative dollar.

If passersby should note the bronze turtle ambling beneath the feet of the general's horse in Hartford's Lafayette Circle, they may accept it as a statement to the flow of traffic, not to the speed by which the sculptor was paid.

America in the cause of liberty. The final versions of both statues depict Lafayette with his sword raised in defense of liberty!

In Paris, and in Hartford, Lafayette rides bare headed, but on the commemorative silver dollar he is dressed in the tricon hat of an American officer. There are other, more subtle differences, particularly in his uniform and horse.

It is the story of the date, however, that presents the most unusual feature of this particular coin. Since the piece was to be the first to portray Washington, the first strike ceremony was scheduled for 11:15 a.m., Friday, December 14, 1899. That day and time marked the 100th anniversary of the death of the first president. The Lafayette Memorial Commission was anxious to offer the coin as soon as possible, but insisted that the piece be dated—1900—the year of the Paris Exposition and the unveiling of the statue. However, U. S. law was paramount and it required that coins be dated the year made, centennial observance of Washington's death notwithstanding.

The Treasury Department refused to postpone its plans for the elaborate first strike ceremony, but it was willing to close an eye and compromise. No year of issue appears on the coin; the year 1900, requested by the commission and seen on the reverse, is the date of the Paris Exposition, not the year of manufacture. This Solomonesque decision satisfied both parties and few were the wiser. But, the letter of the law was broken.

Invitations to the first strike ceremony were limited to a small group of Mint officials, members of the memorial association, and representatives of the press. On cue, at precisely 11:15 a.m. the coin press operator, Miss Geary, pushed the button for the first strike. The coin was handed to Superintendent Henry Boyer, who in turn passed it to Robert J. Thompson, secretary of the Lafayette Memorial Commission. He handed it to George E. Roberts, director of the Mint. The coin was then placed in a small "casket" and forwarded to President William McKinley to give to the president of France, Emile Loubet.

Before the production day ended, all 50,000 authorized coins had been made, along with an additional 26 for good measure. The press was to report an enthusiastic reception for the coin by the public and reported that orders for nearly 60% of the entire issue were received from New York alone.

While the funds sought were raised as planned, a humorous postscript must be told about the Hartford statue. Appearing on neither the Paris version nor on the coin is a bronze turtle ambling carelessly beneath the feet of the horse, with the sculptor placing it there as testament to the speed in which he was paid for his work.

Monetary appreciation of the value of the coin moved with equal tortoisial speed. Released to the public at $2 per coin, the coin had climbed only to a $4 retail listing in Wayte Raymond's *Standard Catalog of United States Coins* by 1935. The first edition of the *Guide Book of United States Coins* by R. S. Yeoman valued the coin at $12.50 in Uncirculated condition in 1947. But, then the pace of appreciation quickened. By the time the Lafayette dollar was 75 years old, it was listing for $450. By 1989, an MS-63 condition coin sold for $2,250. Still, it was too early to say, "Lafayette you have arrived, at least dollar wise!"

AMERICA'S IRISH ROSE

Mary Cunningham's claim to fame was both brief and long lasting! It has been just 20 years short of a century since notice of the pending appearance of her portrait on coins of the United States created national hue and cry. It was not that Mary Cunningham was unpleasant to look at; nor were there any suggestions of impropriety. Her failing was that she was Irish! The assembled delegates to the National Convention of the Order of Independent Americans, held in Harrisburg in

September 1907, voted on a resolution to protest the placement of the face of Miss Cunningham, an Irish-born colleen, upon the obverse of United States coins. Duly adopted, the protest was then forwarded to Washington. Editors had a front-page story to titilate their readers for a few days.

Before her brief moment of recognition, Mary Cunningham had been a waitress in Cornish, New Hampshire, not far from the summer estate and studios of Augustus Saint-Gaudens. The famed sculptor had been commissioned by President Theodore Roosevelt to undertake the task of redesigning the coinage of the United States. The president, comparing the coins of the early Greeks with the mintdesigned discs of the time, felt the need for a "coinage worthy of a civilized nation."

Saint-Gaudens' task of redesigning the coinage became an obsession with him. He set to work immediately on three denominations: the cent, $10, and $20 gold pieces.

He sketched and modeled. He assigned work to his students and assistants, and he studied ancient coins, along with earlier memorials and statues of his own creation. But, Saint-Gaudens was not satisfied with the face of Liberty.

As in plots past and since, fate brought Saint-Gaudens and Miss Cunningham together. She waited on his table one day when the sculptor decided to lunch in nearby Cornish. Immediately, Saint-Gaudens knew that hers was the face that he had been seeking. Hers was not a colleenesque profile, not typically Irish. Her nose line was straight; her features angular, but she was Miss Liberty. The 24-year-old waitress was persuaded to allow the sculptor to make sketches. Mary Cunningham's discovery as the Irish girl whose portrait adorned coins of the United States occurred about six weeks after the death of the sculptor, about two years after she had first met Saint-Gaudens in the Cornish restaurant. Defense for her depiction fell upon the shoulders of the artist's son, Homer Saint-Gaudens. By then, Miss Cunningham was no longer a waitress. She was now employed as a domestic in the Saint-Gaudens household and the young Saint-Gaudens gallantly shielded her from press interviews. He did acknowledge that she would be shown "full length" on either the ten or twenty-dollar gold pieces to be released shortly, but he was unsure which.

Mary Cunningham continues to appear on the coins of the United States. Her current appearance is on the gold bullion Eagles introduced in 1986 and issued annually since.

Cunningham continues to appear on coins of the United States. Her latest appearance on the monetary scene is on the gold eagle series introduced last year in the form of $50, $25, $10 and $5 gold bullion coins copied from Saint-Gaudens' $20 gold piece issued from 1907 to 1933. Her profile was also seen during the same period on the $10 gold coin. Although Saint-Gaudens' death, before he completed his assignment, kept her portrait from the one-cent coin, Mary Cunningham was America's Irish Rose. Sure 'n begorra!

NOTES ON PAPER

THE MAN WHO WOULD HAVE BEEN THE HERO!

Overlooking Colorado Springs, high atop the table mesa—a rise of land that hides the majesty of the Garden of the Gods from downtown view—lies a small, manicured plot that once served as the town cemetery. Today it bears the name Pioneer Park, but for over six decades, beginning in 1857, the grounds that served as the final resting place for many early settlers were known by a succession of names. Officially, the plot had been called the Cemetery on the Mesa, Colorado City Cemetery, Mesa Cemetery, Pioneer Cemetery, and Town Cemetery.

At present, there is a solitary stone marker carrying the names of only 42 of the more than 250 souls believed to be buried in the cemetery. Their identities have been lost to time, as have all traces of the original purpose of the park. Through one of those quirks of fate that give us the interesting anecdotes of the past, one of the unnamed believed to be buried here might well have been a great Civil War hero. Had circumstances been different, his portrait might have appeared on the face of the $10 Treasury Notes of Series 1890 and 1891 and on the back of the Silver Certificates of 1896, in place of the man he had befriended early in life.

The world has taken little note of George Binkley, late of the mining camps of Colorado. Had it not been for an anonymous correspondent for the Denver-published *Field & Farm* newspaper, Binkley's sacrifice in the name of friendship might have gone unrecorded. The old prospector's contribution to posterity's scene manifested itself in the persona of a brilliant Civil War leader: Binkley should be recognized for giving General Philip Henry Sheridan to America and to history.

In the fall of 1874, an unnamed correspondent reported in *Field & Farm* that "Old Bink" had wandered into a mining camp in southwestern Colorado. "How he got into camp no one knew and no one inquired," the writer reported. "He must have climbed the long, toilsome and zigzag burro trail from Del Norte to Summitville on foot, for he was wan and weak from hunger and fatigue when he appeared at the camp and begged for something to eat. 'I'm Old Bink and I'm hungry,' was his laconic salutation as he drew up before a half dozen rough miners who sat about smoking after the evening meal." The reporter's account repeated the oft-told tale of the early miners' proverbial hospitality and how they had placed before Old Bink a big meal. After his hunger was satisfied, he was given a pair of blankets and soon was off the sleep.

Binkley pitched in at camp, carrying his burden of chores. The next pack train from Del Norte with camp supplies replenished the long-depleted supply of whiskey. "A short acquaintance with this article was the key that unlocked Old Bink's lips, and he told the story of his life," the correspondent recorded.

The tale related by Binkley was accepted with a grain of salt and classified with most of the legends of the West under "fiction." The newcomer to the camp declared that his name was George Binkley and that when he was a young man his family had been influ-

El Paso County Memorial Marker.

ential and wealthy. General Phil Sheridan, he told the miners, was his schoolmate, and though Phil's mother was very poor, the two boys were inseparable friends and companions.

An uncle of Binkley's, serving in Congress at the time, obtained an appointment for his nephew to West Point. Binkley said he was delighted initially, but when he told his friend of his promised military career, Sheridan expressed remorse because he, too, had longed for a military career. Old Bink recalled that his family was "astonished" and his uncle "paralyzed" when he declined the appointment and recommended that Phil Sheridan be named in his stead. Sheridan did go to West Point, graduating with the Class of '53. For his part, Binkley tried college, practiced law and drank "poor whiskey," in that order.

The old-timer's visit to Summitville was brief, and he next turned up on the streets of Denver some three years later. At the time, the city was packed with people wanting to see a visiting dignitary—General Sheridan. As the Civil War hero's carriage proceeded down 16th Street, a voice from the crowd shouted out, "Phil! Oh, Phil!" It was Old Bink.

General Sheridan, the reporter related, recognized the voice, ordered his driver to stop, and climbed down from the carriage. Witnesses later reported that General Sheridan pushed his way through the crowd, clasped the old man in his arms, and escorted him back to his carriage. The next day, Old Bink, was seen in a new suit and "a tank filled with Denver delight."

The *Field & Farm* correspondent's story concluded with a footnote explaining that when he was in Colorado Springs a decade later his driver had shown him an unmarked grave, telling him how the man buried there had died of fever and in his delirium kept calling, "Phil! Phil!" Upon inquiry the reporter learned that the remains were those of "Old Bink."

Numismatic scholars have been no kinder to the memory of General Sheridan than fate was to George Binkley. Sheridan's portrait was placed on the face of the $10 Treasury Notes of 1890 and 1891, and he joined General Grant on the backs of the $5 Silver Certificates of 1896. But here too, Sheridan was a substitute. The Treasury Department had wanted to use the portrait of General William Tecumseh Sherman, but felt that he was still too controversial and that the South would object. Even though the figures were changed, several numismatists failed to take note. As a result, early editions of Gene Hessler's *U.S. Essay, Proof and Specimen Notes* identified Sheridan as

$10 Treasury note with Sheridan portrait.

Sherman, in both the portraits and in the index.

Hessler treated Sheridan no better in *The Comprehensive Catalog of U.S. Paper Money*. Sheridan's portrait was identified as that of "Sherman, engraved by Lorenzo Hatch." Although later editions were corrected, Hessler was not alone in his error. In the 1975 edition of the currency collector's bible, *Donlon's Catalog of United States Paper Money 1861 to 1923*, the hapless hero is tagged, "Philip Henry Sherman!"

A LEGEND OF THE WEST COMES ALIVE ON A $10 NOTE!

With the passing of time, legends often become thought of as truth and as such they often give legitimacy to tall tales that cannot be backed by fact. The Old West is full of such fantasies and coin collecting ranks not too far behind. However, when a tale of the West can be paired with one of the hobby, it is a story worth retelling.

The state of Colorado laid claim to being the inspiration for the following song, and, coincidentally, so did the hobby. You may not recognize the words of the Colorado version, but the rhythm should be familiar:

> Oh, give me the hill, and the ring of the drill,
> In the rich silver ore in the ground.
> And give me the gulch where the miners can sluice,
> And the bright yellow gold can be found.

When you hear the more common verse, however, you're sure to recognize the tune:

> Oh, give me a home where the buffalo roam,
> Where the deer and the antelope play.
> Where never is heard a discouraging word,
> And the sky is not clouded all day.

Public appreciation of this folk song, which by now you know is "Home on the Range," did not begin until election eve 1932, when reporters, assigned to cover Franklin Roosevelt's campaign, serenaded the President-elect. The song was to become Roosevelt's favorite and he often requested it be sung at the White House and at his retreat in Warm Springs, Georgia.

Word surfaced that "Home on the

$10 U.S. note, Series 1901.

Range" was the President's favorite, a fact that helped propel it to the top of the music charts of the day. Entertainers also loved it, but for more mercenary reasons. There was no known copyright, no author of record and, therefore, no royalties to be paid.

In the summer of 1934, an Arizona couple, William and Mary Goodwin of Tempe, filed suit and demanded $500,000 in damages. According to their attorney, they had written and copyrighted the tune under the name "An Arizona Home" back in 1905. A fortune was due them in unpaid royalties, they claimed.

"Not so," cried Colorado's newspaper editors. The Leadville *Herald Democrat* reported that the song was written in nearby California Gulch during the winter of 1885. The alleged authors—Bob Swartz, Bill McCabe and Jim Fouts—called it, "Colorado Home." But they were not the only mountainstate claimants. The Crested Butte *Elk Mountain Pilot* said the song was written in Sherman, Colorado, a mining community on the Otto Mears trail to Silverton.

The Lamar *Daily News* credited James Calibran, editor of the Spar City *Spark* with the words and Cy Warman, editor of the Creede *Chronicle,* with the music. In 1945, Colorado Congressman Robert Rockwell had the words entered into the *Congressional Record.* No one could argue with so officious a journal.

Some numismatists, however, believed otherwise. The song, they thought, was inspired by the obverse design of the $10 United States Note, Series 1901, and they expressed rightful indignation through "letters to the editor" columns. The collectors' desire to gain proper recognition matched that of the Colorado press, but was equally incorrect.

Tune detectives traced the origin of the folk song to Kansas, finding that it was written in 1873 by Dr. Brewster M. Higley and published in the Smith County *Pioneer* the following year. Dan Kelley, a member of the Harlan Brothers Orchestra, is credited with the melody. Though neither received a cent in royalties, the Kansas State Legislature belatedly passed an act in 1947 recognizing "Home On The Range" as its own, not only by virtue of resident authorship, but as the official state song. Kansans had the last word, but what about the vocal numismatists?

The $10 United States Note, Series 1901, is not without a legend of its own. Contemporaries called it "The Buffalo Bill," and though it did not inspire "Home on the Range," it was designed to create interest in the forthcoming Lewis and Clark Centennial Exposition held in Portland, Oregon, in 1905. The portraits of Lewis and Clark appear to the left and right of the note's face, a testament to the skills of G.F.C. Smillie, an engraver with the Bureau of Engraving and Printing. A bison, claimed by the Bureau of Engraving and Printing to be the work of its engraver Marcus Baldwin, dominates the center.

"Not so," said Mrs. Catherine Manning several years later. As curator of the philatelic collection at the Smithsonian, she had access to the original art used on many postage stamp issues. A stamp collector had noticed the similarity between the bison pictured on the legal tender note of 1901 and that shown on a 1922 postage stamp and had written Mrs. Manning. In response to the inquiry, she had closely examined a photograph of the original artwork for the stamp and found the credit line, "Chas. R. Knight, 1901."

When contacted, Knight verified the story that indeed he drew the sketch of the bison appearing on the note. He explained that he was on assignment drawing animals for the Department of Anatomy and Osteology at the old National Museum when he noticed Baldwin trying to sketch a stuffed buffalo. When Knight introduced himself and offered his help, Baldwin readily accepted and rushed Knight over to meet Smillie at the Bureau of Engraving and Printing.

Unfortunately, the buffalo on the bill was not at home on any range. The old bull from which the sketch was drawn was grazing instead in the National Zoo at Rock Creek Park in the nation's capital.

THE STORY NOT TOLD ON U.S. CURRENCY!

Officials leaving the Treasury Department by its front steps face a small, well-manicured plot of land centered by an imposing equestrian statue. Erected in 1903 by the Society of the Army of Tennessee, the monument is a tribute to the Civil War successes of William Tecumseh Sherman. Atop its center pedestal, astride his horse, General Sherman surveys the daily comings and goings at the Treasury. If any site in the nation's capital should have been dedicated to the memory of a different Civil War commander, this is it. This ground should rightfully be dedicated to the memory of General Joseph Hooker!

In modern warfare, Sherman's name is synonymous with the powerful tanks of the U. S. Army. Gen. Hooker's name is no less known, but of more dubious honor. It was on this site, in the very shadow of the United States Treasury, that General Hooker gave his name to the painted ladies of the city.

Civil War-time Washington had mushroomed in size, its population doubling, not counting the military stationed there in its defense. Its gentry, civilian and in uniform, was serviced by a reported 5,000 "ladies." Taking care of the "boys" became so free-wheeling, so widespread, that the Washington City Council considered licensing the bordellos, but General Hooker had a better idea. Summoning a number of his trusted aides, Hooker rounded up the ladies and had them bivouacked on this plot, off Pennsylvania Avenue and in the shadow of the Treasury. The area became known as Hooker's Division, and its residents as Hookers!

Perhaps the ghost of a soldier past has had the last word here. Someone has removed the symbolic eagle from the monument's base. Although the eagle has gone, the doves have not. They roost just a few blocks away. Neither general is forgotten, but ask any Washingtonian, he'll probably have more to say on the eponym of the general not honored than the one who was.

THE DOG NOTES OF VIRGINIA

If you ever have the chance to visit the nation's capital on business or for pleasure, forget registering into one of the $150 per night hotels. Plan, instead, on staying in one of the small historic towns nearby—like Leesburg, Virginia. It is just a half-hour drive northwest of Washington, between the Potomac River and the Blue Ridge Mountains. You can stay in any number of bed-and-breakfast inns and be ahead enough on the tariff to rent a car and still have an extra $50 per day to spend on your favorite collectables.

I laid awake for more than an hour in my room at the Laurel Brigade Inn that first evening, wondering if I occupied the same room as the Marquis de Lafayette when he visited here in 1825. It was the Peers Hotel then, and the Marquis was visiting America as "a guest of the nation."

The inn offers many windows to history, beginning in 1758 when the first owner, Peter Gregor, opened an "ordinary," with prices for lodging set by the justices of the parish at six shillings "on clean sheets, otherwise nothing." Today's rate seemed just as reasonable. Twenty-six dollars single, fireplace, antique furnishings, and as a concession to modern mores—a private bath.

The Laurel Brigade Inn takes its name from a later period of history, from a group of local volunteers who donned the grey uniforms of the Confederacy during the War Between the States. Local legend records that the Laurel Brigade, led by Colonel Elijah White, refused to surrender at Appomattox and marched off to nearby Lynchburg, unwilling to be a part of the surrender that brought defeat to the South. It was during this period that Leesburg helped write monetary history and gave us the story retold here today.

During the Civil War, the lack of money was a problem that all southern municipalities shared. Local volunteers had to be armed and equipped, the families of those killed in action had to be supported, and someone had to replace all the metal coins of the Union that had disappeared from circulation.

The Virginia General Assembly met the need by authorizing all cities and towns within the state, with a population of 2,000 or more, together with the towns of Leesburg, Lynchburg and Warrenton, to issue paper notes of "like" denominations not to exceed the amount of state tax assessed on real and personal property. Eighteen months later, the general assembly had a change of mind and repealed the act. However, during the interim, Leesburg issued notes in denominations of 12½ cents, 25 cents, 50 cents and one dollar.

The Leesburg Town Council authorized the mayor, Major John M. Orr, to issue these small notes to the total amount of $5,000. He was instructed not only to sign the notes, but number and register them, as well. The notes were made payable to the bearer in multiples of $5 on presentation at the mayor's office. The money received in exchange for the notes was to be deposited with the treasurer and retained specifically for redemption. To save the mayor from a severe case of writer's cramp, three citizens were authorized to sign the notes on his behalf.

Paper was as scarce as hard money during the Civil War and quality paper for currency was unobtainable. The *Washingtonian*, the local newspaper, printed the currency for Leesburg using buff-colored stock for the 25 and 50-cent notes, and light blue paper for the 12½ cent and one dollar bills. Some notes appear on plain paper, others are printed on rule stock taken from school supplies. All the notes show a dog diligently guarding a safe, its forepaw strategically placed on the key to the lock, canine symbolism at its best. The townsfolk of Leesburg rested, assured that their money was guarded by one not subject to bribes or politics.

Leesburg's dog money is unusual, but not necessarily rare. An occasional specimen can be found in local antique shops, but if you really want to see examples, there is a complete set on display at the Louden County Historical Society Museum, just a few steps from the Laurel Brigade Inn.

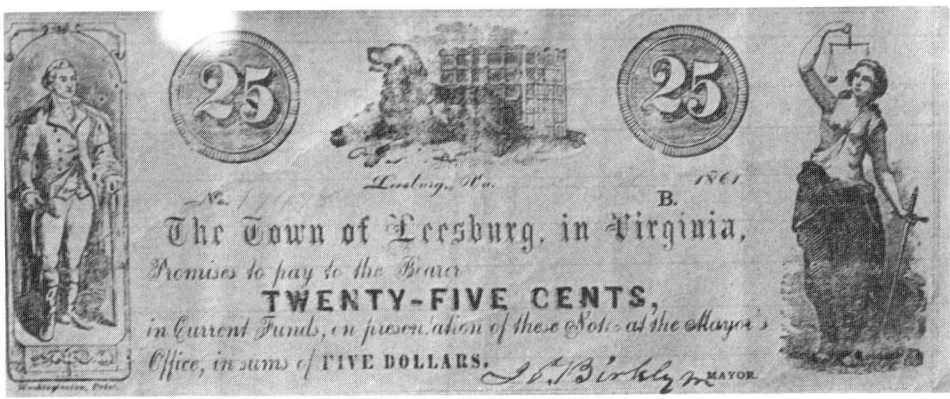

A Leesburg, Virginia 1861 "dog note."

A MAN WHO SEES WHAT OTHERS MISS!

There are countless maxims about the beauty of an object being in the eyes of the beholder. One Georgia gentleman takes the looking one step further and looks for things others miss.

Bill Fivaz, an executive with Nestle Company, focuses his collecting attention on numismatic errors. He has served as a member of the Board of Governors of the American Numismatic Association and during vacation breaks teaches classes on counterfeit detection and coin grading. His true collecting love, however, are those minute differences—overdates, repunched mintmarks, doubled dies—that make rarities out of common coins. So when a rare error is discovered in circulation, no one is surprised to find Mr. Fivaz involved.

What might have passed as a smudged $5 bill to most has turned out to be a rare and unusual find for the former ANA governor. On first glance, the note seems to have been printed twice, with the overprinting slightly out of register from the first. Most noticeable are the signatures on this Federal Reserve Note, series 1985. You can make out one signature over the other. While double printing is rare, it is not unknown. Notes that have been fed through the press twice command premiums of up to $500 for a bill in crisp New condition. Even the most advanced error collectors would have stopped at this point to catalog their find as a "double printing on face" error. But, not Bill Fivaz. For he saw what others missed.

All notes bear position and plate numbers. This helps pressmen locate problems during a press run. Bureau of Engraving and Printing presses are monsters. They are the length of a five-story building. All current presses are "four platers," that is they have four plates of 32 subjects or notes each. Pressmen periodically—about every 500 to 1,000 sheets—pull a sheet for inspection.

At first glance of this error, it appears that the pressman may have placed the sheet back on the yet unprinted stack on the feed end of the press. If that had happened the plate numbers would have coincided and the end result would have been just a "double printing on face error." But that is not be what happened. Bill Fivaz saw that the face plate numbers were different!

Close examination of the $5 bill by Fivaz revealed the check letter and quadrant number at the upper left, to be proper—A 3 over A 3. However, the plate serial number itself, in the lower right hand corner, showed A 98 over A 91! If the single sheet was overprinted a second time at a later date, it certainly meant an almost "impossible error" had occurred. It also means that out

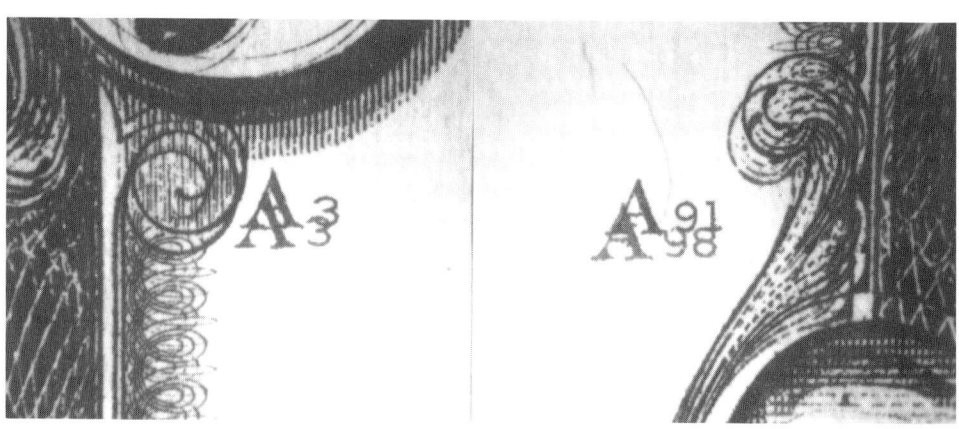

The Twice-printed note.

there, somewhere in circulation, are 31 other companion pieces waiting to be discovered. No catalogs list the value of such notes.

The chance discovery of one of these rare errors may not buy you a new Cadillac El Dorado, but to think of it in terms of putting a good used Ford Escort under the Christmas tree is not be too unreasonable.

THE SECRET OF THE NUMBER IN THE SHADOW!

It is a question often asked. What is the meaning of the secret number—3172—on the back of the $5 bill?

For the authoritative answer to the meaning of the mysterious number, one that many see when they look at the bushes to the left of the stairs leading to the Lincoln Memorial, we asked Robert J. Leuver, the executive director of the American Numismatic Association. Leuver is the former head of the Bureau of Engraving and Printing and it was once his duty to oversee the design and production of United States currency.

"The number goes back a long time in the lore of currency, but it actually has no significance," said Leuver. "The figures are mere quirks of the engraver's art."

We were disappointed, but so much for the numbers. There is special wording on the reverse of the $5 bill that experts turn to first when checking the authenticity of the note. It is lettering that very few realize is even there. Did you know that armed with a magnifying glass, you can find the names of 26 states of the Union? Delaware, Pennsylvania, New Jersey, Georgia, Connecticut, Massachusetts, Maryland, (South) Carolina, (New) Hampshire, Virginia, and New York, are listed in the order in which they were admitted into the Union. These names appear at the tops of the 12 columns fronting the memorial. Arkansas, Michigan, Florida,

Many sharp-eyed collectors can see the number—3172—hidden in the bushes at the base of the Lincoln Memorial.

Texas, Iowa, Wisconsin, California, Minnesota, Oregon, Kansas, West Virginia, Nevada, Nebraska, Colorado, and North Dakota appear on the friezes, at the upper indented part of the memorial. Admittedly, the names are not easy to see, but they are there. "The type is very difficult to pick up in a photograph and, if one is going to make an offset print, they'll never pick it up," Leuver noted.

There is also a design error, one of perspective, on the reverse of the note, one that few, including the former chief of the bureau, have ever noticed. The stair guard at the left casts a long shadow, while the one at the right reflects no shadow at all. "I am not certain," Leuver admitted, "but quite frankly an engraver did this engraving in a bright recess within the Treasury Department, so it would be difficult to say what he was looking at. Probably, he was working from a photograph."

As long as we had Mr. Leuver's attention on the subject of bogus bills, we asked, "What are other points Treasury agents look for in checking for authenticity?"

"One of the most important check points is the portrait and the surrounding area," he responded. "Basically, agents check these points and then look at the 5 in the upper left and right hand corners on the face of the bill—there's a fine dark line. Normally this line is sharp and complete. The fineness alone makes it difficult to reproduce."

We are disappointed that we cannot report to readers that there is some clandestine meaning to the "secret" number 3172 hidden in the bushes. The secret is that there is no secret, but we have made it easy for someone wanting to make a wager that the name COLORADO, or whichever one of the 26 states one wants to use, appears on the back of a five-dollar bill!

AFTER "TOTAL" DESTRUCTION GAS RATION COUPONS BEGIN TO SURFACE

Sixty-three highway miles separate the Pueblo Army Depot from the Rocky Mountain Greyhound Park in Colorado Springs. Although the distance can be covered in approximately a one-hour drive, it has taken three years for an undisclosed number of gasoline ration coupons, supposedly destroyed at the Pueblo facility, to reach the weekly flea market conducted at the Colorado Springs dog track.

The coupons were reported to have been offered by flea market habitues to dealers for resale recently and at very reasonable prices.

The potential need for gas ration coupons occurred in 1973 when most of the oil producing nations of the Middle East embargoed shipments of crude oil to the United States in retaliation for U.S. support of Israel during the Arab-Israeli war. Because the oil embargo led to an acute energy shortage, President Richard Nixon took steps to conserve fuel consumption.

Through an executive memorandum, the president ordered a 15% cut in supplies of gasoline and an even greater reduction in the use of home heating oils. Government thermostats were turned down to 68 degrees. Air conditioning was discontinued. Gasoline stations were asked to close from 9 p.m., Saturdays, through 12:01 a.m., Mondays. Oil companies terminated promotional and ornamental lighting. Congress legislated year round daylight savings time and made 55 mph the maximum speed limit throughout the country.

At first, energy conservation failed to satiate the need for gasoline, and long lines and empty tanks became an increasingly familiar experience. The president named William E. Simon (later secretary of the Treasury) to head a newly established Federal Energy Administration. Simon helped plan a standby gasoline-rationing system, one that required the use of ration coupons.

The rush task of preparing several billion ration coupons fell on the staff of the Bureau of Engraving and Printing. To expedite production, the Bureau of Engraving and Printing simply availed itself of an existing vignette of George Washington used in the design of the current one dollar bill. Although the ration coupons, overall, were one-third the size of the dollar bill, the Washington portrait remained the same size on both. That led to the unforeseen possibility of the ration coupons activating dollar bill changers.

A spiralling increase in the price of gasoline, combined with mandated conservation efforts led to the development of fuel efficient automobiles. The discovery of new fuel sources, and improved relations with Arab nations, negated the need for gasoline rationing. The ration coupons, printed by the Bureau of Engraving and Printing, were reclaimed from the nine strategic storage locations throughout the country and were moved to the Pueblo Army Depot, 14 miles east of Pueblo, Colorado.

In 1984, despite a plea from Congressman Frank Annunzio (D-Ill), chairman of the House Subcommittee on Consumer Affairs and Coinage, that some of the coupons be retained and then sold to collectors to reduce the government investment of more than $15 million in the gas rationing plan, the U. S. Department of Energy ordered all coupons destroyed.

The most efficient and economical method of destruction was to burn the coupons. However, environmental concerns prohibited burning and the coupons were shredded with the residue buried in deep trenches at the Pubelo Army Depot.

The destruction process took approximately three weeks and was completed by June 26, 1984. Officials from the Office of the Inspector General witnessed the destruction as independent observers to the disposal process and to provide assurance to the Department of Energy that all of the coupons were actually disposed of in an appropriate way.

Although Congress was told that the 4.8 billion coupons, printed as part of the Federal Energy Administration plan for gasoline rationing, were sealed in underground bunkers at the Pueblo Army Depot, the coupons were kept in easily accessible storage sheds and some eventually made their appearance and were offered to collectors at nearby flea markets.

The destruction project was managed by the Idaho Operations Office, Department of Energy, headquartered at Idaho Falls. Official records indicate that a total of 4.8 billion coupons were printed, but the records of the Office of the Inspector General show that 19 million more, or 4,819,400 were destroyed or accounted for.

Government records indicate that a 16-subject sheet was forwarded to the Smithsonian Institution on June 25, 1984. On the same day, another sheet was sent to the National Archives. Six additional sheets went to the Federal Energy Administration in accordance with a directive dated April 15, 1975. These eight sheets of 16 coupons each, totaling 128 coupons, were not destroyed and remain accounted for.

A discrepancy exists as to the method and place of storage at the army depot. The Office of External Affairs, Department of Energy, Idaho Operations Office, reported that DOE was not involved until sometime after the coupons were locked and welded inside seven bunkers at the depot where they remained in storage for approximately nine years. The Public Affairs Officer at the Pueblo Army Depot said that the coupons, plastic wrapped and kept in 126,000 boxes, were kept in warehouse sheds on the base and not stored in bunkers as reported to Congress. Regardless of where the coupons were kept on the facility, it appears that an unknown number of gas ration coupons, other than those reserved for official purposes, escaped the shredding machines, as coupons were reported to have surfaced at the weekly flea market held at the Rocky Mountain Greyhound Park dog track, only an hour's drive north of the Pueblo Army Depot.

AFTER THE MODEL-T CAME THE HENRY FORD DOLLAR!

Great automakers have a tendency to see the nation as a machine in need of a tune-up—the country's financial carburetor subject to tinker. Lee Iacocca today, Henry Ford yesterday, both looked to monetary fine tuning as the answer to deficit misfire. Mr. Iacocca suggested adding a surtax to the overseas fuel line energizing American industry; Mr. Ford advocated eliminating the deficits by creating an energy-based currency to finance government-sponsored projects. Muscle Shoals was an example.

It was December, three weeks to Christmas day 1921. Henry Ford, and friend Thomas Edison, had been invited to Florence, Alabama for a three-day inspection tour of Muscle Shoals' nitrate and water power projects. Ford toyed with the idea of running the great power plant under contract for the government. Completed in 1918 to aid in the production of explosives for World War I, the plant and its workers faced postwar idleness. Henry Ford was never a man to disappoint—admirers always found something to cheer; detractors were equally fast to fault. Muscle Shoals was not to be an exception.

Thousands turned out to meet the industrial legend. Crowds began gathering hours before Ford was scheduled to arrive. When he did, Ford made the wait worthwhile, for he had a most unusual proposal to make. He would not only save their jobs, but his plan encompassed the means to fund government projects, including Muscle Shoals, at no expense to the taxpayer. Ford's cure-all would even bring an end to war. The answer was so elementary to Ford that he wondered why others before him had not thought of it. Issue a new currency!

"From the operation of this plant," Ford told his audience, "many great things are possible—greater power production than this country has ever known, greater motor production, the production of aluminum and nitrates in quantities which will make undreamed of changes in many industrial fields and in American farming. But, as far as

I am concerned," said Ford, "all those things are incidental. The one big thing I see in Muscle Shoals is an opportunity to eliminate war from the world."

It was no secret that Henry Ford was hell-bent to end wars. But how, the crowd must have wondered, could a plant designed to produce explosives insure peace without self-destructing? Ford sensed their query. He continued, "The cause of all wars is gold! We shall demonstrate to the world through Muscle Shoals, first the practicability, second the desirability of displacing gold as the basis for currency and substituting in its place the world's imperishable natural wealth. There is profit in war. It is a money profit, profits in gold. Just gold, that is the one and only reason for wars." said Ford. A reporter questioned him, "What, would you destroy all the gold in the world and prohibit mining more?"

"No," the industrialist responded, but without any signs of irritation. Ford went on to say that gold had its place, in the arts primarily, and for certain industrial uses. But Ford believed that gold, through its scarcity, had acquired a fictitious premium far beyond its value as a useful metal. "The people of the world made a mistake which has cost them generations of financial slavery when they consented to making gold a basis for the issuance of currency. They failed to see that, because gold is scarce, its total supply can be controlled—can be got under the dominion of one interest or group of interests. . . and that is exactly what has happened," said Ford.

The automaker believed that a consortium of international bankers controlled the bulk of the world's gold supply, and having gained control of the world's gold, found it to be a heavy burden. "Hoarded gold earns nothing," said Ford. They (the bankers) must keep it turning, making a profit, or lose its control. Peacetime, with stable conditions, does not turn it fast enough. The way to make it work hard and often is to create a demand for it in loans, but always as a currency in lieu of gold."

While many wondered where Ford's dissertation was taking them, they listened patiently. "The essential evil of gold, in its relation to war, is the fact that it can be controlled. Break the control," advised Ford, "and you stop war and the only way to break the control is to smash gold as a basis for currency."

Sensing a touch of impatience, Ford came to the point. "That's just where Muscle Shoals comes in." His audience straightened. They would be the genesis for eternal peace. "Army engineers," noted Ford, "say that it will take $40 million to complete the big dam. But Congress is economical just now and not in a mood to raise the money by taxation. The customary alternative is 30-year bonds at 4%. The United States, the greatest government in the world, wishing $40 million to complete a great public benefit is forced to go to the money sellers to buy its own money. At the end of 30 years, the government has not only paid back the $40 million, but it has to pay $88 million more for the use of the $40 million."

The automaker-cum-economist continued, "Now, I see a way by which our government can get this great work completed without paying a nickel. The government needs $40 million. That is two million $20 bills. Let the government issue those bills and with them pay every expense connected with the completion of the dam. Then retire the bills out of the earnings of the plant."

And to the doubters in the audience, if there were any, Ford planned to back his currency with energy. "The standard American dollar is approximately one-twentieth of an ounce of gold. Under the new currency system a certain amount of energy exerted for one hour would be equal to one dollar. Here we have a river capable of furnishing one million horsepower. It has been here for, say, 100 million years. It will be here as long as there is rain and mountains to shed the rain into rivers. This energy is wealth in a productive form. Now, which is the more secure—this power site and its development, or the several barrels of gold necessary to make $40 million? This site, with its power possibilities, will be here long after the Treasury Building is a ruin."

Many people thought they recognized the genius of Henry Ford that day. Perhaps they wanted to. As Ford talked, Thomas Edison daydreamed. The inventor mentally sketched the designs for this new currency. On the last day of their three-day visit, it was Edison's turn to face the press at Florence. "Now, here is Ford proposing to finance Muscle Shoals by an issue of currency. Very well, let us suppose for a moment that Congress follows his proposal. Personally, I don't think Congress has imagination enough to do it, but let us suppose that it does. The required sum is authorized, the bills are issued directly by the government, as all money ought to be. When the workmen are paid off they receive these United States bills. When the material is bought, it is paid in these bills. Except that perhaps these bills may have the engraving of a water dam, instead of a railroad train and a ship, as some Federal Reserve notes have. They will be the same as any other currency put out by the government: that is, they will be money. They will be based on the public wealth already in Muscle Shoals."

Thomas Edison's fertile mind easily recognized Ford's perpetual motion funding plan. "When these bills have answered the purpose of building and completing Muscle Shoals, they will be retired by the earnings of the power dam. That is, the people of the United States will have all that they put into Muscle Shoals and all that they can take out for centuries—the endless wealth-making water power of that great Tennessee River—with no tax and no increase of the national debt."

The earliest known record of the great shoals in northwest Alabama date to 1793, when the explorer William Tatham, on assignment to the governor of Virginia, reported it as, "nature's masterpiece for an immense and powerful city." But for generations Muscle Shoals was more an obstacle than an asset. In 1824, Secretary of War John C. Calhoun sent a report to President James Monroe recommending improvement of the river at Muscle Shoals. Plans were drawn up, and between 1831 and 1836 a canal with 17 locks was built. Just prior to World War I, the need for nitrate as a component used in the manufacture of explosives was recognized. Under the authority of the National Defense Act of 1916, President Wilson authorized construction of what is now Wilson Dam and hydroelectric power plant, and two nitrate plants. By war's end, 18,000 workers were on site and a formidable city was built to house and maintain these workers. The completion of construction coincided with the cessation of hostilities and the plant units were destined to be mothballed. Henry Ford had a plan to lease, then operate the plants under contract for the government. Realizing that Congress was in an economy mood, Ford's plan entailed self-funding for Muscle Shoals through his energy currency plan. The idea to end wars forever was a fringe benefit of his Muscle Shoals management.

Within days of Henry Ford's visit to the plant sites in Alabama, a National Honest Money Association was formed. North Dakota Senator Ladd called for a monetary conference to discuss agricultural relief through the issuance of a national currency as proposed by Henry Ford. While not supporting Ford, the *New York Times* closed an editorial with, "Still, the 'energy dollar' is likely enough to be made the basis of a new currency system proposed by the agricultural bloc in the House." Others were not so kind. H. Parker Willis, director of the Division of Analysis and Research of the Federal Reserve Bank, described the plan as "old, like a good many of Ford's ideas." Samuel Untermyer, former counsel for the House Banking and Currency Committee, was even more outspoken. He called Ford a "madhatter."

Many, however, took to Ford's ideas. Who wanted to argue against permanent peace? Who wanted to argue for deficit spending or increased unemployment? And, in uneasy comparison to the present, the automaker-for-president clubs sprang up across the country, but Ford's efforts were for naught. He chose to support the next Republican nominee for president, Calvin Coolidge, rather than run himself and, in time, dropped his plans to manage Muscle Shoals, along with a currency whose time may yet to be.

CANADA SAVES THE WHALES BY CHANGING THE SCENE

Was the decision to change the reverse designs of Canada's two-dollar bill a victory for Greenpeace in the ecological war to save the whale?

The year 1986 was to be a landmark year, the year when the International Whaling Commission's worldwide moratorium was to keep the whaling fleets in port. "The year," said a Greenpeace spokesperson, "of letting whales be, of benign study, of strict conservation—a cessation of hostilities that would mark a new beginning for these intelligent and endangered species."

If the removal of the scene depicting Eskimo whalers preparing for the hunt was, in part, due to the influence of the moratorium, it was a small victory in a year marked by major defeats. Several nations, Iceland, Japan, Norway, Russia, and South Korea included, opted to ignore or postpone participation in the moratorium. Even the United States turned its back on those dedicated to save the whales when the Supreme Court ruled that the president did not have to impose economic sanctions legislated by Congress against violators of the moratorium.

The Canadian currency note bearing the whaling scene is a relatively new design, having been introduced 11 years ago, in 1975. The money design had been adapted from a news photo shot several years earlier, on Baffin Island, of an Eskimo crew about to launch a kayak to hunt whales. Spokesperson Joyce McLean commented that while Greenpeace did not have a direct effect on the removal of the scene, changing Canadian attitudes, affected by the Greenpeace policy regarding whales, certainly contributed. "I am happy to see the Bank of Canada

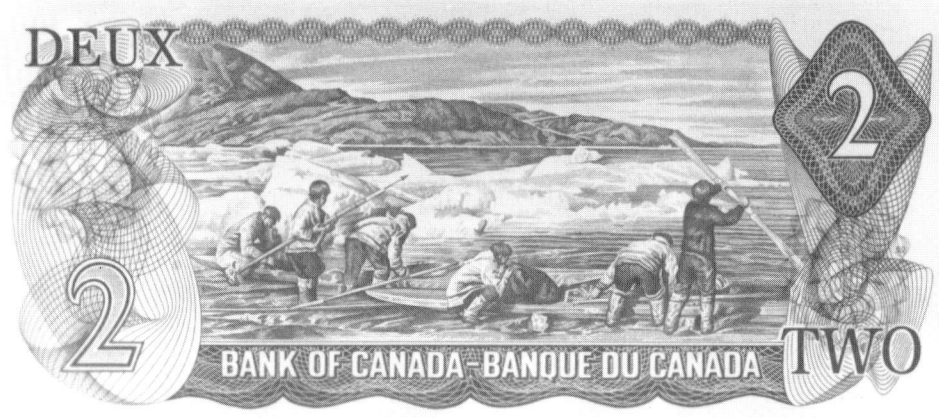

The whale hunting scene on the reverse of the Canadian $2 bill has given way to a more ecologically secure robin.

move away from scenes of resource exploitation and move toward scenes of natural beauty or animals in the wild," she added. The replacement bills depict a robin.

Bank of Canada notes date from 1935, the year following the bank's authorization to be solely responsible for the management of all Canadian paper money in circulation. The first currency consisted of two separate series, one in English, the other in French. Two years later, in 1937, the bank turned to bilingual notes as an economy measure. By 1969, counterfeiting of Canadian currency reached such proportions that the bank turned to more extensive use of color and deeper engravings, giving the notes a special "feel." The whaling scene on the $2 bill was printed in a basic terra cotta color. Other denominations ranged from blue to bright red in color. Of the current designs now in circulation, the $2 bill being replaced was the most recent issue. They were not placed in circulation until 1975. There are no great rarities, but early issues of the two, with two-letter prefixes to the serial numbers, sell for double face value in crisp, New condition.

"Greenpeace," Ms. McLean emphasized, "has never opposed subsistence hunting of marine mammals or other animal species, provided their deaths do not form the basis of commercial enterprise." Perhaps the public relations specialists with the Bank of Canada felt the wrong message was being conveyed in this time of ecological awareness. But, whatever the reason, collectors now have a new note to add to their collections.

THE LAST OF THE BIG BUCKS

The news release was straight to the point, "Treasury officials admit that dollar coin and $2 bill fail to win public approval. Bureau of Engraving and Printing facilities being monopolized by production of $1 bills!"

The story has a familiar ring. After all, we recall these words being bantered through the press not too many years ago. True, but the recent releases were mere echoes of similar plaints voiced more than 60 years ago.

In 1926 a traveler was likely to receive a standard-sized silver dollar in change only in the West and Southwest. In New England it would not be unusual to tender a $2 bill. Elsewhere in the country, though, both forms of currency were shunned.

The silver dollars were deemed too heavy, the cause for holes in men's pockets. The prejudice against $2 bills was attributed, then as now, to the ease with which it could be mistaken for and handed out as a one. It was a bum rap. No one ever gave a $20 bill in place of a $10!

Solutions to the problem, then and now, remain strikingly similar. In 1926 the Secretary of the Treasury announced a reduction in the size of the paper dollar. In 1979, a half century later, Congress authorized the reduction in size of the dollar coin.

On July 10, 1929, new bills, one and one-half inches shorter and a half inch narrower, were placed into circulation. On July 2, 1979, eight days short of the 50th anniversary of new sized bills, the Treasury released a greatly reduced sized dollar coin. Both times, the Treasury heralded the action as a means of saving the country money.

Following World War I, rapid growth of both the economy and the population created an increasing demand for money. At the time paper money was manufactured through a tedious, more costly method known as "wet printing." The paper had to be kept damp and was hand fed into presses, one sheet at a time. If the dollars could be made to last longer, Treasury officials reasoned, demand on the production facilities at the Bureau of Engraving and Printing would ease. At the same time a reduction in the size of the notes would conserve millions of tons of high-grade, specially prepared currency paper.

The Treasury went so far as to forecast longer life for the new bills by pointing out that the need to fold only once rather than twice as with the old saddle blankets, promoted longevity. It was an illustration on par with the latter-day pitch through cartoons showing that a dropped small-sized dollar coin will fall to your feet, whereas a dollar bill is liable to blow away.

While the earlier solution offered no answer to the problem of the unacceptability of the $2 bill, the Federal Reserve did offer to support legislation to discontinue production of the $1 bill coincident with the introduction of the mini-sized dollar coin. It was an offer not accepted by the Carter Administration, although the Bureau of Engraving and Printing resumed production of the $2 bill. Most of these remain in government vaults along with the Susan B. Anthony mini-dollars the public refused to accept.

TOKENS AND MEDALS
HAVE TALES, TOO!

"COINS" OF THE ALASKA COMMUNE

A Token Reminder of the American Communist Experiment

The age of Utopian societies had passed, but some of Franklin Roosevelt's New Deal touched upon radical ideas. Not the least was FDR's Federal Emergency Relief Administration's (FERA) plan to transplant 200 farm families (approximately 1,000 people) from the depressed areas of Minnesota, Wisconsin and Michigan to Alaska and assist them in making a fresh new start.

Site of the pioneering government-run project was a 140,000 acre fertile valley called Matanuska, 35 miles from Anchorage. The unusual experiment of a government-sponsored commune was not without critics. Senator Arthur Vandenberg assailed the colonization plan as a "crazy experiment." The Michigan Republican called the idea, "an utterly untenable and ridiculous proposition." Many of the first settlers concurred.

In their rush to find a new and better life than rural America offered in 1935, the settlers overlooked their agreement to forego freedom of choice. Their contract with the government required that their crops be sold through a cooperative. They not only surrendered their right to choice of crop, but even the pricing and how to market the produce. Participants were expected to pay the costs of maintaining their commune from the profits of the cooperative. The communal system was planned to last for at least the 30 years allocated to repay the $3,000 assessed each family. In fact, Matanuska Valley Colony lasted for only three years, but the American experiment with communism was not without its successes.

Still, high expectations brought disappointment to both the colonists and their government planners. When the first contingents of settlers sailed from Seattle aboard the rusty old Army transport, *St. Mihiel,* they had hopefully left behind the memories of drought, dust storms, foreclosures and financial ruin. Bands played, crowds waved, as they sailed north from Seattle. At the time the settlers did not know that numbered among their fellow passengers were the very workers who were going to build the shelters they expected to be waiting for them on their arrival. And, little did these work-

No date appears on the tokens of the Alaska Rural Rehabilitation Corporation (ARRC), but the tokens were made and used in 1936. Issuance was discontinued when nearby localities started accepting them in lieu of cash.

ers realize that while the ship's hold contained the necessary lumber to build the shelters, someone had overlooked ordering tools. There were horses to pull the lumber, but no wagons to load the lumber on. Someone remembered that horses needed harnesses, but no one thought of collars to attach the harnesses to. An emergency requisition on arrival in Alaska for the necessary transportation was answered by a 5-ton shipment of paper towels.

The government theory of selecting hardy families of Scandinavian decent, for their eagerness to work and their being accustomed to cold climes, went awry when those doing the screening failed to recognize the Smiths and the Jones from the Swensons and Johansens. For the most part, however, the gala sendoff buoyed enough spirits for the majority to stick with the experiment.

Forty-acre lots were assigned by the luck of the draw. In the excitement of the moment, the settlers voted to rename Palmer to Valley City, but, like the commune idea, the name change was shortlived. It remains Palmer to this day.

One reason for the failure of the Matanuska colony experiment was bungling bureaucracy and government mismanagement bordering on corruption. In the rush to get underway, the settlers were shipped to Alaska before the most rudimentary preparations had been undertaken. The land had not been cleared, roads not built, hospitals and necessary services unavailable. The government's army of Civilian Conservation Corps volunteers, recruited from federal transient camps to build a temporary city of tents with board floors and walls, were paid room, board and $30 per month. Their pay was doled at the rate of $2 per week, the balance held in escrow to eliminate the danger "of their becoming dependents of the Territory." Disillusioned, the workers fell behind schedule. With the short Alaskan summer reaching an end, settlers panicked. One dissident group telegraphed Washington, "Six weeks passed. Nothing done. No houses, wells, roads. Inadequate machinery, tools, government food undelivered. Commissary prices exorbitant. Educational facilities for season doubtful. Apparently men sent to pick political plums." A former Michigander wrote to her hometown newspaper, "Pray for us, dear folks at home. We need the mighty hand of God in this undertaking."

While not all families feared doomsday, there was justified concern. Of the original 200 families, six quit early on. A federal investigator, Eugene Carr, substantiated their complaints, in particular those concerning the management of the commissary and the construction of adequate shelters. Carr's first act was to fire the commissary manager and give him 24 hours to quit the territory. He then took over the duties of resident manager.

The federal investigator found the commissary's accounting system in disarray. With little or no money available, the commune was without a circulating currency. All transactions were mere bookkeeping entries and debits. Carr found that prices were not only exorbitant, but that settlers were often charged for merchandise never purchased. He immediately started issuing sales slips with purchases. And, in the following year, 1936, he introduced a unique but unimaginatively designed currency for Matanuska Valley. It was as utilitarian as a coinage could be. Both sides were the same. The values were noted in Arabic numerals in the center and in words around the edge. The "coins" bore the initials of the official name of the community—ARRC—the Alaska Rural Rehabilitation Corporation. Denominations ranged from one cent to one dollar and included 5, 10, 25, and 50 cent pieces, all in aluminum. In addition there were 5 and 10 dollar coins in brass. With the exception of the one-cent piece, all the minor denominations matched circulating legal tender coins in size and shape. Since the one-cent piece was of the same color as the others and between the nickel and dime in size, it was struck on octagonal planchets.

Each family received a monthly allowance of the currency in return for service to the community, including payment for clearing one's own land. Although everything at the commissary was priced in dollars and cents, only tokens could be tendered. These soon became known as "bingles," from the name given them by the poker players of the community. When the special money gained acceptance in nearby Palmer, the government ceased their issue and the end of 1936 marked the end of this money for America's communist experiment.

Today a modern road connects the former commune to Anchorage. Many of the colony houses remain standing in various degrees of repair and disrepair, but there remains one common bond with all the farmsteads. The government had designed only one plan for their barns.

As a colony, Matanuska disbanded within a few years of its founding. More than two-thirds of the original settlers eventually returned to the Lower 48. Still, those that stayed became the backbone of the valley's farming community. Today, Matanuska provides the rest of Alaska with most of its milk, eggs and produce. An annual fair champions Bunyanesque vegetables: 15-lb. cauliflowers, 6-lb. heads of lettuce, 70-lb. pumpkins, 35-lb. squash, 24-lb. turnips. Prize winning celery stalks stand taller than a young boy and rhubarb grows to more than three inches around. The legacy of Matanuska is not one of failure, but of success. To Alaska it provides a major source of its produce; for the numismatist—an unusual series of collectibles.

THE GHOST OF PECK HOUSE

When the late William C. Henderson related his tales of the Old West, he seldom failed to spice his stories with little known anecdotes. To the citizens of our town—Colorado Springs—Bill was a man of varied talents and countless interests. On the local scene, he is best remembered as a former mayor and member of the city council. To the city's financial community, Bill was a founder and one-time president of the Pike's Peak National Bank. But, to us at ANA Headquarters, Bill was not only our treasurer, but an articulate and spellbinding raconteur of legends about the crusty, old individualists who helped settle the frontier that was to become the Rocky Mountain West.

Reminiscences bring to mind the time Bill learned of our plans to spend a Thanksgiving weekend at the Peck House in Empire, Colorado. My wife, Mary Ann, and I had picked it as the site of a brief vacation not because of James Peck, the man once known as the "Emperor of Empire," but because the place was billed as the "oldest hotel in continuous operation in Colorado." To have served so long in such competitive company boded well for the property. Besides, we were intrigued with the idea of adding our names to a guest register that boasted the likes of Ulysses S. Grant, Gen. William Tecumseh Sherman, not to mention Phineas T. Barnum.

Before leaving on our trip, Bill not only treated us to a history of the property, but admonished us to watch for the one guest not listed in the register nor mentioned in any promotional literature—the Ghost of Peck House!

James Peck arrived in the area 45 miles west of Denver in 1859. He needed little urging when the first word of gold in the Rockies reached his ears to quit the polluted climes of then-primitive Chicago and try his luck at a promising new endeavor. The death of his first wife, two infant sons and a little daughter, gave Peck all reason he needed to become one of the gold seekers heading west. He sold his profitable shipping business and joined the rush to the Rockies.

Dame Fortune smiled on James Peck. He had since remarried and started raising a new family. The former Chicago shipping magnate struck paydirt early on. He developed his claim on Silver Mountain into the Atlantic Mine, one of the finest and most fully developed in the district for the period. He helped found the town of Empire, a name that fit his ambitions well.

Peck built a cabin for his growing new family, then he helped build the first church in the district. Turning his attention to his home once again, Peck soon expanded his cabin into a four-room residence. Recognizing that nearby Union Pass could emerge as a major route west, Peck quickly added seven more rooms to attend to the needs of the anticipated traffic over the pass. Peck House opened to its first paying guest in 1862.

Peck remained in Empire for the rest of his life. Ore mills were added to his mine holdings, as well as a general store and a post office. James Peck soon became known as the "Emperor of Empire." Most of his family stayed, too. But, Dame Fortune did not always smile on the man from Empire. James Peck was killed when he fell from his buggy one day in 1880. The operation of Peck House passed to his son, Frank and then tragedy struck again.

In 1885, Gracie Peck, granddaughter of James, succumbed to ravages of tuberculosis. She was just 14 years old. Although Gracie was laid to rest in Denver's Riverside Cemetery, her ghost returned to Empire and to this day is believed to roam the house that she never wanted to leave.

But the Ghost of Peck House is not the only fantasy willed to us of present time. A century after the opening of the hostelry, eight decades after the death of James Peck, a charlatan of the present concocted a series of tokens alleged to have come from James Peck's Empire. The series comprises three denominations, each in two metals, six tokens in all. Marked "Colorado Gold'" on the reverse, these pieces, as far as is known, are fabricated in brass and copper only. The tokens have been marketed to collectors in face values of $2½, $5 and $10 and bear the identification "Empire City Mine/1876/Empire, Colorado." While there was an Empire City Mine, no records substantiate the issuance of any tokens.

Did we meet the Ghost of Peck House? I believe that we came as close as anyone can come to meeting a ghost—face to face. Sleep did not come easily at the hotel. Not for fear of the unknown, but for the mere fact that while the property has been restored several times over the years, the mattresses appear to be originals. Unable to sleep, I tossed and turned that Thanks-

giving night. The bright moonlight lit the room with an eerie pallor. Then I noticed the doorknob turning ever so slowly. Curiosity overcame fear and I jumped up, opened the door, and found myself face to face with someone looking for the restroom down the hall!

FIRST THE COINS, NOW THE STICKS!

When Tennyson wrote, "So sad, so fresh, the days that are no more," he never guessed that some might use his words in eulogy to the passing of the twin-sticked Popsicle. We have lost another reminder of the days we called childhood. A recent announcement by Popsicle Industries that it is phasing out the twin-sticked Popsicle in deference to mothers' wishes for a smaller-sized, bullet-shaped, single-stick confection reminds us of the evolution of the summertime treat.

Like many of the great creations of the past, Popsicle's entry into the product world was strictly by accident. It happened in New Jersey in 1923. Frank Epperson, a traveling lemonade salesman from Oakland, California, was on a sales blitz of the East Coast. On a cold winter evening, Epperson unthinkingly left a glass of lemonade on his hotel room windowsill overnight. By morning he found that the New Jersey night air had frozen the lemonade around the spoon left in the glass. Voila—an "Epsicle!"

Epperson patented his "Epsicle," and, during the following year sold the patent to the Joe Lowe Corporation, a food-processing company. The name was soon changed to the more palatable "Popsicle." During the great Depression, the twin-stick variety was introduced. "The company thought it could win over customers by selling the treat for a nickel and saying it could be split with a friend," noted Paul Kadin, Popsicle's current marketing director.

There were other sales stimuli—the company pioneered "instant winner" games with premiums dispensed by local vendors on "proof" of winning. Luck came on the stick. Random imprints indicated the prizes won—a toy, a whistle, a piece of costume jewelry, even a coin!

The "coin" was one of a series of small aluminum, quarter-sized medals depicting the famous movie stars of the day, and were adapted from designs by Adam Pietz. The artist was an engraver with the United States Mint at Philadelphia at the time. Pietz is best known to coin collectors for his design of the Iowa Centennial commemorative half dollar. However, in the field of medallic art, Pietz earned recognition for his

A typical Popsicle game prize from the 1930s.

portrait medals, including a commissioned series featuring prominent movie actors and actresses. Pietz was a prolific artist but unfortunately kept so few records that collectors today fail to realize that some innocuous premiums of yesteryear are the work of a former assistant chief engraver of the United States Mint, a designer of a commemorative half dollar and one whose designs for the Jefferson nickel and Washington quarter were considered, though not used.

Popsicle premiums ceased, we are told, in the name of economy. We suspect otherwise, that too many young friendships were temporarily strained when generous youngsters went "halvsies" with playmates and found that they had given the newest acquisition to their coin collection away. All is not lost to history, though. One can still buy twin-sticked Popsicles at convenience stores, amusement parks and from bike-carts, but not from grocery stores. And, the premium pieces of one's childhood recall can still be found in coin dealer junk boxes, but those giveaways no longer come free with the Popsicle, even at today inflated prices.

LUCKY CENTS GAVE BIRTH TO A MAJOR INDUSTRY

While Joseph Koenig practiced thrift, he intentionally overlooked his maxim "Keep Me and Never Go Broke." While he placed the motto on the aluminum novelty rings for the encased cents he manufactured, Koenig's ambition in life was far greater than to be recognized as the "Father of the Lucky Cent."

Joseph Koenig inherited the work ethic of his Old World German parents. When the elder Koenig died in the 1860s, pre-teenaged Joseph helped his mother gather up the Koenig brood of nine siblings to cross the Atlantic and half the United States and settle in Two Rivers, Wisconsin.

Life in the small community, 175 miles north of Chicago, offered so little to satisfy the youngster's imagination and ambitions that by the time he was 15 Koenig was off the see that part of the world contained within the American Midwest.

Beginning as an itinerant painter and decorator Koenig soon became a factory manager, then turned to land speculation before accepting positions as teacher and lawyer. His big break in life, however, came with the World's Columbian Exposition in Chicago.

In 1892 Koenig accepted an offer to be the legal representative of a German aluminum novelty manufacturer exhibiting at the fair. When the show closed in October 1893 he purchased the remaining merchandise and exhibited at other fairs. When Koenig found that he had sold every single item, and made a profit in the process, he knew the direction of his future.

Aluminum was still a novelty metal at the turn of the last century. Fifty years earlier its price exceeded that of silver or gold. It was so rare that King Christian X of Denmark ordered a crown made of the magical metal. Napoleon commissioned an aluminum watch chain to be made for presentation to the King of Siam as a gesture of goodwill and esteem. It was not until 1886, with the discovery of an electrochemical process, that the cost of producing aluminum dropped drastically enough to make it commercially feasible. Still, its use remained minimal and the metal was used primarily for novelty items like medals, tokens, encased cents, and pocket combs.

Koenig saw that his golden opportunity rested with silver colored aluminum. Returning home to Two Rivers, he opened his first plant in a small back room of the Hollywood Type Company. His first two products were encased cents and combs.

He made the latter one at a time, sawing each tooth individually. The costly process made importing them far cheaper than making them in the U.S.

But, Koenig experimented. First he devised a gang saw but that heated the comb to such temperatures that the metal warped. He then invented a rotary drum so successful that his combs were soon selling for only a few cents each.

Next, Koenig added key tags, medals, tokens, salt and pepper shakers, cigar cases, mustache cups, and ash trays to his line of combs and "lucky" cents. By 1895, he found that a two hour sales spiel in Chicago netted more in orders than he could produce in three months.

By mid-1895, Koeing knew that it would be necessary to expand his facilities. In need of capital, the Bank of Two Rivers magnanimously loaned Koenig $500 on the condition that the owners of the bank received a half interest in the company and that Koenig's half be paid out of earnings. But, as conservative as the bank was, the town council of Two Rivers was just the opposite. Recognizing the company's potential, the council voted to approve a $2,000 expenditure on condition that the company would not move from the city. Two Rivers was one of the first cities in the country to recognize the value of economic development incentives to attract industry.

Koenig may have been a great innovator, but a congenial boss he was not. He often quarreled with his best two tool and die makers, Herman Schwab and Henry Meishner. One day he invited them to take a walk. They did—for the seven miles it took them to get to Manitowoc to start their own business.

Koenig's open door policy soon became a ritual. He would fire an employee and a new competitor would soon be in business. Eventually, the whole of the Manitowoc Valley, between Lake Winnebago and Lake Michigan, bustled with Koenig-trained aluminum novelty manufacturing companies. Most included encased cents in their product line.

The banking panic of 1907 killed the market for nonessentials. The price of aluminum novelties dropped to a point where most of the companies faced bankruptcy. In self-preservation moves, several merged and names like Mirro, West Bend, Leyse, and Wear-Ever emerged. Realizing that novelties could no longer sustain their industry, more essential products had to be considered. Pots and pans for example.

In 1913, Mirro, a firm that included Koenig's original company, began the manufacture of cookware adapting the same procedures used to stamp novelties. Their first major order was from the Quaker Oats Company, to produce a pan called "a double boiler." It was to be used as a premium in a national advertising campaign.

West Bend landed Sears Roebuck and Company as their prime customer and soon the Chicago-based mail order house accounted for more than half the company's production.

F. W. Woolworth asked Koenig to build a separate plant to make pots and pans for his stores. Ever cantankerous, Koenig refused. He offered instead a "special department." Woolworth said, "no," and another of the old German's employees added "former" to his job description. He built a competing plant at Chilton to make aluminum pots and pans solely for the nickel and dime emporium.

By 1920, every other aluminum pot and pan found in an American kitchen had been made in the Manitowoc Valley of Wisconsin. The whole industry owed its existence to one man—Joseph Koenig, the man who decided not to continue making "Keep Me and Never Go Broke" encased cents, but to make aluminum pots and pans instead and become "very rich," instead.

IN SEARCH FOR THE TRUTH (ABOUT SOME "OLD" TOKENS)!

I never thought that I would find myself visiting a house of ill-repute. However, on occasions, inhibitions must be shunted aside while in pursuit of a story, especially if it is in the name of numismatics!

It was too late to ask Dirty Neck Nell, Bilious Bessie, or the madame, Pearl De Vere, if tokens had ever been used in lieu of cash. The infamous painted ladies were long gone. Questions, instead, had to be directed to Phyl and Vic Heyliger. Neither could answer from first-hand knowledge.

As a bawdy house, the doors of the Old Homestead have been closed to clientele for a half century. Once the classiest bordello in Colorado's greatest gold camp—Cripple Creek—the house welcomes guests today only as visitors to the country's sole parlor house museum. The Heyligers operate it, along with Harold and Lodi Hern.

The Old Homestead is one of the few buildings still standing on East Myers Avenue, once the glittering midway through the city's lusty red-light district. For a while, the street bore another name.

During the twilight years of mining activity, *Collier's* magazine writer, Julian Street, visited. Town fathers, hoping for a favorable review, hosted and toasted the author, but he repaid their kindness with a blistering condemnation of the town and its citizens. The town fathers fallaciously reciprocated in kind and renamed the thoroughfare through the red-light district Julian Street, in his honor. The name stuck for as long as the hurt remained. But, today, the name reverts back to the original Myers Avenue, so named for one of the town founders.

The doors closed on the Old Homestead not for any change in mores or morals. The gold mines of the area played out and shut down. Both entertainee and entertainer moved on.

While the feminine tenants of the place have long since departed, the furnishings remain. From the front desk, where visitors once made their appointments, one can now see the three parlors where the ladies of the house displayed and bargained their wares—for cash, sometimes gold nuggets or dust—but never for tokens, we are told.

The Old Homestead, once one of the West's classiest, now welcomes visitors to the only museum of its type in the country.

Today, mannequins, dressed in the finery of the past, have replaced their flesh and blood sisters, but their hearts remain just as hard and cold.

One of the parlors boasts a grand piano and an old Edison talking machine, complete with its huge "morning glory" speaker. The Old Homestead was a class operation, and there was entertainment while being entertained. The museum has a large collection of antique bottles and old glass displayed on an antique but ornate etagere, but nowhere are there any tokens to be seen.

What of those brass checks we see pandered at flea markets, souvenir stores, and even under-the-counter by some who like to play alchemist by turning cheap brass disks into solid cash tokens?

Most, if not all of the larger-than-a-silver dollar sized brass checks are latter-day fantasies designed to titillate the imagination of the purchaser and turn an eight-cent investment in the cost of manufacture into a several dollar sale for the benefit of the wallet.

Genesis for the flood of brass checks led to a former Denver resident, now deceased, who reveled in the bawdy tales of the Old West.

On one occasion, we find, he had two different versions of one madame's card made. One variety was a giveaway, a conversation piece, its spurious origins readily admitted to. The other, however, was for show. Its pedigree never mentioned. Seldom was it offered for sale. But, it has been said that more than one prominent collector paid upwards of $30 for a specimen of the alleged "original."

Many of the brass checks were manufactured in Denver. The firm remains in business today, but its old original Larimer Square area location has long since given way to urban renewal. The company delivered the tokens, bright and shiny, to those who ordered in quantity. Most had "years of service" added to their surfaces shortly thereafter, aged with the help of blow torches or chemicals, before finding their way to the souvenir counters of junk stores, tables at flea markets, or behind the bourse of a few dealers.

So, if you are ever offered such a token, bear in mind that it may not be as old as the profession.

A HA'PENNY'S WORTH OF PROTEST!

Psychiatrists often like to play word games with their patients. Word association, as it is called in layman's terms, gives the doctors the opportunity to analyze their patients by responses based on the first thoughts that come to mind when given a specific word. But no one's sanity can be tested with, "April 15th!" The universal answer is—"income tax." Well, it is now April. It is deadline time for tax returns and time for another article. Perhaps we can combine the two.

The Legend of Lady Godiva is one story that comes to mind. It has been told that the fair lady of Coventry so nagged her husband, Leofric, Earl of Mercia, over his oppressive taxes, that he agreed to meet Godiva's plea for lower assessments if she would ride naked through the streets of Coventry. This titillating legend has not only given us the tale of Lady Godiva's ride, but an annual re-enactment at the Coventry Fair, an expensive brand of chocolates, another tale about "Peeping Tom," and a trade coin depicting Godiva in the nude. The coin carries the inscription, "For the Public Good."

During the late 18th and early 19th centuries, England experienced chronic shortages of small coin. In order to do business, merchants often resorted to having their own coins made. This private token coinage consisted of bronze or copper farthings, halfpennies and pennies, and there were a few silver shillings made, too. Naturally, the merchants added their names, both for identification and for purposes of advertising. In Coventry, from 1792 through 1795, the ribbon-making firm of Robert Reynolds and Company chose the Godiva story from the town's history and issued halfpenny tokens bearing, or baring, the figure of Godiva astride her horse. She was featured as legend remembered her.

There was a real Godiva, but her name was Godgifu. History tells that in the year 1043 she founded the monastery at Coventry. History, however, fails to substantiate the charge that her husband taxed his subjects unmercifully. It is believed that at the time no taxes were levied, save those on horses. The earliest mention of Godiva's ride is to be found in chronicles written more than 200 years after the event was supposed to have taken place. And, it was another 300 years before the story of modesty dictating that the townspeople shutter their windows on the morning of Godiva's ride was added. Then, in the 17th century the tale was further embellished by the introduction of "Peeping Tom." Godiva's horse whinied, it was said, and Citizen Tom peeked. In just retribution for this indiscretion, Tom immediately went blind.

The Coventry Fair dates from the year 1218 with the granting of a royal charter by King Henry III, but the fair's Godiva ride dates from 1678 and continued through 1826, when it was discontinued in the name of propriety. With the passing of the Victorian period and in recognition of present day mores, the ride has been revived in recent times and is once again the highlight of the fair. While Britons are sticklers for historical accuracy, even though this tale is more legend than fact, the young lady chosen to ride as Godiva must wear a body stocking. If her tresses are not of sufficient length to satisfy British modesty, a wig must be worn.

As noted, the tokens of Robert Reynolds were issued between 1792 and 1795, but there is a much rarer Coventry halfpenny. It was issued in 1797. The story of this token is equally intriguing and relates to the ride of Lady Godiva. The token was designed by Robert Sharpe and depicts a personification of Industry on one side. On the other side of the coin stands a Georgian house. You need a magnifying glass to see him, but there is a man peeking from a niche. The figure is supposed to represent the unfortunate tailor blinded by Godiva's nakedness. Thomas Sharpe depicted his own home, for the story goes that he was born in Peeping Tom's house on

Long before taxes took one's shirt off one's back, a young lady shed hers on behalf of others.

Smithford Street in Coventry, on November 7, 1770. The 27-year old Sharpe, a coin collector, had 48 coins made. These today remain very expensive and very elusive specimens to obtain for one's collection. The earlier Godiva tokens command more modest premiums, not because of their scarcity, but for their demand by American collectors who would very much like a peek of their own.

ADVERTISING GOES TO THE DOGS!

Every age has its dog! Current honors for Canine of the Year go to Spuds McKenzie, Anheuser-Busch's promulgator of Budweiser beer. Elmer the Wonderdog had his day barking for Diet Coke. And, in years past, advertising moguls gave the likes of Tighe to Buster Brown and Bingo to Sailor Jack, the Cracker Jack kid.

Currency buffs can identify a number of the hounds on obsolete currency, but the best known canine publicist was a listener, or so we are told, waiting to hear his master's voice. That was RCA Victor's Nipper. Of mixed breed, with recognizable traces of bull terrier, Nipper really listened for, but not to, his master's voice. And, as long as we are correcting popular misconceptions, the talking machine Nipper originally posed by was neither a Victor nor the parent company's Gramophone. Nipper was partial to the competition, he cocked his head for an Edison talking machine. Incidentally, Nipper was English, not American.

The early day canine huckster was born in 1884. Adopted as a very young pup, Nipper became the companion of a scenery painter working at the old Princess Theatre in the English seaport town of Bristol. Nipper's acting career started at an early age. He gained local recognition for his walk-on parts at the old Princess, trotting on stage with his master whenever the scenic artistry merited a curtain call. The pooch loved the applause. When the scenery painter died, Nipper was adopted by his late master's two brothers—Philip and Francis Barraud. The two were professional photographers and operated a small studio in Liverpool. Philip was fond of fine music and Francis had a penchant for painting during his spare hours.

Whenever Philip put a record on the phonograph, the dog would jump up and listen to it. The Barraud's theorized

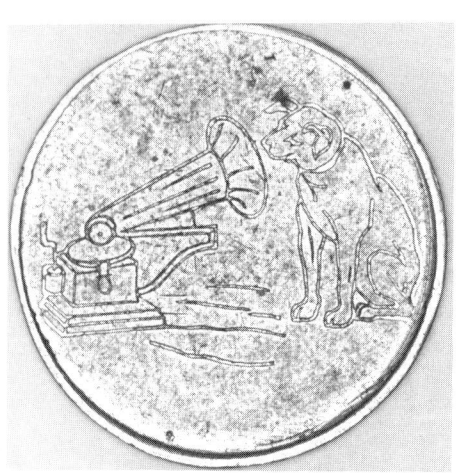 

A French jeton is one of the few numismatic items to portray what is probably the world's most enduring advertising canine.

that Nipper may have been hoping to hear their late brother's voice. They surmised that the sound of music evoked recall of the dog's theatrical days. Francis, the more commercial of the two, sensed a commercial value to the scene of a dog listening to a phonograph. He captured the dog's faithful pose on canvas and then showed it to the distributors of Edison phonographs. The result may explain why the Edison name is no longer seen on musical reproduction equipment. They were not interested.

Disappointed, Francis Barraud hung the painting in the photographic studio. Customers looked and smiled and thought it was cute. Then, one day, a customer suggested a slight change. Why not make the horn larger? Perhaps, the customer went on, Barraud should look at one of the new Gramophones, recently introduced in Liverpool. Francis Barraud took the painting down, wrapped it, and called on William Owen, district manager for the Gramophone Company. The rest is what history is made of.

Owen was more than willing just to loan a new instrument, he insisted on buying the painting, on condition that Barraud remove the Edison name and replace it with the Gramophone label. The painter readily agreed. The year was 1899, but the pooch was not able to take any bows. Nipper had passed away four years earlier.

For the next 25 years, Francis Barraud was to enjoy the recognition that came with the creation of an advertising masterpiece. Until he died in 1924, Barraud was busy earning a comfortable living painting reproductions of the original.

Even though Nipper's portait began appearing in 1909, on millions of labels, album covers, advertisements, signs, and papier mache models, it was not for another two decades, not until 1929, that he officially became the RCA trademark. In the meantime, coin collectors were treated to an unusual addition for their collections. A small, nickel-sized token, engraved with Nipper on one side and a store card on the other, appeared. Regrettably, it was issued neither in England nor in America, but in France. Here, nickelodeons worked to one-franc pieces. Smart merchants drummed new releases by giving customers a token for a sample listen.

The greatest recognition, though, came not in the form of tokens, scrip, or even in papier mache models. There is a bronze plaque to Nipper's memory on the front of an English bank building, built on the site of an old Mulberry tree where Nipper often stopped to answer a call of a different nature.

THE TOKEN ISSUES OF THE RADIO PRIEST

Modern-day evangelists appreciate television as a prime means of building huge followings, but even the former Nielsen ratings of Jerry Falwell and Jimmy Swaggert pale in comparison to those of the one who pioneered the broadcast pulpit. More than 50 years ago the "Radio Priest," Reverend Charles E. Coughlin, boasted a listening audience of more than 40 million faithful, at a time when the total population of the U.S. was half what it is today.

Originally, Father Coughlin used the airwaves to reach the religiously faithful and to focus attention on his small, financially troubled Shrine of the Little Flower in the suburban Detroit community of Royal Oak, Michigan. Coughlin soon abandoned his parochial teachings, turning instead to a social-economic program of his own design, one that "guaranteed to solve the financial ills of the Great Depression."

An ardent supporter of Franklin Roosevelt in the 1932 presidential campaign, Father Coughlin became disillusioned with the New Deal and by 1936 had formed his own political force—the Union Party. Counting every adult listener as a potential vote, Coughlin spearheaded the nomination of Rep.

William Lemke of North Dakota to be his party's 1936 presidential candidate.

The Radio Priest promised his listeners, "If I cannot swing at least nine million votes to Mr. Lemke, I will quit broadcasting." Lemke polled no more than 891,858 votes, but Father Coughlin went right on broadcasting. But Coughlin did do something different, however, he turned to numismatics as a new way to raise funds for his Shrine of the Little Flower. He commissioned the striking of a medallic, silver dollar-sized piece to present to donors in recognition of their radio response donations.

The Royal Oak shrine was as much a memorial to the Coughlin family as it was to its patroness, St. Therese Martin, the "Little Flower of Lisieux." While Father Coughlin claimed to have been inspired by the young girl's desire to be a missionary and named his church after her, he dedicated its four main entrances to his family. The northwest entrance was reserved in memory of his mother, Mrs. T.J. Coughlin; the southeast portal memorializes his father; the southwest is dedicated to the memory of a sister who died at an early age; and for himself, he reserved the northeast entrance.

While promising to remove from his listeners' hearts "the roots of prejudice," Father Coughlin failed to ignore his own. His radio talks became increasingly stained with anti-Semitism. Accused of being pro-Nazi, his ecclesiastical superiors banned him from further radio talks. In 1942 the U.S. government charged Coughlin with "giving aid and comfort to the enemy." The Post Office revoked the mailing privileges for his magazine, *Social Justice,* and the Radio Priest was effectively silenced.

In 1966, a second numismatic issue was prepared portraying Father Coughlin and recognizing his 50th anniversary of ordination to the priesthood. The pioneer of the airwaves lived on in quiet retirement for another 13 years, passing away two days after his 88th birthday, in 1979. Time has thinned the ranks of his loyal followers and tempered the memory of his radical broadcasts, but two medallic issues remain, reminders of the power of the pulpits of the air.

One of the Rev. Charles E. Coughlin's tokens.

WHEN BAKED BEANS WERE IN BAD TASTE!

The medals committee for the 57th anniversary convention of the American Numismatic Association can be forgiven for choosing the outline of a bean pot for the 1948 convention badge. Boston is, after all, the ubiquitous Bean Town of America. Boston baked beans are an inheritance from colonial days, a way of life in the Bay State. But, there was a time, less than a generation prior to the meeting, when Boston baked beans were held to be in bad taste. It all had to do with molasses!

In the days of Puritan Boston, the Sabbath lasted from sundown Saturday until sundown Sunday. Work was not to be performed and baked beans were the answer to not disturbing the time of prayer with mundane labor of the kitchen.

Beans could be kept warm over the slow heat of the fireplace and served both as Saturday night supper and Sunday morning breakfast. If the family was large or the chores many, the local baker called for the family pot on Saturday to bake the beans in a communal oven and return them in time for supper, along with a brown bread or two.

Saturday night baked beans were still a tradition when the ANA met in Boston, August 21-25, 1948. But it was not a tradition without a break. There was a time when the smell of molasses did not mean beans baking in the pot.

If one were to list all horrible plots of the Class B horror movies, you would not find one so chimerical as the Great Molasses Deluge. Imagine, if you can, a 15-foot tidal wave of molasses engulfing a city, destroying buildings and drowning people in its gooey wake. It happened in Boston on January 15, 1919.

It was 20 minutes after the hour of noon. The day was mild for mid-January, close to 40 degrees Fahrenheit. What snow had been on the ground was gone. Molasses in Boston had two main purposes—the making of rum and the flavoring of baked beans. True Boston baked beans are one part molasses for every six parts beans.

Ratification of the 18th Amendment—Prohibition—was still 24 hours into the future. So the principal use of molasses was still legitimate on that day.

There stood within sight of *USS Constitution*—"Old Ironsides"—a huge steel-sided, five-story tall, 90-foot diameter, concrete-based storage tank. It had been built by the Purity Distilling Company in 1915 and sold two years later to the United States Industrial Alcohol

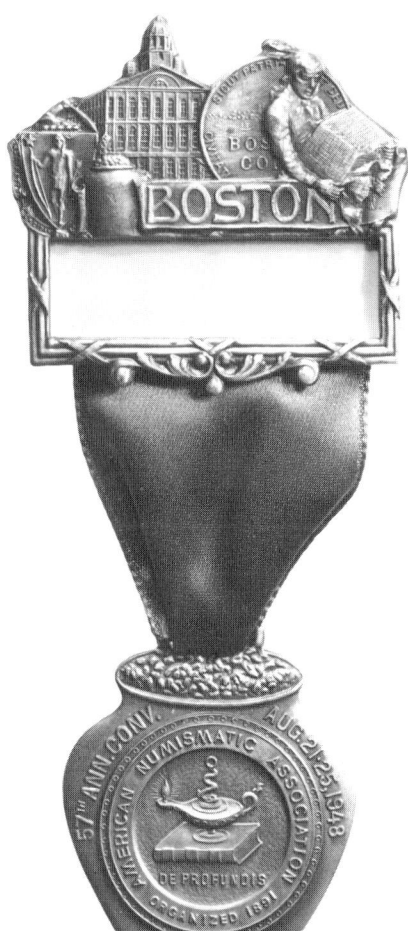

The badge for the 1948 American Numismatic Association convention featured a pot of Boston baked beans.

Company. On the previous afternoon, the tank had been filled, topped with almost 2.5 million gallons of molasses.

The only warning of imminent danger was a muffled sound not unlike distant thunder. The seams of the huge tank split and in what appeared to be slow motion at first, a huge brown wave, two and one-half times the height of a man, swept downtown Boston.

Homes and buildings in its path seemed to lift, then disintegrate in its path. The molasses spread for several blocks, thinning only in height and with it took the lives of 21 people, injuring 150 others.

Horses at the time were as prevalent as the chain-driven, hard-rubber-tired trucks that worked the harbor district. So many horses died that the figure was given only as "a number"!

Litigation, as with most major disasters, was not to be an exception in Boston. Three probable causes of the accident were investigated—an anarchist-planted bomb; fermentation of the molasses causing an explosion; and, a structural failure in the tank.

The company, United States Industrial Alcohol, would be liable only in case of the latter. The courts subsequently found structural failure to be the cause and six years and 3,000 witnesses later, United States Industrial Alcohol agreed to pay more than three-quarters of a million dollars in damages.

But, long after the lawyers and the courts went on to other cases, the smell of molasses lingered. It was years before baked beans found favor again as the Saturday night repast. Boston baked beans were once again in good enough taste to be included on the Plaza Hotel's menu during the 57th anniversary convention and to wear as proof of registration during the days of the ANA show.

FROM OUT WEST

THE LAST WORD ON MILLIONS FOR DEFENCE

The guru of current day study on the issues commonly called Hard Times tokens is Russell Rulau of Iola, Wisconsin. His revisions and updates of Lyman H. Low's classic reference are standards for the serious collector. Rulau's complementing works on early American tokens and U.S. merchant tokens spark a genuine collector curiosity into, as Rulau notes, "a period of peculiar interest in the numismatic history of the United States."

A recent foray through the bookshops of San Francisco and the finding of a broadside dating from the period of the California Gold Rush of 1849 caused an immediate referral to Rulau's *Hard Times Tokens*. The broadside's headline played on a prominent motto from this particular series of the substitute coinage, the one with the words, "Millions for Defence, Not One Cent for Tribute."

The motto of the broadside had been abbreviated to "Millions For One Cent!" To fully appreciate the comment is to know the story of the slogan. Some Frenchman past was making a vain attempt to have the last word.

The slogan "Millions for Defence," predates the era of the Hard Times tokens, 1832 to 1844. It even predates the period some scholars attribute it to, that of the war with the Barbary Pirates, 1815. Origins for the first use of the rallying cry can be traced to 1797, to a time when American negotiators helped spread a little omelet on the faces of their French adversaries. History books record the event as "The XYZ Affair." Whether these exact words were uttered is a matter of conjecture, but the episode surrounding its use made a great contribution to American legend.

During the Revolutionary War, the U.S. entered into an alliance with the French in return for aid in defeating the British. Later pro-French sentiment was to dissipate with the excesses of the French Revolution. After French privateers started seizing American ships at sea, adding insult to an injury over an embargo against American goods, relations between the two countries reached a point of near hostility.

George Washington named Charles Cotesworth Pinckney to go to France to try to resolve the situation. After Washington left office, Pinckney was joined by John Marshall and Eldridge Gerry. The three man commission was refused an official meeting with French foreign minister Talleyrand. Through

Imitations of the large cents of the day, these tokens circulated as money for a short-lived period.

DES MILLIONS POUR UN SOU!

MINES D'OR DE LA CALIFORNIE

NOUVEAUX DÉTAILS.

O vous, qui traversez la grande ville avec des bottes éternellement éculées... qui fouillez les coins les plus obscurs, les plus ignorées de ses maisons innombrables, pour trouver à force de labeurs le pain noir et le maigre potage qui vous permettent d'arriver au lendemain!

En route pour les mines d'or de la Californie!

O vous, jolies filles, qui, privées de dot, seriez éternellement privées de mari!

En route pour les mines d'or de la Californie!

O vous, chanteurs, aboyeurs ambulants, escamoteurs de contrebande, baladins de plein vent et arracheurs de dents malsaines... qui passez votre existence dans la frayeur du gardien de Paris!

En route pour les mines d'or de la Californie!

O vous, juifs, usuriers, agents de change, avoués, huissiers, gens d'affaires, avocassiers, notaires, lèpres de l'humanité, fesses-matthieu mâles et femelles, vous tous qui passez votre vie à barboter en eau sale comme les canards, gâtés par la civilisation, le tout pour amasser des écus!

En route pour les mines d'or de la Californie!

O vous, éternels solliciteurs, avides et gavés sous tous les gouvernements, qui ne mourrez jamais que d'indigestion!

En route pour les mines d'or de la Californie!

O vous, vaudevillistes crétins, qui ne semblez écrire que pour montrer jusqu'où peut aller la bêtise humaine!

En route pour les mines d'or de la Californie!

O vous, pauvres maris, qui ne pouvez parer les pauvres épaules de vos pauvres femmes que de pauvres cachemires pauvrement fabriqués pour vos douze pauvres francs!

En route pour les mines d'or de la Californie!

O vous, pauvres artistes, qui couvrez vos toiles de chefs-d'œuvre sans parvenir à vous couvrir vous-mêmes, par les temps froids, d'un bon paletot de laine!

En route pour les mines d'or de la Californie!

compatriotes à s'exterminer les uns les autres sous couleur de patriotisme!

En route pour les mines d'or de la Californie!

O vous, propriétaires au désespoir de ne plus recevoir vos loyers, abandonnez vos baraques aux communistes, proudhonnistes, cabétistes, simplistes, boulimistes, quiétistes, fouriéristes, et autres équilibristes!

En route pour les mines d'or de la Californie!

O vous, enfin, honnêtes coupeurs de bourses, assassins consommés, banqueroutiers émérites, que l'ingratitude des hommes envoie pourrir au bagne de Brest ou de Toulon!

En route pour les mines d'or de la Californie!

Partez!

Il n'est pas nécessaire que vous preniez de lourds bagages : une cassette et une bonne pioche vous suffiront. Ne vous laissez pas décourager par la peur d'une navigation de cinq mois... elle sera peut-être périlleuse... mais le résultat est si consolant : de l'or!... toujours de l'or!... Qu'importent la colique et les fièvres doublées d'un mal de mer brutal... de l'or!... toujours de l'or!... Qu'importe d'être noir ou jaune en mourant, du moment qu'on se repose dans un linceul d'or pour l'éternité!

Partez!

Ne regrettez pas l'asphalte et les arbustes rabougris de nos longs boulevards!

Partez!

Ne regrettez ni le musée, ni les omnibus, ni le braillards dramatiques et forains du quartier du Temple, ni l'esprit-calembour-dindon de M. Clairville et consorts, ni les ours du Jardin des Plantes... Quittez Paris, et d'ailleurs l'orang-outang est mort!

Partez!

Et ne vous arrêtez qu'au bord de la rivière Sacramento!

Sacramento! le Pactole d'aujourd'hui!

Ce n'est pas trois francs, quatre francs, cinq francs

que vous arracherez par douze heures de travail à la terre généreuse qu'on nomme Californie!

Une fois là, ne soyez pas difficiles sur les gens que vous y trouverez... Ne vous heurtez pas du voisinage des Anglais; il faut souffrir parfois la mauvaise compagnie... Vous y verrez aussi des Chinois, des Tartares, des Baskirs, des Allemands, des Arabes, des Russes, des Espagnols, des Portugais, des Suédois, des Italiens, et surtout des Américains... Car le monde entier se met en route à cette seule pensée de déterrer de l'or.

O nobles aspirations de l'humanité!

Une fois là, ne vous amusez pas à suivre de l'œil les oiseaux revêtus d'un plumage d'azur et d'or... courbez-vous vers la terre et fouillez-la!... N'admirez pas les horizons lointains, qui laissent derrière eux les plus beaux décors de l'Opéra... courbez-vous vers la terre et fouillez-la!...

Par exemple, ne vous attendez pas à jouir de toutes les douceurs de la vie... Vous n'y trouverez ni biftecks au beurre d'anchois, ni dindes truffées; car les aliments y sont rares... Mais les racines y sont en grande abondance... Vous vivrez un peu à la manière des anachorètes pour un temps... seulement, vous déterrerez de l'or... ce qu'ils ne faisaient pas, que l'on sache...

Oubliez, en vous dirigeant sur ce point, le goût des petits pains au beurre; car on les vend quatre-vingt-dix francs la pièce, vu l'absence des pâtissiers!

Partez, afin de revenir au plus vite, car vous pourrez compter alors parmi les élus de ce monde. Vous pourrez, fussiez-vous laid comme Vulcain et de travers comme lui, trouver une Vénus pour votre moitié... Quant au désagrément qui en fut la suite, rien, pas même votre or, ne saurait vous prémunir contre ça.

Mais n'importe, le bonheur ne tient pas à si peu.

En route donc, et rapportez-nous de l'or!... de

French intermediaries a round of negotiations was carried on with X (Jean Conrad Hottinguer, a Swiss), Y (an American banker named Bellamy), and Z (Lucien Hauteval, also Swiss). They suggested that a bribe of some $250,000 would help open the doors to Talleyrand's office and to improved relations with France. Pinckney was alleged to have replied, "Millions for defence, sir, but not one cent for tribute."

While differences were finally settled in 1800, the response remained an American rallying cry. A few years later, when Congress realized it was cheaper to build a navy than pay tribute to the Barbary Pirates, the reply was recalled. Both in Rulau, and in the original opus on Hard Times tokens by Lyman H. Low, it was noted that "Not One Cent For Tribute," was still, "a phrase to conjure with when placed upon these tokens, where it was used to serve as a protection for the coppers issued during the suspension of specie payments in Van Buren's Administration, so that they might be truly said to declare their character, as not a legal coinage."

Even though war with France was averted, the French bristled with indignation whenever the phrase was expressed. Frenchmen took it as a personal affront, for many refused to believe the allegations of bribery. Decades later, when the rush to the goldfields of California materialized, drawing the fortune seekers from Europe, the French took a caustic view and recoined our own slogan. "Millions For A Cent!" they cried.

Handbills, purporting to give latest details of the California Gold Rush, were posted throughout France:

> O you, who would travel the big city with your shoes so worn ... who search the most obscure corners, the most ignored of unnumbered houses, to find hard work, black bread and the most meagre porridge, permitting you to last another day! Head for the gold mines of California!

Remark after sarcastic remark continued on the poster, up to its final words:

> Leave now, so that you may retire even quicker, so that you can be counted among the world's elite. You can, even as ugly as Vulcan, and as dishonest as he, find a Venus for your share. And when the disagreements, that are sure to follow, even your gold cannot protect you. But, never mind, that happiness is not stopped by so little. Go then, and bring us back gold—gold—and forever gold!

Second thoughts surely haunted the author of the broadside. For among the many who did go, some indeed returned with their fortunes, their "millions." Perhaps this was a fitting last word for a slogan that began with patriotic indignation and ended with financial retribution.

THE TWO HORSE RACE & THE CLARK, GRUBER PURSE!

Of all that has been written about the bank and private minting firm of Clark, Gruber & Company of Denver, there has been little mention as to one reason for the far greater scarcity of their coins dated 1860 compared to those of the following year. True, the first year of issue was made of pure gold and subject to greater wear. In 1861, however, although alloyed, Clark, Gruber coins contained more gold than their official U.S. counterparts.

A contributing factor to the disappearance of many 1860-dated coins was an event held during the six-day celebration in May 1861, marking Jubilation Week. It was an event taken little note of by numismatists.

The story of brothers Austin M. and Milton E. Clark, who together with Emanuel Henry Gruber, traveled from Leavenworth, Kansas Territory, to Denver to establish a private mint, is fairly well known to serious collectors. Their plant produced gold pieces for two years, 1860 and 1861, coins that were used to meet the needs of commerce throughout Colorado Territory and the Rocky Mountain West. The production was far from minimal, contemporary reporters noting "their press works round the clock to supply the demand for coin." The coins were issued in denominations of $2½, $5, $10, and $20 gold pieces.

On May 27, 1861, the much heralded territorial government became a reality. Jubilation Week was inaugurated with the installation of the newly arrived William Gilpin as the first territorial governor. He brought with him a semblance of law and order, a lessening of the Indian threat, and a promise that the area would remain under the Northern banner during the War Between the States. Already the Confederacy was casting a covetous eye toward the gold fields of the Rockies as a means of financing their secession.

However, with the formation of a territorial legislature came an ordinance prohibiting the use of private coin in commerce. Unfortunately for the commerce of the day, and for collectors in future years, it was the celebration of the installation of the territorial government that led to the destruction of a large quantity of Clark, Gruber & Company coins then in circulation.

For one day, during the week-long celebration, a horse race to match latter day events like the Preakness, the Belmont Stakes and the Kentucky Derby rolled into one, was set. It was just one event of many that marked Jubilation Week. It was a race where too many bet too much on just two horses. One was named Rocky Mountain Chief and the other, Border Ruffian. The race was scheduled by the citizens of Denver to demonstrate to the new governor that the territory had class.

Local citizens, and Denver had less than 3,000 at the time, were asked to create a winner's purse. Miners emptied their leather pouches, and the business community, from parlor ladies to shopkeepers, contributed a generous

Clark, Gruber & Company's bank and mint building in Denver, Colorado, circa 1861.

share of gold coin. Since little official U.S. currency circulated, the coin donated was primarily the product of Clark, Gruber & Company. The purse, no small sum even to this date, amounted to more than $95,000—in gold!

The race's promoters were not so crass as to want to give the owner of the winning horse, bags of gold coin. They took the prize money, instead, to the mint of the brothers Clark and Emanuel Gruber, located at the northwest corner of McGaa and G streets in Denver City, back to where most of the coin had originated. Their suggestion was accepted. The coins were melted down and a giant gold nugget was cast. It weighed almost 500 pounds. The gold was as pure as the race was not.

The race was set for three heats of one mile each. The winner was to take all. In addition to the purse, more than $100,000 was bet on the first heat alone. The outcome, though, was to mean political victory as well as monetary gain. Rocky Mountain Chief's owner, Bill Greer, was known for his Unionist views; Border Ruffian's master, Col. A. B. Miller, for his Southern sympathies. The race was as much a skirmish in the War Between the States as it was a contest of speed and endurance.

Border Ruffian won the first heat, but not without justified cries of "Foul!" Bill Greer's trainer had secretly bet against his boss' horse, as had his jockey. At the starting line, the trainer intentionally held the horse back after the starting gun was fired. The trainer lamely explained that he had not heard the signal. Greer's jockey appeared to be on just for the ride, never once forcing the horse to run.

The owner of Rocky Mountain Chief warned his two employees that they had better exhibit greater concern over the outcome of the second race. The jockey was told, "use the whip." The start was unspoiled, but again the jockey seemingly preferred a leisurely jaunt. So incensed did one of Greer's staff become that he jumped on his mount, caught up with the jockey and gave him his choice—"use the whip or taste lead." The revolver in the staff members' hand left the jockey little doubt about the seriousness of the situation. The rider whipped his mount forward, but as he was about to pass Border Ruffian, the other jockey lashed him across the face with his whip. But, this time Greer's horse won and now it was the other side's turn to cry foul. They claimed interference, but the judges ruled in Greer's favor. Col. Miller was so incensed over this decision that he refused to race the last heat. Rocky Mountain Chief ran alone and was declared the winner.

The race proved an unintended boon for the Union. Col. Miller and his supporters left the area and headed south to join the Confederate cause. For latter-day collectors, the purse increased both the premium and the rarity of an issue already destined to become scarce. For Bill Greer, winner of the huge nugget made of Clark, Gruber & Company coins, the race proved that he was a far better judge of horseflesh than of card table partners. He lost his entire winnings before the sun set on the day of the last race.

WHEN WOMEN WON THE RIGHT TO VOTE IN COLORADO, COLLECTORS LOST THE CHANCE FOR AN UNUSUAL COIN

Colorado was a good choice for the Home and Headquarters of the American Numismatic Association, for it is an area rich in minting history. Three well-known private mints and two of lesser recognition, plus the world's most productive coining facility (the United

States Mint at Denver), have contributed to the hobby lore of the state.

But one chapter in Colorado's numismatic history has escaped the attention of hobbyists—the time when Governor Davis H. Waite urged a boycott of U.S. Mint products. He planned to ship Colorado silver to Mexico to be coined into pesos, which then would be returned to the state and used as legal tender! Historians dubbed Waite's scheme, "Colorado's Fandango Dollars."

One has to understand the times to appreciate the reasons for the governor's action. In the closing decades of the 19th century, silver was the very lifeblood of Colorado. One half of the total production of silver in the United States flowed from the mineral veins in Aspen, Leadville and Creede. The value of the metal was sustained, in part, by the Sherman Silver Purchase Act of 1890, a law requiring the government to buy 4.5 million ounces of silver every month to be coined into dollars, whether there was a demand for the coins or not.

Farmers, merchants, laborers, all depended on the flow of this precious metal for their prosperity. However, overproduction of silver and the repeal of the Sherman Act diminished the value of the metal, the price collapsed, and with it fell the state's economy.

In 1893, Colorado's total population barely reached 500,000, and by the summer 45,000 men were unemployed. Banks and businesses of all types failed. Many people believed that the "Panic of '93" was a conspiracy by Eastern bankers and Wall Street financiers to subjugate the working class by reducing the amount of money in circulation. Some had a ready answer to the dilemma—restore the monetization of silver at a ratio of 16 to 1, and the price of silver would rise in value to $1.29 per ounce. Prosperity would be just around the corner.

Governor Waite was swept into office in 1893 on just such a platform. He was a Populist and the only member of that party ever elected as Colorado governor. Waite had a number of imaginative ideas about how to get silver working for the economy of the state once again, among them was a plan to establish a state bullion depository and issue certificates of deposit for use as currency throughout Colorado. But, his most unique scheme was for the issuance of "Fandango Dollars!"

In January 1894, Governor Waite called a special session of the Colorado General Assembly and proposed that the state send its silver to the Mexico City Mint to be coined into pesos. Waite would then have the legislature declare the pesos to be legal tender, and the Colorado-mined, Mexican-made, coins would circulate throughout the state despite the monometallists in the East.

When the legality of the proposal was questioned, Waite asked Colorado's attorney general, Eugene Engley, to investigate. Engley found that although the Constitution of the United States forbade states to issue their own coins and paper money, it preserved their right to make gold or silver coin, either domestic or foreign, legal tender for the payment of debts.

The attorney general interpreted this as a go-ahead, and correspondence was initiated with Mexico's President Porfirio Diaz inquiring as to "what terms

Governor Davis H. Waite.

the mints of Mexico would receive and coin for us our bullion silver." Diaz was receptive, but Waite first had to secure the approval of the state legislature.

Waite offered the special assembly 32 proposals on a variety of topics, most of which failed, including his plans for certificates of deposit and "Fandango Dollars." However, one of his proposals unrelated to silver passed, making Colorado a pioneer in a different area. The Assembly approved the governor's request to allow the people to vote on the question of equal rights for women.

The vote was affirmative and Colorado became the second state in the Union to grant women equal political rights. Though women received the right to vote thanks to Governor Davis H. Waite, numismatists lost what might have been an unusual collectible.

TOKENS OF THE LAST WAR BETWEEN THE STATES!

It was not even a memorable little war; in fact, the war is hardly remembered at all. But history should not be deprived; recording it is a must—for this was the last war between the states.

The battle was "fought" 61 years after Appomattox. Texas and Oklahoma were the adversaries and if victory can be measured in achieving objectives Oklahoma was the victor, Texas the loser. The engagements were void of bloodshed, the battle cries less than forgettable. There was no, "I have just begun to fight," nor "Remember the Alamo," let alone a "Remember Pearl Harbor." There was not even a "Don't shoot until you see the whites of their eyes," but there was one shibboleth uncommon to military men even today, "Hold the fort, but keep the expenses down."

In almost every sense, it was war. Oklahoma summoned its National Guard, Texas called out its Rangers. Commanders-in-chief were named, a "war zone" proclaimed, the home front mobilized, and a corps of correspondents sent to the front lines.

While no medals were issued, a series of tokens represented the cause celebre—free access across government-financed highway bridges or pay-the-toll passage over private bridges. It was a war of minor consequence, as many wars are, but the argument was one of "principles," so justification was claimed. If there was any hero, it was Oklahoma's governor, W. H. "Alfalfa Bill" Murray. For a brief moment of glory he played Patton, visiting the front with a rusted old horse pistol in hand. And, for those brief few hours of glory, he became known as "Cocklebur Bill."

Wars of shorter duration have been fought but none had fewer casualties. The press dubbed it, "The War of the Bridges," and the whole cockamamie event started over the issue of opening free bridges to span the Red River border dividing Oklahoma and Texas.

New federal highway bridges competed with privately owned toll crossings. Oklahoma espoused the cause of the motorists. Texas sided with the bridge owners, promising that toll bridges would remain open to traffic until the toll span proprietors had been compensated. Texas offered to buy the toll bridges, but the state's attorney general ruled the contracts illegal. Texas could buy only half of each interstate bridge.

Impatient with Texas legislative delays, Oklahoma moved first by removing the construction barriers to the new bridges. Texas kept the southern accesses closed and turned back motorists from the Oklahoma side. Oklahoma retaliated by bulldozing sections of state highways leading to the old toll bridges. Texas responded by seeking a federal injunction.

No sooner was one injunction granted that another would overturn it. The argument became heated. Gov. Ross B. Sterling dispatched armed Texas Rangers to patrol the Texas side of the free bridges and to turn back "trespassers." With the Texas side of the free bridges closed and the Oklahoma side of the toll bridges blocked, interstate traffic was at a standstill.

One week after the initial skirmishes, Oklahoma placed a strip of border under martial law. Passes were required to enter the area. Lt. Col. John A. McDonald was given command of the Oklahoma National Guard on site. His orders from the state attorney general, "Hold the fort, but keep the costs down!"

Hostilities erupted when Capt. Tom Hickman, in command of the Texas Rangers, chased a pedestrian across the free bridge. Hickman charged that the man had "cursed" the governor of Texas. Citizens of Denison, Texas, feeling the pinch of restricted trade, sympathized with the "enemy."

The war was not going well for Texas. A judge in Houston ordered the state to cease impeding traffic. Barriers were removed and motorists given the choice of free access or paying a 75-cent toll over the privately owned competing bridges. There was little doubt about that choice—the toll bridges were without paying passengers. The Texas legislature continued to argue solutions for compensation and on November 2, 1931, ninety days after it began, the last war between the states ended.

A federal judge decreed that the Oklahoma National Guard had to withdraw or federal troops would be used to drive them out. Gov. Murray hung up his horse pistol and ordered his boys home.

No record exists indicating that these toll bridges used tokens, but a number of bridges connecting the states' borders did, including Chouteau Bridge. But these particular tokens were issued when Oklahoma was still a territory and were used on the more tranquil border with Arkansas. The toll was 5 cents for foot passengers, and 25 cents for wagons, buggies and sizable loads. A later token represented a 10-cent fare.

Today, these tokens are as rare as the memory of the "War of the Bridges." Both provide an insight into a sidebar of American history.

Chouteau Bridge token.

THE BIMETALLIC COINS OF THE HERMIT OF ARBOR VILLA!

It was almost 50 years ago that Frank Gimlett launched his campaign to change the coinage of the United States. While unsuccessful in this endeavor, he nonetheless provided colorful copy for regional reporters. As the self-proclaimed Hermit of Arbor Villa, Gimlett often made the wire services with his philosophical meanderings that bore the imprimatur of a mountain guru.

Cantankerous, opinionated, scraggly-bearded and pot-bellied, with his sole companion an equally obstreperous burro, Gimlett turned to letter writing to vent his outspoken views. His opinions were many and varied and they included such subjects as the "fiscal irresponsibilities of the demonetization of gold." Gimlett's letters were seldom addressed to anyone in particular; some were sent to local editors and most were saved and later published in a series of booklets he entitled, *Over the Trails of Yesterday*.

Gimlett's letters were long on unendowed reason, often expounding the evils of modern woman and the perils of fiat currency. He had all the time in the world to write as Gimlett was the last and sole resident of the once boisterous Colorado mining town of Arbor Villa.

As hermits tend to, Gimlett professed not to miss feminine companionship and wrote that he had to stretch far back into time to find a woman worthy of mention. "Modern women," he once said, "are no longer like the women of a thousand years past, 200 years ago, (or for that matter) 60 years ago as I knew them."

Still, the solitude of the mountains failed to erase thoughts of womanly pulchritude from the old hermit's mind. There came a time when he viewed his surroundings and saw not the majestic peaks of Colorado's Collegiate Range, but the imagined voluptuousness of his fantasy woman—actress Ginger Rogers. Such excitement generated an inimitable idea, one that he shared in an exchange of letters with President Franklin Delano Roosevelt.

Gimlett campaigned to have one of the Rocky Mountain peaks renamed "Ginger." Roosevelt sympathized with the hermit, diplomatically replying that Ginger Peak was indeed a fine name for a mountain, and that Miss Rogers

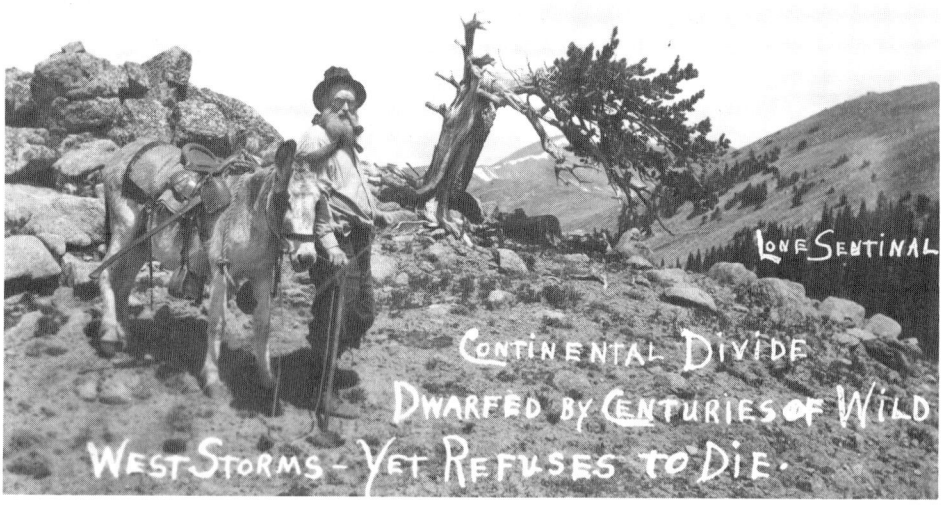

Frank Gimlett, the Hermit of Arbor Villa.

was equally deserving of the honor of having a peak as a namesake. However, Roosevelt admonished, the renaming of even a single peak would cause the government undue expense and trouble in reprinting signs, maps and atlases.

"Great expenses," fumed the old hermit. He would show the government that it did not pay to rebuff worthy suggestions of a devoted citizen. Gimlett calculated the time he had spent in the mountains ever watchful for vandals and trespassers. He then submitted a bill to Washington for $50,000 for his vigilant guarding of the snow and ice. Under his guardianship, Gimlett told Roosevelt, not a shovelful of snow or ice had been taken from the mountains. Records fail to indicate whether Gimlett's bill was ever paid. Perhaps the amount remains a part of today's national debt.

Though numismatists may scoff at Gimlett's eccentricity in wanting to rename a mountain peak or billing the government for keeping an eye on the ice and snow, few collectors would fail to delight in finding one of the coins Gimlett contemplated on producing as his answer to sound currency.

It had been almost seven years since Roosevelt entered the White House and his first Congress passed the Emergency Banking Act. The president controlled banking transactions and foreign exchange, and Congress prohibited the hoarding and export of gold. Much to Gimlett's chagrin, all private gold holdings had to be surrendered to Federal Reserve banks and exchanged for other coin or currency.

It was not that the hermit had much, if any, gold to surrender. He simply felt that such action was an infringement of his constitutional rights. He editorialized against paper and championed the restoration of gold and silver money. By early 1940 Gimlett thought that he had found an equitable solution to the problem.

In a series of letters addressed to Colorado's congressional delegation and to Treasury Secretary Henry Morgenthau, Gimlett offered this solution:

> I am enclosing you a design of money, the kind our forefathers once did use, of a certain weight, size and fineness.
>
> It will be an honest money with

The Hermit of Arbor Villa's bi-metallic coins.

the proper number of grains of precious metal, and thus the intrinsic value will be contained therein.

There will be no change in the coins except the 1c, 5c and 10c pieces, who in the 'ell ever conceived the idea of a penny and a nickle (sic) being larger than a dime, and the metal itself worth nothing, must have been a crack pot for sure.

148 years ago, the men who framed our constitution also designed a money to go with it, and at that time our beautiful gold and silver coin was fixed with a certain weight and fineness, even the lowly nickle (sic) and a 3c piece had enough silver to make them worth their face value in metal, and now these phony, germy, microby paper money advocates want to repudiate this honey money and go on a managed currency basis.

Now I want these paper money agnostics and infidelists without a conscious (sic), that cannot stand the 'In God We Trust,' stamped on our money, to also advocate the elimination of the oath in all courts and congresses, in fact, anything that pertains to God in the heavens, and even rewrite the Constitution itself which is pretty well sprinkled with reference to the almighty. Now in lieu of this, place in our halls of Congress an image, not of a gold or silver calf, but an idol (a paper idol) entirely made up with these spurious, fiat, germy greenbacks and shinplasters, so they (the pagans) may worship this paper or false God of their own choosing, and may God have mercy on their souls, as for myself I would prefer to see them in 'ell. Now is the time to go back to a metallic base, and as a creditor Nation the whole world would soon adopt our standards of money, weights and fineness, and for the sake of the Nation quit buying that foreign gold at the inflated price of $35 per ounce. Wipe out that mythical seven billions of value and restore it to its former and honest price. Raise silver to $1.29 per ounce, and if the raise in silver will not compensate for the drop in gold, pay the misled domestic gold producer a bonus of ten dollars per ounce, providing the mine will not pay a profit otherwise.

Yours truly the Hermit of Arbor Villa.

Gimlett's accompanying coin designs adhered to the principle of a half century earlier—parity between gold and silver at a ratio of 16 to 1, as expressed in a bimetallic coinage. To Frank Gimlett, gold and silver coin was the "Key to the Pearly Gates of Heaven with its Silver Chariots and Streets of Gold."

The U.S. Treasury accepted Gimlett's proposition with the same enthusiasm shown by the Department of the Interior when the Hermit of Arbor Villa campaigned to rename one of the Rockies "Ginger Peak."

HISTORY FIBBED ABOUT THE GOLDEN SPIKE CEREMONY

On a bronze plaque at Promontory Point, Utah, at the Golden Spike National Historic Site, we are told that "On May 10, 1869, a crowd gathered at this site for a momentous event—about 1,800 miles of railway between Omaha, Nebraska, and Sacramento, California, had been laid and at 12:47 p.m. a golden spike was driven into the last tie. The news was instantly telegraphed across the nation that the East and West coasts were at last linked by rail."

One hundred years later the United States Mint issued a congressional medal honoring this event. The medal was designed by Frank Gasparro, chief engraver of the Mint, and struck at Philadelphia. Copies were made available in two sizes—34mm and 64mm. Bronze versions were struck in both sizes, but silver was used in the smaller version only. The obverse depicts the engines Jupiter and No. 119 nosing together against the mountain backdrop at Promontory and carried the legend, '' '. . .The Pacific Railway/is Completed.'/May 10, 1869.''

The reverse shows a section of rail bearing the dates ''1869-1969,'' with the Golden Spike separating them. There is a small mintmark ''P'' along the shank of the spike. A cynic might say it stands for ''phooey,'' for what is reported is not exactly what happened on that date.

Yes, the rails met. Chinese workers laid track eastward from Sacramento for the Central Pacific. The Irish moved the iron for the Union Pacific westward. The crews worked right up to the last minute. Just as they were about to put the last tie in place, a photographer decided to record the event for posterity. He set up his black box and, as that last tie was being set, his assistant yelled, ''shoot!''

While the Chinese did not have a great command of the English language, their experience blasting a trail across and through the mountains, plus their run-ins with their Irish counterparts, that singular word ''shoot'' did have significant meaning. It scared the celestial daylights out of them.

Pandemonium broke loose as the Chinese scattered. It took a great deal of persuasive argument before they would agree to return to work. Already delayed, the time had passed for the official ceremony to start.

The president of the Central Pacific, Leland Stanford, governor of California as well, was not unlike collectors of today. He wanted a few ''commemoratives'' from the event.

Stanford brought with him a number of golden spike replicas and the Golden Spike original. The latter was cast from U.S. $20 gold pieces. On this singular piece he had engraved, ''The Last Spike''; the terminal dates of construction, ''July 10, 1865 to May 10, 1869''; and the words, ''May God Continue the Unity of Our Country as this Railroad Unites the Two Great Oceans of the World.''

General Grenville Dodge, representing the Union Pacific, had no love for such sentimentality, but he went ahead with the golden spikes. Few knowledgeable numismatists are unaware of what would happen to a soft

A 1969 U.S. Mint medal repeats the fallacy that the East and West coasts were linked by rail on May 10, 1869.

metal cast gold spike if it were hit with a sledge hard enough to drive it into a railroad tie. General Dodge had the foresight to consider such consequences and had ordered a special laurel tie with a pre-drilled hole put in place. A special telegraph table was set next to the spot where the gold spike would be driven. The world awaited the word.

Governor Stanford raised his hammer, struck—and missed! The workers had a good laugh.

Again, he tried. His aim was consistent. He missed again, and again. In exasperation he handed the special silver-plated hammer to Thomas Durant, vice president of the Union Pacific. His aim was no better. The waiting telegrapher lost all patience. Taking matters into his own hands, he signaled the country "It is done!"

In Philadelphia, they rang the Liberty Bell. In Washington, a special magnetic ball set atop the Capital dome dropped. In Chicago, a band struck up the music and began a seven-mile parade. In New York, a 100 gun salute signaled completion, and the whole nation cheered. But, the spike had not yet been driven!

Then, only to the knowledge of those present at Promontory, General Dodge strode to the rescue. He picked up the hammer and tapped the spike in.

History records that on that day the two great oceans—the Atlantic and the Pacific—were joined by rail. That, after all, is what was inscribed on the Golden Spike and, 100 years later, repeated on the congressional medal struck by the United States Mint.

History fibbed!

The rail tie between the coasts was not completed and would not be for several years. One could not travel coast to coast by train alone. Regardless of the direction traveled, there was a barrier called the Mississippi. On reaching the river, one had to quit one train, board a ferry, cross the river, and then continue their journey on a different train. And it remained so until the river was bridged many years later.

DEAF SMITH—A GOURMET BRAND OF NOTE!

If you ever find yourself traveling northeast along a lonesome stretch of highway known as US 70, between Roswell and Clovis, New Mexico, during the early days of late summer or early fall, watch for the town of Portales. As you approach it, forget the heat of the highway, turn off your air conditioner, open your car windows and savor the aroma of roasting peanuts. You are experiencing a gourmet treat. You are in Roosevelt County where Tennessee red peanuts are specially grown to make Deaf Smith peanut butter. Gourmands hold Deaf Smith in the same high esteem as do Texas paper money collectors, for notes bearing his portrait.

Deaf Smith is a genuine southwestern legend and ranks high along with Stephen Austin and Sam Houston. While the latter had cities named after them, Deaf Smith was given a whole Texas-sized county.

Smith's real first name was Erastus. When he was given the opportunity to change it to "Deaf," following a trail accident, he eagerly took advantage of the chance. Smith's shining moment in history came during the Battle of San Jacinto, the most critical battle of Texan independence. Smith destroyed a bridge at Vince's Bayou, thus cutting off Mexican general Santa Ana. When the fledgling Republic of Texas issued its early currency, Smith was remembered and portrayed on the five-dollar note.

While the rationale for Smith's portraiture is understandable, the balance of the design, the central feature of the note, has left students of currency puzzled. The Texas notes were printed by the engraving firm of Rawlon, Wright and Hatch of New York. Good at engraving, the artists were poor historians. Perhaps they believed that the Texans were too busy with the problems of independence to notice and might accept the design as one of an Indian overlooking the ruins of the Alamo. To the engravers, a ruin was a ruin, and it mattered not that what was pictured was taken from J.G. Chapman's painting of the ivy clad rubble of Jamestown, in Virginia, site of the first English settlement in America. To disguise the scene, the engravers added the Indian, one taken from Benjamin West's painting of the death of Wolfe on the Plains of Abraham above Quebec. The same scene later appeared on the notes of the Exchange Bank of Norfolk, Va. And the engravers were right: Texans did not seem to mind as long as their hero, Deaf Smith, was being given fitting honors.

Deaf Smith notes are hard to find these days, and so is the peanut butter. Forget looking for the spread on the shelves of regular grocery stores—it's unblanched and unhydrogenated. You'll find it in the specialty shops and health food stores. Likewise, forget to look for Deaf Smith notes in regular coin shops, unless by accident. Only the paper money specialists can help you.

A TALE OF OSTRICH FEATHERS!

The *Guinness Book of Records* fails to take note that one of our own—a prominent numismatist—is the largest purchaser of ostrich feathers in the world. Numismatists themselves fail to appreciate that the sum total of his topically related collection is just two items: a 1913-dated stock certificate of the African Ostrich Farm and Feather Company and a receipt for the purchase of the same.

Edward Schuman, erstwhile editor of *The Shekel*, the official journal of the American Israel Numismatic Society, is looking forward to a 50% increase in the size of his collection the day he finds a special 1-peso note of the Argentine Banco Solanas y Cia., which depicts gauchos herding ostriches. But acquisition of this bill may be a long time coming. Banco Solanas currency was never released, and only two printer's proofs are known to exist.

E. Schuman, president of the P.R. Schuman Duster Company, (which produces 99% of the feather dusters sold in the supermarkets of America today), believes that most people think ostriches live in Australia. "But those are not ostriches," he explains; "they

Famed scout Deaf Smith appears on the $5 notes of the Republic of Texas. His name is equally admired by gourmands and notophilists.

are emus, wild, scavenger birds whose thin feathers are good for nothing." Most ostrich feathers once came from South Africa, but a farm on the shore of the Sea of Galilee is now Schuman's primary source.

Today, few people can recall that ostrich farming had its ties to the history of the Old West; in fact, the high hopes of ostrich ranchers once matched those of the cattle barons of the past. The galloping goonies formerly strutted a range that has since given way to becoming metropolitan Phoenix, Arizona.

Toward the turn of the last century, ladies' fashion dictated plumage, ostrich feathers, in particular, for bustles, bonnets and boas, in addition to fans for hot weather and dusters for household chores. The source for this fashion necessity was, at the time, solely through import. That is, until 1887, when Josiah Harbert, of rural Phoenix, Arizona, read a newspaper account of the huge profits being made by ostrich ranchers in South Africa. Harbert had never visited the country, but his mental picture of South Africa differed little from his own arid surroundings.

It was worth a gamble, Harbert decided, and he proceeded to invest in and import to America the first commercial flock of these big birds. Most survived the arduous journey across the Atlantic, through the Drake Passage around the southern tip of South America and up the Pacific Coast to Pasadena, California. The birds even seemed to relish the railroad trip to Phoenix. It was the last few miles, from the railhead to Harbert's farm, that almost brought a premature end to the experiment.

Few Phoenix residents had ever seen 350- to 400-pound birds before, let alone anything ornithological that could run a mile a minute covering as much as 25 feet in a single stride. The public asked Harbert to put the birds on exhibit, and it was a full two weeks before their curiosity was sated. It was mid-August when Harbert finally moved his flock to the farm. To protect his birds from the blazing summer sun and the 110-degree heat, he covered his wagon with a tarpaulin. Then, having read that the best way to calm agitated birds is to put something over their heads, the ostrich-rancher-to-be rounded up all his farmhands' spare socks and put each bird in a world of darkness for the short trip. All but three birds, one female, one male and a chick of undetermined sex, perished during the last few miles of their 15,000 mile odyssey.

Discouraged, Harbert put the survivors to pasture. The female mistook a piece of barbed wire for an edible, new world caterpillar, and then there were

Never released, the obverse of the 1-peso note of the Banco Solanas y Cia. depicts gauchos herding ostriches.

two. But fate was not so unkind to Harbert as to deem the surviving chick to be other than female. On reaching maturity, the pair lost little time in producing more than 100 descendants. The start of the American ostrich business was well underway by 1891.

Others copied Harbert. Soon, investors flocked by the thousands to buy stock in the likes of Big Five, Pan American, Phoenix American, and the Tempe and Mesa City Ostrich Companies. The owner of the San Marcos Hotel in Chandler turned the land adjacent to his posh hostlery into range for ostriches. Even the Pima Indians joined in the raising game.

Soon the birds were providing more than just feathers for market. Their eggs proved to be a delicacy, one alone was equal in volume to three dozen pullet-style fruit of the hen. The ostrich business boomed. Top breeding birds soon sold for as much as $1,000 a pair. Business became so promising that Congress voted to appropriate funds for research at the University of Arizona.

It was about this time, in 1906, that a 16-year-old salesman started making turkey feather dusters in his basement in Philadelphia. He then traveled by streetcar to deliver and sell his product to grocery stores. This was the inauspicious start of the P. R. Schuman Company that today has 35 sales representatives throughout the United States and Canada.

The Schuman Company currently is the world's largest purchaser of ostrich feathers. Still, it was fortuitous that Ed's father, Philip, used turkey feathers when he began his enterprise in his teenage years. For by 1914, depression had hit the ostrich market. Ladies' fashions, too, had changed. Ostriches were no longer plucked, but crated instead and shipped to market for restaurant menus. When the price of the birds dropped to $10 a pair, there were no takers. The last recorded transaction of the Pan American Ostrich Company was the sale of their last 2,500 birds to the British-American Mercantile Company for $7.50 per head.

The Roaring '20s brought a brief revival. Devotees of burlesque cheered on ostrich-feather fan dancers, but then, they wanted to see more. The few remaining markets included the makers of Kewpie dolls; however, they did not take many feathers.

Today, the story of ostrich ranches in Arizona is relegated to the pages of obscure history books. But the business of feather dusters continues. Perhaps the world's largest purchaser of ostrich feathers, while waiting to find the ever so elusive note of the Argentine, should turn his attention to the ephemera dealers of the Southwest and look for names like Big Five, Pan American, Phoenix American, and Tempe and Mesa City Ostrich companies. Stocks certificates were indeed issued.

THE THIRD LITTLE TRIANON!

Brad Williams' and Choral Pepper's *The Mysterious West*, includes a fascinating tale about the two Petit Trianons of the American West—replicas of the French palace at Versailles.

The authors state, "There are the remnants of the two French monuments in northern California that have almost been forgotten by all. Although several miles apart, both of these monuments were once vast estates and both were patterned after the famed Trianon of Marie Antoinette. Both were built for women. One, according to legend, was built for an empress; the other for an infanta. Today there is little physical evidence of either Petit Trianon replica, yet each retains its mantle of mystery."

There is a third Petit Trianon. It, too, was built for a woman, but unlike its companion copies, the building remains standing, decked in much of its original splendor. Through an interconnecting chain of events, this Trianon made a major contribution to the history of the

American Numismatic Association. Along with the ANA, the third replica of the palace at Versailles calls Colorado Springs home!

The first of the three American Trianons was built around the turn of the century by a Frenchman named Alexander Duval. It was said that he made his fortune building railroads in Peru and Chile. Duval built his palace in an area that later became Marysville, California. He dubbed it Chateau Bellevue, but he always referred to it to friends as "my daughter's house," or "the infanta's home" to everyone else. His neighbors were far more realistic and simply called it "The Petit Trianon." Legend tells that when the young girl blossomed at the age of 18, she eloped with her tutor. Her widowed father died shortly thereafter and the property fell into ruin. Today, only traces of the foundation remains.

The second of the little Trianons was also built in California by another French emigre, Paulin Caperon, at about the same time. Made on a grander scale than the first, legend tells that the mistress of this property had lived in the original. She was Empress Eugenie, widow of the exiled Napoleon III. Caperon originally planned to name the estate La Petit Trianon, but on completion he changed his mind, calling it, instead, Ayreshire Farm. Today, little remains of this Trianon, as well. It was built in a town called Mayfield, which ceased to exist when it was incorporated into the growing campus of Stanford University. Though the main building has long since vanished, the building that once housed the estate's library is now used by the Arts and Architecture Department.

Colorado Springs' Petit Trianon has fared much better than its California counterparts, although, it too, has seen rough times. The 40-room replica of the Versailles palace was built to one-eighth scale for Charles Baldwin in 1907. It is reported to be the only true replica of the Trianon and architect Thomas MacLaren was sent to France for a year to study the original.

Baldwin had the home built for his wife, Virginia, after the family had relocated to Colorado Springs for her health. Although he was an heir to the Baldwin Locomotive Works fortune, his funds had been fairly depleted by the time he moved to Colorado Springs. Still, money was not a problem.

Baldwin had married Virginia Hobart in 1896, namesake of Virginia City, Nevada, where through her father, Walter Scott Hobart, she was able to call a sizable portion of the Comstock Lode fortune "hers." Like his California predecessors, Baldwin called his Trianon by another name—Claremont. And, through his wife, royalty was eventually to move in.

Charles Baldwin died in 1934 and 15 years later his widow, at age 74, shocked local society by marrying a man 20 years her junior. He claimed to be a Russian nobleman, Prince Tchkotoua. The new princess kept a tight rein on her money, though. It was reported she turned down the heat in her Colorado Springs palace to the degree that she had to wear a fur coat day and night to keep warm. The royal couple soon quit Colorado Springs and moved

The Petit Trianon. *(Photo courtesy Local History Section, Pikes Peak Library.)*

to San Francisco but, shortly before her death in 1958, the two separated and the princess moved into an elegant suite in the Golden Gate city's Fairmont Hotel.

Before quitting the Colorado scene the former Mrs. Baldwin had sold her property to Bleven Davis, a New York art patron, for a reported $250,000. She included the bulk of the furnishings and antiques in the sale price. One of Davis' first acts was to rename the place The Petit Trianon and to put the property in his wife's name.

In 1952 the New York court handling Davis' now deceased wife's estate ordered that he give the place to the Poor Sisters of Saint Francis, a local religious order, in accordance with the dictates of her will.

The Poor Sisters of Saint Francis proved too poor to maintain the property and it was soon on the market for resale. In 1957 the Petit Trianon found an anonymous Texan seriously considering its purchase for use as the Summer White House for President Dwight D. Eisenhower. Whether it was for fear for lack of adequate security or the lukewarm reception to the idea by the neighboring community, the plan never materialized. In 1960 the nuns disposed of the property to the newly created Trianon Foundation.

In order to sustain the property, the foundation started a search for a new resident-owner. It was at this point that overtures were made to the American Numismatic Association to consider the property as the site for its permanent home and headquarters. Ralph Cleaver, then president of the local Pikes Peak Numismatic Society, led a delegation of local supporters to the ANA's 1961 convention in Atlanta. Armed with a model of the Trianon and a prospectus, the 26-acre estate was offered to the ANA for a reported $250,000. The sale price was to include the art work and furnishings, then valued in excess of $1 million. The asking price was exactly a quarter of a million dollars more than the Association had in its building fund. Cleaver suggested a one dollar subscription from every coin collector in the country as a means of raising the money.

The dream of buying the Trianon faded with the close of the 70th anniversary convention in Atlanta, but the idea of a permanent home and headquarters remained. A committee was formed to study the feasibility of such an endeavor. Later it reported favorably and within a few years a building fund drive was underway.

In the meantime the Trianon suffered rejection from one potential suitor or another. By 1962 it was an art school, and the following year, 1963, the Petit Trianon became an art museum. The surrounding acreage was subdivided and sold for residential development. The Trianion's land shrank to six acres and then, in 1964, a Save the Trianon Committee was formed. Its main task was to raise $175,000 for the purpose of moving the building to a site near Denver, Colorado, 70 miles distant. That endeavor failed, and for the next three years a succession of auctions to sell the art collection and the furnishings resulted in a mere shell remaining. The library, with more than 10,000 volumes described as "the finest and largest personal library ever assembled in Colorado," found a new home at Colorado State University at Fort Collins.

The disposal of the assets of the Petit Trianon lowered the value sufficiently to find a buyer. In 1967 it became the Colorado Springs School for Girls. The only change that the past two decades has brought was a decision to go coed. In the 1970s the building that had been built as a palace for a young lady and later had become a school for young ladies, dropped the latter requirement and survives today as The Colorado Springs School.

The ANA's brief affair with the third of the American West's Petit Trianons sowed the seed of thought for a permanent home and headquarters. Ralph Cleaver went on from his presidency of the local coin club to become an elected member of the ANA Board. Enlisting the aid of fellow resident-collectors like

Al C. Overton and William C. Henderson, then mayor of Colorado Springs, Cleaver's dream for a permament Association home in Colorado Springs culminated in success, although it was not to be within the walls of the only remaining American replica of the French palace at Versailles.

FROM THE LIGHTER SIDE
OF THE COIN

"COME UP AND SEE ME SOMETIME!"

She was the parody of the femme fatale of pre-World War II America. Too blowsy to be called "blonde," too hefty to be considered "svelte," and so buxom that seamen named their inflatable life jackets after her, still Mae West was the sex symbol of the 'thirties. She was the first to do the shimmy on stage, her one liners became folkloric. "Come up and see me sometime," she used to say and every vamp echoed it.

By the mid-thirties, her movies earned Mae the paycheck of the highest paid woman in America. The public loved her films and the press revelled in her witticisms. Few of her caustic comments escaped reporters' note; Mae West even made the pages of *The Numismatist*.

Coffee, toast and the morning newspaper was the breakfast ritual in the home of ANA district secretary, Charles F. O'Malley, of Rahway, New Jersey. He would scan the paper, then clip and forward any item of numismatic interest to his friend, Frank G. Duffield, business manager and editor of *The Numismatist*. Friday, September 28, 1934, was no exception to his routine. The following news brief caught his eye:

Mae West has wired Secretary of the Treasury Morgenthau at Washington asking him to help her find some young descendant of the American Indian who posed for the original on our Buffalo nickel. She wants to have the handsomest descendant of this handsome brave appear with her in the early sequences of her next film, "Now I'm a Lady," in which Mae plays a cowgirl on a ranch near an Indian reservation.

Mae was informed the Indian she sought probably would turn up on a Montana reservation, so she asked the studio traffic manager to find out the cost and time required to make the trip there.

"I want to see my Indian in person," she smiled, "and see if we would go all right together in my picture." In subsequent sequences of her story, Mae the cowgirl is transplanted to Newport society and then to England. Her studio tries to give her anything she wants, and if she wants Sopwith's yacht *Endeavour* to carry her from Newport to London, a Paramount henchman probably will be in Rhode Island pricing the America's Cup challenger tomorrow morning.

The imaginative district secretary immediately clipped the story and sent it to Frank Duffield. Not one to miss a chance to expound on numismatic

Mae West wanted the model for the Buffalo nickel to star in her next film.

Mae West—darling of the young at heart, bane of hypocrites.

history, O'Malley penned a letter to Mae West informing her that sculptor James Earle Fraser used not one, but three different Indians to produce a composite portrait. The ANA district secretary magnanimously suggested that West rewrite the script to substitute a 260-pound Irishman (named O'Malley) for the part.

The star's reply held true to form, "Dear Mr. O'Malley: Yours is a good idea—pure and simple. Well, anyway, simple."

Perhaps her screen writers should have paid heed to O'Malley's offer. The star did go on to make her movie, but the title was changed to "Goin' To Town." Instead of a cowgirl, West played the role of Cleo Borden, a cattle baroness.

Mae West never found her descendant of the Indian on the Buffalo nickel, although she kept the part in her film. Joe Frye played the role of Laughing Eagle. As for Charles F. O'Malley, the erstwhile ANA district secretary, there was no part in it for him at all. It was just as well, for critics panned the film pointing out "that not everything Mae West did was perfection, and 'Goin' To Town' was proof of that pudding."

REAL COLLECTORS DON'T EAT NUTS!

Of late, if you are one who has started your morning by fortifying yourself with eight essential vitamins and minerals and breaking fast on crispy wheat and rice flakes, lightly sweetened with brown sugar, chances are that you're a ragpicker in search of one of the 18 foreign banknotes packaged in the specially marked boxes of Ralston Purina's Almond Delight. But, real collectors shun the opportunity to load their bodies with 25% of the daily recommended allowance of sodium ascorbate, coupled with a nutritious sprinkling of niacinamide, zinc oxide, reduced iron, thiamine mononitrate, pyridoxine hydrochloride, folic acid, and a little "BHT added to packaging material to preserve freshness." Real collectors start their mornings by adding an ounce of 100% grain neutral spirits to their orange juice and thereby adding a collectible of intrinsic value to their collections.

Wyborowa (those in the know pronounce it "Veeba-rova,") is a premium vodka produced by The Polish State Spirits Industry in Warsaw and export-

The Polish State Spirits Industry provides collectors with a glowing way to add to their Mint State coins.

ed to the United States in return for hard currency. Attached to the neck of each bottle is an "authentic Polish coin, no longer in circulation." The accompanying brochure adds, "It is a collector's coin, and believed to bring good luck and good fortune." The good luck is yours immediately for the coin will not affect the insurance premium covering the value of your collection. The coin is an Uncirculated one grosz last issued in 1949.

The denomination was discontinued when the cost of manufacture far exceeded the face value. When I was in Poland a few years ago, a grosz was equivalent to one-thirtieth of a U.S. cent, 300 to a dime, 3,000 to an American dollar. Although the coin is no longer minted, there is a demand for the grosz in Poland, primarily at weddings. It is often thrown to brides following the ceremony in lieu of rice. It is not that the grain is more expensive, but that the throwing of rice is symbolic of fertility and productiveness, no longer a bride's principal objectives of marriage. The grosz is construed as a symbol of "good luck, good fortune."

The demise of the grosz—plural is groszy or grosze—paralleled the degeneration of the once proud coin from a solid silver piece issued under good old King Wenceslaus II (1278-1305) and popularly called a prager groschen, to copper, then to brass when the Polish republic was re-established following World War I, to bronze (1923), to zinc during the German occupation of the Second World War (1939), to aluminum for the last year of issue in 1949. But its demise never cost the coin the "good luck" it imbued on those who kept the piece as a talisman.

Leave the search for Bulgarian three-leva notes or Indonesian one sens among the wheat and rice flakes of Almond Delight to the ragpickers. Settle instead for a growing collection of groszy. Start your day with a glow—be a real collector—a coin collector!

GOD TOOK CARUSO AWAY, BUT LEFT HIS COIN COLLECTION FOR OTHERS!

They began arriving in cabs, on foot, and in chauffeured Rolls Royces and Pierce Arrows. They came wearing business suits, spats and homburgs; some were in evening dress. Their number included opera lovers, the press, and the just plain curious. But the majority were coin collectors.

The fanfare was not unlike that of an opening night of a great production. The show was staged to run four days, with afternoon and evening performances. On this gala evening—March 5, 1923—the public witnessed the first blending of grand opera and a great hobby. This was the night of the legendary sale of The Enrico Caruso Collection of Foreign and American Gold Coins.

Henry Chapman conducted the sale for the American Art Association at its galleries at 30 East 57th Street in midtown Manhattan. The sale of the coins followed an auction of other items belonging to the noted tenor, among them an accumulation of ancient Greek

Enrico Caruso on the title page of a quaint music sheet of the period.

and Roman glass, dating from 200 BC and described at the time as "one of the finest ever offered at public sale." The third part of the sale, held in the afternoon of the second day, consisted of Caruso's collection of antique glass dating to the 12 and 13th centuries. Buyers included representatives of major museums.

The late tenor's opera costumes were part of the following session, offered along with his collection of Limoges enamels, fine bronzes, and watches. The final session brought forth recognition of the singer's talent for drawing. Caricatures, including a number of self-portraits, plus books from his personal library, made up the last session. In all 1,350 lots realized a grand a total of $151,147.90.

However, it was Caruso's coin collection that captured a large share of the public's attention. On this first evening, just as the coin sale was about to begin, a tall distinguished "foreign-looking" stranger stood up and asked those in attendance to "rise and stand for a few moments in silent prayer for the great Italian-American whose collection is about to be sold." Immediately everyone responded, remained reverently silent for a few moments, then sat down.

The *New York Times* was to report the incident as perhaps the first time that an auction sale ever opened on a prayer. Those bending their heads in common that evening included such numismatic luminaries as Moritz Wormser, John Casimer, Julius Guttag, C.W.E. Clarke, Thomas Elder, and Henry Chapman, who catalogued Caruso's collection.

As the evening progressed, Clarke bid lot number 475—an Uncirculated 1915 $50 Panama-Pacific commemorative gold piece—to a record $160. For the next lot, an octagonal version of the same piece, he paid $170! Wormser was particularly interested in the listings of foreign gold, buying a very fine 1751 8-escudos of the Lima mint for $22, and spending $100 for a 1681 gold ducatoon of Holland, described in the catalog as "sharp and beautiful, excessively rare, as it is stated that only three examples are known."

Guttag invested $22.50 for an Extremely Fine 1801 $10 gold piece, and $8 for a gold angel of Henry VII (1485-1509). Elder, always the shrewd buyer, raised eyebrows when he bid $120 for a $2½ dollar gold piece. It was dated 1798 and described as one of the finest known examples. The heaviest buying of the evening was left to Henry Chap-

At the Caruso sale, C.W.E. Clarke purchased an Uncirculated octagonal 1915 Panama-Pacific $50 gold piece for $170.

man, the auctioneer. He paid $37.50 for an 1822-dated 320 reales of Spain's Ferdinand VII. (He originally sold the coin to Caruso for $22.)

Although Caruso had acquired an extensive collection of gold coins, he focused special attention on the private gold issues of the United States. Chapman bought Caruso's Augustus Humbert 1851 $50 gold piece for $400. The collection also contained six Clark, Gruber & Company gold pieces, as well as specimens of Mormon gold. It was Caruso's collection of pattern coins, however, that would cause today's price-comparing collectors to suffer a breakdown. Two 1879 dollar specimens—a goloid-metric and a metric—together realized the grand sum of $4!

All together, Caruso's coin collection raised less than $7,000. Though it contributed little to the final value of his estate, the collection had brought much solace to its owner. We will never know how often the singer turned to his treasured coins to escape personal problems and career pressures, but he often took parts of the collection on tour. His conductor and constant companion, Alfred Hertz, often judged the tenor's moods by the amount of time spent with his coins.

Hertz once related a humorous incident involving the collection. As a child, Caruso's greatest fear was that Mount Vesuvius would do to his hometown of Naples what it did to Pompeii 1,800 years earlier. When it erupted again in 1906, Caruso was on tour in the United States. He considered himself fortunate to have missed the eruption, but his seismic premonitions did not cease.

April 18, 1906, found him ensconced in San Francisco's Palace Hotel. It was the day of the Great Earthquake and Enrico Caruso, half a world away from Vesuvius, was in the epicenter of destruction. Forsaking his collection, Caruso sought only to rescue an autographed photo given him by President Theodore Roosevelt. He looked to it as his passport to aid and rescue.

Hertz ran to Caruso's suite to find him on the verge of hysteria. "Sing," cried Hertz, "Sing!" The tenor complied, forgetting his fear. His voice calmed most who heard him, and Caruso was credited later for his brave performance as one of the heroes of the disaster.

Caruso was rescued from the Palace Hotel by a police officer who arrived on the scene with a horse drawn wagon. Caruso climbed aboard, just in time to see four Chinese workers carrying his trunks from the hotel. Believing that they were not only stealing his collection, but his precious little black books in which he logged every expenditure, from purchases of coins to tips to bellhops, Caruso grabbed a pistol and yelled for them to stop or he would shoot. Only then was he informed that Hertz had arranged for them to save his belongings.

Once his trunks were loaded on the wagon, Caruso joined the others as they fled the advancing flames of the burning city. He sought refuge at the top of Knob Hill, where he calmly sat down and sketched the devastation below him.

As much as Caruso loved his coins, a few years before his death in 1921 at the age of 48, he lost all interest in them and became melancholy, reliving happier days. His collection had been his escape from the woman who dominated his life. Although she refused to marry, opera singer Ada Giachetti bore him four children. Faithless to him, she devoted her attention to her voice and an occasional passing fancy.

However, Giachetti did take Caruso's name just in time to share in the proceeds from the sale of his collections. It must be said in her favor that her share of the prices realized was donated to the Caruso Foundation for Needy Musicians.

A PENCHANT FOR THE PACHYDERM!

There was a time around the mid 19th century when the passenger trains of the New York & New Haven Railroad slowed as they passed through the agricultural suburbs of Bridgeport, Connecticut.

The trains' engineers eased their throttles as they traveled along one particular six-acre stretch paralleling the tracks. The purpose of the slowdown was to allow passengers the opportunity to witness the "phenomenon of the ages," an elephant plowing the fields belonging to one Phineas T. Barnum, entrepreneur. Although the delay was not scheduled on the road's timetables, Barnum's farm manager timed his chores to the trains' passings.

Barnum was never a man known for idle undertakings. His ulterior intent was to call attention to his American Museum in New York City. This was just another of his legendary advertising gimmicks.

The railroad loved it. Increased passenger load included a number of reporters sent to cover the "story" for their papers and magazines. Barnum added to the mystique by never granting an interview or being available to answer any questions about his pachyderm-powered farm. He preferred to leave the details to the fertile imaginations of the press. And, as usual, his intuitions proved correct.

Reporters strived to outwrite one another. Not content to leave the mammoth to the rough labor of the fields, reporters had it washing windows and watering lawns, irrigating other crops, playing school transport, picking fruits from the orchards—and with a real stretch of the imagination, milking the dairy herd. The result was a marked upswing in traffic, both on the rails of the New York & New Haven and through the doors of Barnum's New York museum.

But, the penchant for promotion by pachyderm was nothing new, not even to America, let alone New England!

Under the guidance of the Duke of York and his brother, Charles II, the Royal Company of Adventurers was founded in 1662 in London. Granted a monopoly on the British trade in West Africa and the right to coin from the metal obtained in trade, some believe that the company struck a series of copper tokens bearing an African elephant on the obverse. The shield of London was imprinted, along with the words, "God Preserve London," on the other side of the coin. Several years later, the obverse of this token was muled with a new reverse that simply read, "God Preserve Carolina and the Lord Proprietors, 1694." This issue was soon followed by another with a simpler legend, "God Preserve New England, 1694."

Both are believed to have been made to heighten speculative interest in the American colonies, Perhaps, if this advertising was to believed, our forebears expected to find elephants tending the meagre corn crops of New England or watering the tobacco plants of the Carolinas. Only latter-day numismatists were not disappointed.

The New England Elephant Token of 1694.

IN DEFENSE OF ANTHONY COMSTOCK!

The promotional genius of Harry Reichenbach is a textbook classic. He made his mark during the era of silent films. Hired as the publicist for the first Tarzan movie, Reichenbach paraded a live ape, dressed in a custom tailored tuxedo, through lobbies of several posh New York hotels. While the property managers ended up presenting him with bills for broken furniture, the press gave him the news coverage he wanted for the picture.

Long before Boston became the banning capital for books, Reichenbach secured the publicity needed to make *Three Weeks,* a tawdry film based on Elinor Glyn's novel, a box office hit. He made sure that Anthony Comstock, founder of the New York Society for the Suppression of Vice and special agent of the U.S. Post Office, received a copy. The easily shocked Comstock banned the book from the mails, and in so doing, helped create a best seller.

Reichenbach's classic, however, was a promotion that he undertook more to heckle Comstock than for any financial return. This supreme example of the publicist's genius had its genesis on the streets of Brooklyn. One day in 1912, while passing a small art gallery, Reichenbach's eye was caught by a painting of a young nude. It was the work of a yet-to-be-discovered French artist, Paul Emile Chabas entitled *September Morn.*

After discussing his plan briefly with the gallery owner, Reichenbach bribed a group of street urchins to stand in front of the gallery and giggle. Anonymously, he had called Comstock, who soon arrived to find the youngsters crowded around the window frolicking and uttering obscene remarks amongst themselves. Indignant, Comstock, as guardian of the morals of youth, had both the artist and the gallery owner arrested. The pair was quickly acquitted of the charge of contributing to the delinquency of minors, but the resulting publicity helped generate the sale of more than seven million copies of the painting. The scene is reprinted to this day and sold as "calendar art of old."

"Vile books and papers are the branding irons of hell, and used by Satan to sear the highest life of the soul. The world is the devil's hunting ground, and children are his choicest game," bemoaned Comstock, the patron of moral purity. For more than 40 years he played official censor and self-appointed guardian angel to youth of all ages.

In one year alone, 1896, Comstock's agents caused 2,044 arrests to made, 19 tons of gambling paraphernalia and 47 tons of "obscene" matter to be seized and destroyed. One risque play was suppressed and Comstock cited, as testimony to his Puritan diligence, that "no (New York) newspaper was found to contain unlawful or obscene matter."

The following year the Society for the Suppression of Vice observed its 25th anniversary and engaged Carnegie Hall to conduct its annual meeting. Comstock boasted of the group's successes

$5 U.S. silver certificate, Series of 1895.

and accomplishments since its founding in 1872. What was noticeably missing from the report was any mention of the "new" series 1896, $5 silver certificate. This omission is particularly troubling as latter-day numismatic historians credit, or blame, Comstock for the removal of these notes from circulation. Gene Hessler, in his well-researched reference *U.S. Essay, Proof and Specimen Notes* writes, "Mr. Anthony Comstock, head of the Watch and Ward Society, had demanded recall of these dirty dollars because of the lewd unclothed females."

Still, within weeks of the society's anniversary meeting, the *New York Times* was to report:

"GAGE CANCELS CERTIFICATES
A Total of Over Fifty Millions to be Supplanted by Other Bills
Washington, May 3 (1897)—Secretary Gage has determined to cancel the new one-dollar, two-dollar, and five-dollar silver certificates outstanding as they come into the Treasury. The total foots up $16,280,000 ones, $8,144,000 twos, and $30,000,000 fives—$54,424,000 in all. It may take years to wipe out the entire issue and substitute bills.

It can be said authoritatively, however, that no more of the so-called "new certificates" will be printed. Neither will fresco painters be called in to make designs for substitutes. The Bureau of Engraving and Printing has been endeavoring to force these certificates into circulation."

Subsequent press releases from the Treasury appeared throughout the rest of the year, but no mention of credit for the change was attributed to Comstock. Nor was there any mention of criticism of subject matter. Quite the contrary. The press was to note, "All judges of good designs and workmanship have admitted the superiority of the new notes to anything ever before produced by the Government."

Blame for the discontinuance was placed on complaints that new notes became "smudgy and suspicious-looking with little use." The Bureau of Engraving and Printing studied the possibility of "cleaning-up" the design. One essay extant even shows the offending female clothed. But, it was Secretary of Treasury Gage who had the final word, "I have reached the conclusion that it was not worth while to try to experiment with the picture certificates any longer."

Thus ended the most imaginative and beautiful issues of United States currency ever produced. Dubbed "Educational Notes" by collectors, the series terminated even before the designs for all denominations were completed. Other than a coincidence in timing, there is little to prove that Anthony Comstock was responsible for their demise. Perhaps it is just as well, had the output of the notes matched that of *September Morn* the notes would never have reached the collector value or appreciation enjoyed today.

SMILE, SUSIE B., THERE MAY STILL BE A NEED FOR YOU YET!

My grandson Jesse is at that trusting age, too old not to anticipate Christmas without anxiety, too young not to believe in Santa Claus. He is just at the age where the shedding of a baby tooth brings a largesse in the form of a tooth fairy dollar from an imaginary lady.

I did not know there was such a coin.

"Yeth," I was informed. Emphatically, sincerely, and with a front-tooth-missing lisp. "And, the toots fairy's picture is on it, too."

Immediately, I mentally pictured a dollar-sized aluminum token bearing the picture of a lithesome, evening-gown clad, magic wand holding feminine princess—a beautiful star-spangled Glinda, the good witch of the East on one side; a dental supply firm message on the benefits of good hygiene and brushing on the reverse.

It was something I would want for my accumulation of advertising tokens, as would Dr. Radford Stearns, the 1987 Atlanta convention's general chairman for his collection of medals and tokens relating to the dental profession. Jesse promised to bring his "collection" of tooth fairy dollars with him the next time babysitting responsibilities fell our way.

Slightly larger than a quarter, somewhat smaller than a half dollar, I was surprised to find that tooth fairy dollars bear not the beautiful smiling face of a lovely Billie Burke, playing Glinda, but of a stern visaged character that one could conceivably pass off as the wicked witch of the West.

Jesse's highly touted tooth fairy dollars were real dollars—albeit Susan B. Anthony ones. It will be bad enough to be around in a year or so when he finds that he has been duped into believing in Santa Claus, but his faith in adult man will be shattered when he eventually learns that the tooth fairy is none other than the unloved matriarch of the mini-dollar. A suffragette of a bygone era enlisted as a dental assistant. To think of it, the idea has merit!

If there are more than 20 million children coming into the age of losing their temporary deciduous, or milk, teeth and each of these children possesses the correct number—20 baby teeth in all—two central incisors, two lateral incisors, two canines, and four premolars in each jaw, the cost of storage and the problem of distribution of the unloved, unwanted Susan B. Anthony mini-dollars has been solved. The Bureau of the Mint could concentrate on educating the dental profession to prescribe, as balm for lost baby teeth, the placement of Susan B. Anthony mini-dollars under the pillow as gifts from the tooth fairy.

In spite of the Madison Avenue promotional blitz, Americans failed to accept Susan B. Anthony mini-dollars into their circle of acceptable circulating coin.

WHEN HE FAILED TO COUNTERFEIT GOLD, HE CREATED A MAN!

George W. Hull once listed his address as Colorado Springs. Fortuitously, it was during pre-American Numismatic Association days; otherwise Hull would have found some way to take advantage of another golden opportunity. His sojourn in the Centennial State left its mark—on an earthen mound near Beulah, on a newspaper's masthead in Ouray, and on the state as a whole.

George Hull once attempted to turn base metal into gold. When that effort failed, he turned to changing rock into man. Success here was but fleeting, but the attempt would insure that he would go down in history as one of the great con men of the 19th century.

Circumstances found Hull visiting a sister in Ackley, Iowa, in June 1866 to discuss the repayment of money he had borrowed from her husband. A Reverend Turk also was visiting at the time, and one evening the front-porch discussions touched on religion. Hull was as much a nonbeliever as the minister was a fundamentalist. When the topic of conversation turned to Genesis 6:4 ("There were giants in the earth in those days; and also after that. . ."), George Hull impiously schemed. If the reverend believed in giants, Hull would give him one.

For two years the idea of turning stone into a giant man brewed in Hull's fertile mind. On a return visit to Iowa in 1868, he detoured through Fort Dodge and ordered from a gypsum quarry a block of stone, 12 feet long and 4 feet square. At the expense of several bridges and a wagon axle, he had the 10,000 pound stone trucked to the nearest rail depot. From here it was shipped to the studio of sculptor Edward Burghardt at 940 North Clark Street, Chicago.

The Solid Muldoon.

Burghardt, with two trusted assistants, Fred Mohrmann and Henry Salle, devoted three months of labor to the creation of a reclining giant. By the time the mammoth man was finished, Hull had spent $2,600 in borrowed money, too great an investment for a mere practical joke.

Hull surreptiously shipped the giant to the region that gave America Mother Ann Lee and her Shakers and Joseph Smith and his golden plates of Mormon. The stone man was buried on a farm near Cardiff, New York, where he slept for a year before being "discovered" in October 1869.

For months following the discovery people poured into Cardiff via excursion trains and special stagecoaches. Thousands paid 50 cents a head for a peek at the petrified man from the past. Even when the giant was exposed as a fake, the curious still came to Cardiff, including none other than Phineas T. Barnum. However, Barnum balked at paying $60,000 to lease the stone man for one of his attractions. A syndicate eventually bought the Cardiff giant, and to this day people pay to see Hull's first creation, on display at the Farmer's Museum in Cooperstown, New York.

George Hull chose Colorado as the perfect place once again to turn stone into man. By the time he had established residence in Colorado Springs, his reputation was such that he had to resort to using an alias—Davis. He cut his hair short, shaved his beard, donned spectacles and walked stoop-shouldered. Hull, after all, was preparing for a repeat performance of his classic hoax. It would do him no good to be recognized as the father of the Cardiff giant.

Created on a smaller scale, measuring only seven feet tall and weighing 500 pounds, the Solid Muldoon, as he was dubbed, was a piker in comparison to the Cardiff giant. Hull invested his own money this time—$11.45 for Portland cement and a cast-off medical school skeleton.

Buried in a shallow grave near

Beulah, Colorado, 18 miles southwest of Pueblo, the Muldoon was to be "discovered" by an innocent passerby in the fall of 1877. This time, the intrepid P.T. Barnum was in on the hoax. By "coincidence" the showman was in Colorado Springs visiting his daughter at the time of the discovery. He rushed to buy the Muldoon for a reported $20,000.

Charles Darwin's theory of evolution had recently made the press and was hotly debated in public forums. The Solid Muldoon was billed as the "missing link between man and ape." Again, gullible hordes flocked to Pueblo, then to Colorado Springs and Denver, to see the stone marvel. As with its predecessor, the Muldoon was exposed as a fake, but, unlike the Cardiff giant, it disappeared from the scene. Its location, if it still exists, is unknown.

Although George Hull experimented with make-believe giants and counterfeit metal, he was never charged with making false coin. In fact, when he died in 1902, Hull was without coin, real or otherwise. The man with the million-dollar ideas died a penniless pauper.

THINGS COULD BE VERSE!

Thankfully, the designs of today's currency notes occupy the full surface of both the front and back of the paper. But, such has not always been the case, especially during the days of pre-Civil War era obsolete currency. Many bills sported blank backs and there were those who could not pass up an opportunity to practice their imagined talent for verse.

The would-be Longfellows filled the backs of notes with creative doggerel or iambic pentameter, forcing their words on later recipients of the money.

Imagine, if you can, your reaction to this penned little addendum to a currency note received in trade:
  Ye ugly, dirty little scrap,
  To look at hardly worth a rap,
  And yet I'll give my hearty vote
  None can produce a sweeter note!
Amused? Perhaps, but no more so than a Scottish cousin would have been on receipt of this ditty, penned on the back of an English one pound note:
  It's odd that any man should wish
  A dirty, scrabbit rag like this,
  Yet mony a mane would cut a caper
  To get a ween sic bit o'paper.
Frank G. Duffield, editor and business manager of *The Numismatist* during the late teens of this century, referred to this type of monetary graffiti as the scribler's itch.

But, long before there was an American Numismatic Association or a journal called *The Numismatist*, even before there was a United States of America, there was a poet who could lay claim to the "laureate" honors of the hobby. He was Joseph Addison, born in England in 1672.

Addison was both poet and statesman. Some might even say diplomat, in a polite way. His poem, "To The King," written when he was 27 years old, caused William III to blush and earned Addison a sizable annual pension allowing him to travel the Continent.

The poet put his talents for rhyme to

Joseph Addison, poet laureate of numismatics.

continued good use. A 1704 work celebrating the victory of Blenheim was recognized by a commissionership of excise. Recognition allowed him to be elected to Parliament later that same year and he kept the seat for the rest of his life. One contemporary biographer gushed that as a light essayist, Addison had no equal in English literature.

Lord Macauley said of Addison, "For never . . .had the English language been written with such sweetness, grace and facility." S. Austin Allibone, in the 1875 edition of the his *Dictionaries of English Literature*, published in Philadelphia, was even more generous, allowing four full pages of praise the poet.

Allibone, in selecting a number of prose quotations from Socrates to Macauley, on a score of subjects, allowed for more than a half dozen on the topic of coins—all by Addison. But the poet had another admirable quality, he was a coin collector, a numismatist true.

Allow one's self to savor ''the sweetness, grace and facility'' of such proofs as:

> There is great affinity between coins and poetry, and your medallist and critic are much nearer related than the world imagines.

> Among the great variety of ancient coins which I saw at Rome I could not but take particular notice of such as relate to any of the buildings or statues which are still extant.

> You will never, with all your medallic eloquence, persuade Eugenius that it is better to have a pocketful of Othos than of Jacobuses.

Or, what could be more succinctly put than—"Old coins are like so many maps for explaining the ancient geography."

Addison certainly tops the bit of banknote verse found in John Gibson Lockhart's *Life of Sir Walter Scott*:

> Farewell my note, and where soe'er ye wend,
> Shun gaudy scenes, and be the poor man's friend.
> You've left a poor man; go to one as poor.
> And drive despair and hunger from his door.

I do not know how appreciative numismatic readers will be of poetry, but let's be thankful, at least, that Joseph Addison was a collector of ancient coins and not of obsolete currency.

WHY CHESHIRE CATS GRIN!

"All right," said the Cat; and this time it vanished slowly, beginning with the end of its tail, and ending with the grin, which remained some time after the rest of it had gone.
(Alice's Adventures in Wonderland.)
And the grin remains to this day.

Long before Lewis Carroll borrowed the old tale, English folk speculated as to the reason why, in all the feline world, Cheshires alone grinned. The Cheshire's grin is true, the reason may not be. But an old tale repeated by essayist Charles Lamb says that Cheshire was a county palatine, and that their cats, when they thought about it, were so pleased that they could not help grinning.

In England, counties palatine (or palatinates) date to the Middle Ages and were designations given to counties whose lords had been awarded rights and powers usually considered regal privileges, including the right to coin money. Cheshire gained this right in 1241, when the earldom, created and presented by William the Conqueror to Hugh of Avranches in 1071, passed to the English crown and the county became a palatinate with control over its own legal and fiscal administration.

During the reign of Henry VIII all these privileges were withdrawn, save the name and the palatine courts. The courts, too, disappeared in 1830 and today only the title, County Palatine, serves as a reminder of more independent times past.

The most intriguing series of coins struck at Cheshire date to the English Civil War. Chester, seat of the local government, was a Royalist stronghold, faithful to Charles I. Parliamentarian forces unsuccessfully attacked the city in July 1643, before returning to lay siege 18 months later. For a year the Royalists held out, but by Christmas 1645 the situation was desperate. Food was low, morale no better, and Cheshire finally surrendered in February 1646.

During the seige a series of half crowns was struck, converting the silverplate of the city to coin. Still extant records indicate, "that as much of the ancient plate of this citty as will amount to ye summe of one hundred pounds shall be fourthwith converted into coyne for the necessarie use and defence of this city and towards the payment of the citty's debts."

No specimens of silver service plate prior to the Civil War remain, mute testimony to the extent that it was used to coin money. Today, these coins, called "declaration half crowns" are extremely rare and valuable. They may have been remelted later and made into new coin. Cheshire cats' grins may be one of smugness, knowing that not only did Cheshire coin its own money, but in doing so, made extremely valuable, eagerly sought-after pieces, not just the ordinary "run of the alley" variety used by the rest of the country.

A half crown struck from silverplate at Chester during the siege of Parliamentarian forces in 1645.

IN OTHER WORDS

THE ORIGIN OF THE SIGN OF THE DOLLAR

Surprisingly, the true story of the development of the dollar sign is a Colorado Springs story. The years of research, the study of thousands of early documents and the compilation of the evidence to support the findings was accomplished within a stone's throw of the headquarters of the American Numismatic Association. The story was written by Dr. Florian Cajori, professor of physics, and later professor of mathematics and dean of the department of engineering at Colorado College. His period of study happened long before the ANA found a permanent home on the college campus.

Like many of the early residents, Professor Cajori came to this high altitude community for reasons of health. Quitting the steamy climes of Tulane University in New Orleans in 1887, where he was a professor of applied mathematics, he accepted a teaching assignment at Colorado College. During his 29-year tenure here, Cajori published a great number of scholarly papers, ranging from *The Study of Diophantine Analysis in the United States* (Colorado College Studies, 1891) to *A History of Mathematics* (New York, 1894). Some of his works were translated into Russian, Japanese and Italian.

However, it was the professor's article, "The Evolution of the Dollar Mark," published in the December 1912 issue of *Popular Science Monthly*, that attracted numismatic interest. His study shattered many of the myths about the origins of the familiar symbol. In the article, which was reproduced in part in *The Numismatist* in 1929, Dr. Cajori stated, "There are few mathematical symbols the origin of which has given rise to more unrestrained speculation and less real scientific study that has our dollar mark $. About a dozen different theories have been advanced by men of imaginative minds, but not one of these would-be historians permitted himself to be hampered by the underlying facts."

The doctor first investigated a number of ancient and religious hypotheses. For example, around the turn of the century, the *Standard Dictionary* suggested that the dollar sign was a monogrammatic form of "IHS," (a symbol representing the Greek contraction for "Jesus") or a combination of "HS" or "IIS," abbreviations used by the Romans for "sestertius," a small-denomination coin. "If (that is) so," wrote Cajori, "(then) we should expect the supporters of these hypotheses to endeavor to establish an unbroken line of descent from symbols used at the time of Nero to the symbols used in the time of Washington."

Cajori also noted that others of theological bent tried to give the dollar sign Biblical meaning. One saw a scroll intertwined with two pillars reminiscent of those of Jachin and Boaz in Solomon's Temple, while some felt the pillars were similar to "the device that was stamped upon the coins of the people who built Tyre and Carthage." Although Dr. Cajori jokingly conceded that such religious origins might account for the modern phrase, "the almighty dollar," he found nothing to support these unique claims.

The Colorado College professor saved his scurrility for those who advocated that the origin of the dollar sign

Dr. Florian Cajori.

evolved from the Pillars of Hercules, the two points of land, Gibraltar and Jebel Musa, that flank the Strait of Gibraltar. "All flights of fancy were eclipsed by those who carried the $ back to the 'Pillars of Hercules,' " he wrote. "These pillars are strikingly impressed upon the 'pillar dollar,' the Spanish silver coin widely used in the Spanish American colonies of the 17th and 18th centuries. A Spanish banner or scroll around the pillars was claimed to be the origin of the dollar mark."

Cajori was kinder to noted historian T. F. Medina of Santiago de Chile for suggesting that the dollar mark perhaps was derived from the mintmark of Bolivia's Potosi Mint in Bolivia—a monogrammed "p" over "s." The professor argued that forms of "p" and "s" were used as abbreviations for "peso" long before the establishment of a mint at Potosi. He also debunked the "US Theory," the belief that the dollar sign was comprised of the intertwined letters "U" and "S" (signifying to some, "United States," and to others, "Uncle Sam").

The first documented use of the dollar sign by a high-ranking American official occurred in 1792 in several letters written by Robert Morris, the great financier of the Revolution. Examination of a number of these letters, and others penned by Morris' secretary, revealed that the sign had but a single downward stroke through the "S." (If Morris meant the symbol to be a monogrammatic "US," asked Cajori, "what happened to the second downward stroke?")

Perhaps T. F. Medina was on the right track but failed to pursue his hypothesis to its logical conclusion. In tracing various account books and ledgers, Cajori found the first abbreviations for "dollar" were used in Spain in 1500, but the actual development of the symbol spanned 300 years of bookkeeping. Maybe it evolved from the word "peso" after all. When the "p" of "ps" (the abbreviation for peso) was changed to one long stroke through the "s," the dollar sign took on the form as used by Robert Morris. (Cajori discovered that before 1800, "dollar" was seldom symbolized by $ but rather spelled out or abbreviated as "Doll" or "Ds.")

Florian Cajori established that the dollar sign was the lineal descendant of the Spanish abbreviation for "peso" and that "the change from the florescent ps to $ was made about 1775 by English Americans who came in business relations with Spanish-Americans, and that the earliest printed $ dates back to 1797" (in Chauncey Lee's *American Accomptant*, an arithmetic book published that year.)

The curative air of Colorado Springs apparently helped Dr. Cajori, for he left Colorado College in 1918 to become head of the mathematics department at the University of California at Berkeley. He died in 1930 at the age of 72. Though no bronze markers on the campus of Colorado College recognize this distinguished educator, a scholarship fund bears his name. Numismatists who wish to see where Cajori carried out his extensive research about the origin of the dollar sign will find that his home at 1110 Wood Avenue has given way to a modern Gamma Phi Beta sorority house.

THE USE OF COINS HAS LED TO COUNTLESS INNOVATIONS AND CONTRIBUTED TO OUR LANGUAGE!

Numismatists can legitimately claim that the commercial use of the objects of their prime interests has led to the development of many innovations of utilitarian nature. Coins led to the development of cash registers, fare boxes, piggy banks, counters, weighers and vending machines, a great hobby and a major industry, to name a few. But, one of the most obvious creations devised, caused by the need for small coins, is one most taken for granted—

the pocket.

Pockets did not debut on wearing apparel until coins had been in use for more than 2,000 years. The idea of attaching pockets to clothing coincided with Christopher Columbus' preparations to try to discover a new route to the Indies. One, however, had nothing to do with the other.

Not too many years prior to Columbus' departure, coins in particular, along with keys and whatever else man felt that he must carry with him, were wrapped in cloth and placed in diaper-like accessory called a codpiece. Needless to say, a handful of coins could be downright uncomfortable.

Men, more concerned with comfort than style, returned to dropping such coin into cloth bags they called purses and hung them from their clothing. Such use gave rise to a whole new occupation—cutpurses—precursors to pickpockets. It is not that purses were new, their use preceded the invention of coinage, but by the 15th century the age of the purse inside the clothing, as a pocket, had not dawned.

Security dictated that a safer way to carry coin be devised than by hanging money in an outside pouch. First, a slit was made in the side of men's trousers into which the cloth purse could be placed and hung. In due process some forgotten tailor sewed a purse on the inside and thus the pocket was born. From trousers, it took another generation of tailors and couturiers to add pockets to the likes of capes and coats. With the latter, the pocket was added at the hemline which meant pulling up the coat to reach in the pocket, or more foolishly to kneel or stoop down. It was a long time before someone thought of slitting the cloth and adding the pockets at hip height.

While it was the need for small change that gave us pockets, it was the purse that gave us the name of the coin show sales area—bourse. The first purses were made from hide that the Greeks called byrsa. A small drawstring was added at the top to secure the contents. The byrsa was copied by the Romans, only they called it bursa. The French came along a little while later to make it bourse and literally gave the word the meaning of "coin in the purse." Afterwards, when the first stock exchanges were established in Paris in the 16th century, they borrowed the name, and eventually most European stock exchanges came to be called bourses. These exchanges became synonymous with "money markets" and so it should not come as a great surprise that coin collectors would want to appropriate the name of where money is sold for their own use.

Renaissance man generally carried his coin in a diaper-like "codpiece," worn front and center!

CARPETBAGGER, ANOTHER OF OUR WORDS APPROPRIATED!

The public cannot be blamed for conjuring up the unsavory image of a sleazy politician when they hear the term "carpetbagger" mentioned. After all, few abridged lexicons disagree with the standard definition, like the one that appears in the *American Heritage Dictionary*:

"carpetbagger - 1. A Northerner who went South after the Civil War for political or financial advantage. Compare scalawag.

2. A nonresident politician who represents a locality for political self-interest.—carpetbaggery, carpetbaggism."

Political satirist Thomas Nast's caustic caricatures of Union general Carl Schurz as the epitome of a carpetbagger emblazoned the image in everyone's mind. Nast did much to lose the original meaning of the word, but managed to keep the name synonymous with those mostly unsavory characters who originally earned their living—carpetbagging. The term was borrowed from a numismatically-related occupation that saw its heyday prior to, but not after the Civil War.

During the period that extended from the expiration in 1836 of the charter of the Second Bank of the United States to the introduction in 1861 of government currency, the nation endured a free banking system. Critics of the times pointed out that a plethora of banking institutions were organized for the sole purpose of issuing currency, paper money redeemable for hard currency on demand, the caveat being that the currency could only be redeemed at the issuing bank's "principal" office. The central offices were most often situated in places not easily located nor readily accessible. Many word historians trace the origin of the name "wildcat banks" to the location of these institutions.

Others claim the term "wildcat," as applied to currency, can be traced to bounty certificates issued in Missouri during its territorial days. Wildcats and other predator animals were hunted and county treasurers paid the bounties in scrip that could be used for payment of county taxes or levies. The scrip, often called "wildcat certificates," or "wildcat money," came into circulation due to shortages of regular tender.

While financial scholars disagree as to the origin of the term "wildcat," as it applies to paper money, there is unanimity of opinion among them that the word "carpetbagger" had its introduction with those employed to redeem the notes of banks headquartered in the backwoods of the beyond.

It was to the advantage of the wildcat bankers to keep their money in circulation. One way to accomplish this was to see that as much as possible was introduced as far away from their home office as imaginable. One method of accomplishment was to hire men to travel into distant states and purchase farm commodities—beef, corn, barley—paying either in the bank's currency or by making arrangements with another bank, of equal notoriety, to exchange the worthless notes of one for the worthless notes of the other. The farm produce would then be sold for specie and the winners would be the banks

Thomas Nast's post-Civil War caustic caricatures of Union general Carl Schurz served as the epitome of the carpetbagger.

involved. Circuitously, they received hard cash for their near worthless paper. The bag men in these cases carried enormous sums of their bank's paper in carpetbags and thus earned for themselves the byname, "carpetbaggers."

But, like the bounty hunter of the past, not everyone considered carpetbagging an unsavory occupation. There were those who looked upon the men with the large cloth bags as avenging angels. While some sought their livelihood by dispersing the "wildcat" currency to the far corners of the country, others earned a respectable living bringing the money back to its point of origin. A certain percentage of the "carpetbaggers" were employed by exchange houses to return the notes of issue to the wildcat banks of issue and demand payment in gold or silver, for a percentage of the redemption, of course.

Since such currency was taxed out of existence during the Civil War, there is no need for collectors to reclaim the term "carpetbagger" as one of theirs—give it to the dictionary writers and to those who took part in the second invasion of the South, but at least, let us numismatists take credit for the origin of the term.

THE LOST AND GENTLE ART OF LOBBYING!

The growth of the annual conventions of the American Numismatic Association, from single hotel self-contained meetings, to multi-facility mega-footage events, has brought an end to the delightful convention practice of "lobbying."

Once upon a convention a number of familiar registrants would stake their claims to particular seats in a hotel lobby, and for the remaining days of the show, hold court. Gone is the softer pace and more pleasant time when smiling faces of collectors like Al and Sally Kirka, of Manchester, Connecticut, and Mr. and Mrs. Steve Penzes of Detroit, Michigan, would greet us every time we passed through the lobby.

Hobby "lobbying" was more than a friendly greeting, a familiar face, or a numismatic ritual. As much business was transacted in the hotel lobby as on the bourse floor. I recall that my first encounter with the practiced art of "lobbying" happened at the ANA convention in Boston, Massachusetts, back in 1960. The show was self-contained in the old Statler-Hilton Hotel on Park Square. The late Mike Powills from Chicago was doing a little trading in Carthaginian silver pieces—the pillow of the settee was his bourse table, the antique Persian throw rug on the floor his kneeling place. On spotting my wife and I sitting across the way, Mike scooted, without ever rising to his feet, across the width of the lobby to drop a handful of coins in her lap. Not an eyebrow was raised for such familiarity was in keeping with the gentle art of "lobbying."

Gone, too, are the days when appointments were set to "meet in the lobby." Those of you who have lodged in the latest hostelries like Atlanta's Marriott Marquis, one of several convention hotels used in the convention city, can appreciate the problem caused by such latter-day generalities. What lobby? In the Marriott there was one on the 42nd floor, the "Concierge Level," for the wheeler-dealers and big traders in ANAC's papers. Another lobby was to be found on the 10th floor, transfer level for the banks of elevators operating between the first and 17th floor, the 18th to 30th floors, the 31st to 41st, and the 42nd to 49th. Then again, one could meet at the CL, LL, or GL floors, roughly translating to convention level, lobby level, and garden level. Then, of course, there were lobbies at the Georgia World Congress Center, too, one at the entry level, and one on each of the four floors escalating down to Hall F, the bourse room.

The gentle art of "lobbying" should never be confused with that of political buttonholing. Though both practices bear the same origins, one is as pleasing as the other is galling. Webster describes the latter as "to address or solicit members of a legislative body in the lobby, or elsewhere, with intent to influence legislation." The *Oxford English Dictionary* attributes the verb "lobby," and the practice of "lobbying," to American origins and usage. And John Morris, in his *Dictionary of Word and Phrase Origins,* writes "I should think it would be obvious that the first lobbyists were men who hung around lobbies of statehouses and other places where legislators assembled, in order to persuade them to pass legislation favorable to the interests the lobbyists represented." Morris, along with all other etymological cataloguers, fail to credit the man pictured on the $50 bill for first coining the word, "lobbyist."

The honor for this contribution to the American language belongs to Ulysses S. Grant, 18th President of the United States. And the "lobby" in question was not that of any statehouse or Congressional chambers but that of the old Willard Hotel at 14th and Pennsylvania Avenue in the nation's capital.

Ever since the first hotel was built on that site soon after Washington became the capital city, it was a meeting place for congressmen, officials of varying degrees of importance, and would-be office seekers. Because of its proximity to the White House and list of distinguished guests, the Willard became known as "the Hotel of the Presidents." It was a favorite escape for President Grant, who frequented the hotel enough to warrant a special leather chair set behind a screen in the lobby. Office and favor-seekers haunted the Willard lobby hoping to secure a few words with the President causing him to denounce them as "lobbyists."

But for the fate of time, the word "lobbying" today often suggests derision. Had wordmongers first attended a coin convention, the term "lobbying" may have been far more endearing.

THE ART OF SPEAKING EMPHATICALLY NUMISMATICALLY!

If your feelings have been hurt, your feathers ruffled, so to speak, and you must return an insult, do it with class. Do it numismatically!

The master of creative retaliation was also the master of paint and palette—James Abbott McNeill Whistler. His responses to slights, real or imagined, were legend enough to warrant the autobiographical *Gentle Art of Making Enemies,* published in 1892. Numismatists, however, need not peruse the entire 340 pages of copy to fully appreciate Whistler's deadly sarcasm. Collectors need only visit the Freer Gallery of Art in Washington, D.C.

The Freer is on the Mall, part of the Smithsonian complex. The gallery may not attract as many visitors as other facilities in the national museum complex. Yet, its showcase exhibits are as worth seeing as any other. The Freer houses one of the world's most renowned collections of Oriental art, as well as an important Egyptian glass and early Christian manuscripts. But, it is the works of Whistler that relate best to the numismatic mind.

Frederick Richard Leyland was a British shipowner of legendary wealth. He was Whistler's first important patron. When Leyland purchased the artist's "Rose and Silver: The Princess From the Land of Porcelain," he was so pleased with his aquisition that he commissioned a leading interior decorator of the day, Thomas Jeckyll, to redesign the dining room of his London townhouse to showcase the painting. Jeckyll was given three requirements: (1) provide an appropriate setting for Whistler's masterpiece; (2) cover the walls with a tooled and decorated Spanish leather reported to have been brought to England in the early 16th century by Catherine of Aragon, Henry VIII's first wife; and (3) to incorporate shelving in the room design to exhibit Leyland's famed collection of oriental porcelain.

When Whistler first viewed the newly completed room for Jeckyll, he suggested a "few" changes to his sponsor. Whistler asked for permission to "tone down the room a bit." The American artist started by painting over the rare antique wall hangings. Then, feeling that the red border of the priceless Oriental carpet clashed with his intended color scheme, he cut the border from the rug. Aesthetically, Whistler's changes were an improvement, but not in Leyland's view. He was appalled.

When Whistler requested payment of 2,000 guineas for his work, Leyland refused, offering instead payment in pounds. Whistler was incensed. The slur did not escape him. English aristocracy regarded remuneration in pounds suitable for mechanics and tradesmen, but reserved payment in guineas for themselves and artists.

Tales of the quarrel titillated London and overshadowed the artistic improvements, albeit at the expense of some priceless items. If one is to visit Leyland's dining room on exhibit at the Freer, he should carefully examine the large panel over the sideboard. Called "The Fighting Peacocks," one can identify the bird on the left—poor, calm and docile—as the artist, Whistler. The angrily strutting peacock on the right, greedily clutching a hoard of silver shillings, its body smothered in gold sovereigns, is, of course, Frederick Leyland. The American artist, forbidden ever to set foot again in Leyland's home after the project was completed, wrote to Leyland's wife, "I refer you to the cartoon opposite you at dinner, known to all London as 'L'Art et l'Argent' or 'The Story of the Room.'" Whistler was not about to let the subtlety go unnoticed.

Charles Lang Freer acquired "The Princess From The Land of Porcelain" in 1903. The following year he purchased the Peacock Room and brought it from London to be reassembled in his Detroit mansion. After Freer's death in 1919, the room was again dismantled and reinstalled in the present Freer Gallery of Art in Washington, D.C.

Guides, conducting free public tours through the galleries, seldom fail to recount the story of the room, the quarrel between patron and painter, and to point to the coins on the wall as symbols of the Ultimate Insult!

AT ODDS WITH THE ENGLISH LANGUAGE!

Editors pride themselves on being letter perfect. Why, then, do many persist in calling their publications "journals"? To be strictly accurate, the name "journal" should apply only to publications issued daily, the word "journal" means daily! We can correctly have our *Wall Street Journal*; Lafayette, Indiana, its *Journal and Courier*; Rockville, Maryland its *Montgomery Journal*; and Syracuse, New York, its *Herald-Journal*; but etymologically speaking, a monthly journal, such as *The Numismatist*, the ANA's official publication, is an impossibility.

The word "journal" is derived from the French word "jour," meaning "day." What it took a day to accomplish, whether it be travel or production, was called a "journee." When the word was exported to England, it became "journey," more specifically the distance of 20 miles, the measure that a man could be expected to cover in one day's walking. If the distance a person was to travel measured 60 miles, London to Northampton for example, it was referred to as "three journeys, or "three days journey."

"Journal" became a term used to describe a daily record of commercial transactions. In the church it came to mean a book containing the daily Hours (prayers to be said at specific times), and in transportation it meant a record of notices concerning the daily stages of a route and other information for travelers. But nowhere did it mean more than a day. In fact, in 1611, Shakespeare penned, "So please you, leave me, Sticke to your Iournal course." And Spencer wrote, ". . .his faint steedes watred in ocean deepe, Whiles from their iournal labours they did rest."

Even Charles Earle Funk, Funk and Wagnalls' good word doctor, pointed out that, ". . .in strict accuracy, in this sense of a written or printed record, the term should still apply to the occurences of a single day, though many technical publications, perhaps issued not oftener than once a month, contain the word journal in their titles."

The Numismatist, often referred to as the official journal of the American Numismatic Association, is no exception, but, don't blame Dr. George Heath for the the malapropism. There were journals of numismatics, medicine, archaeology and countless other disciplines, long before the good doctor from Monroe, Michigan, set his first page of type by hand.

The *American Journal of Numismatics and Bulletin of the American Numismatic & Archaeological Society* was introduced in May 1866. That pilot issue noted that prior to its debut, the subjects of numismatics and archaeology existed without an organ or means of introduction to the public, or to those who make their study a specialty. The editor, Frank H. Norton, said, ". . .the only means for instruction, for the spread of information, or for the advancement of these sciences, in a literary point of view, has been an occasional paragraph in a weekly newspaper, or an account of some coin sale or the discovery of some ancient relic, transiently made public in the newspapers, and perhaps cut out and preserved by interested collectors."

Norton then went on to say that the *Journal* would be ". . .punctually issued on the first day of every month!" Norton should have known better—he was a professional librarian for the Brooklyn Mercantile Library. Time evolved the numismatic-archaeological group into the American Numismatic Society.

Misuse of the word "journal" continued. In 1876, Scott & Company of New York City launched *The Coin Collector's Journal*; its publication continued for 13 years. After a 46-year respite, Scott, now Scott Stamp and Coin Company, resumed publication in April 1934, with a new volume 1, number 1. At the beginning editorship was shared by Wayte Raymond and Prescott H. Thorp, and, once again, they called their publication *The Coin Collector's Journal*. As chance would have it, the magazine lasted for a like 13 years before succumbing to a more appropriately named competitor, *The Numismatic Scrapbook*.

The Numismatist remains, as it has for now for more than 100 years, the monthly word of the Association.

DON'T BET YOUR BOTTOM DOLLAR!

From the time of the establishment of the United States Mint in 1792 to the outbreak of the Civil War, the grand total production of United States silver dollars was a mere 3,169,962 coins. For more than half of those 69 years, no silver dollars were made for circulation. It was not to be for another decade, until 1871, that annual production reached one million coins for the first time. This miserly production record of the coin representing the nation's basic unit of exchange led to the use of an expression heard to this day—Don't bet your bottom dollar!

In fairness to Mint officials, there were sound reasons for the low-mintage figures. Gold was the coin of trade in the East, silver served the West. America's population centered along the Eastern seaboard. In the West and Far West, wealth and trade were more often measured in terms of raw materials than in coin of the realm. Furthermore, there was a period, particularly in the early 1850s, when the intrinsic value of the silver dollar exceeded its face value. Few people brought silver to the Mint to be coined, especially during the period when it was worth more than they received in return. The one dollar coin was subjected to export as bullion as fast as it was produced.

The silver dollar was the coin of the realm of the West. Its popularity was evidenced by the fact that at the end of 1854, in answer to urgent demands from San Francisco businessmen, the United States Mint forwarded fully one-third of the year's production of silver dollars in a single shipment. The coins were immediately placed in circulation.

In St. Louis, Missouri, particularly, the coin was an enigma. The gentry of the town fancied themselves "Easterners," lobbying to have manufacture of silver dollars discontinued. Gold was the proper medium of exhange for "civilized" folk. Still, St. Louis was the gateway to the West and the headquarters for countless fur traders and buffalo hunters. While barter might sustain these men in the field, silver was their coin of exchange while visiting civilization. Paper money, consisting of private bank issues, was favored by neither the gentry nor the roughshod.

Men who had been on the trail for months at a time, either trading for furs or hunting buffalo for their hides, preferred to be rewarded for their labors in silver dollars. It was an expedient method to account for their wealth or monetary reserves. Few of the men of the West bothered to count how much they had on hand. They would simply stack their supply of silver dollars and, as funds were needed, draw from the top of their stack. When they reached the bottom dollar, they knew that it was once again time to head out west—to their traps along the lakes and rivers, to meet with the Indians at the trading posts, or to hunt the herds that roamed the plains.

The country's meagre supply of silver dollars gave the men of the West a means of measuring when it was time to return to their commercial pursuits. Today, long past the period of fur traders and buffalo hunters, the term bottom dollar has come to symbolize the end of one's resources. Thanks to the production records of the United States Mint.

ONE SHOULD START AT THE VERY BEGINNING!

Even though it was mid-August, the day before the ribbon-cutting cere-

During its first seven decades of production, the U.S. Mint struck a little more than 3 million silver dollars.

monies opening of the American Numismatic Association's 1962 convention in the sweltering motor city of Detroit, I found myself being given a heavy padded jacket to wear. Then I signed a release of liability, donned a steel helmet and descended 1,138 feet below the streets of Detroit in search of a story for *Numismatic News.*

Far under the hustle of metropolitan Detroit is another city, complete with roads, traffic, rules, regulations, and, at one time, even a bank. The city below the city is the Detroit Mine of International Salt Company and from here is gathered one of the earliest currencies known to man—salt. If one is going to write about numismatics, one should start at the very beginning.

Collectors are familiar with the oft-repeated tale that Roman soldiers were paid in salt and thus the origin of the word, salary. The etymological facts are a little different. When Roman soldiers were sent to foreign provinces, they were given, in addition to their regular pay, "salt money," a sum specifically for the purchase of salt. In Latin, it was called salarium. The amount differed with each country and was based on the dearness of salt. By the time of Augustus (27 BC-AD 14), the foot soldier was forgotten and "salarium" became the sum paid officers and civil-

ian authorities to purchase any necessary supplies available in the territories under their command. By the third century AD, "salary" came to mean "payment of money at specified intervals."

Marco Polo told of cakes of salt, bearing the seal of the great Khan, being used as money in Tibet. He related that the Chinese considered salt second in value only to gold.

Salt, through the ages, has been a currency. Both Quiggins and Einzig, in their primitive money anthologies, cite several instances of the currency uses of salt, primarily in Ethiopia. When Mussolini's troops occupied Addis Ababa, the country's capital, in 1936, they found that the Central Bank held its reserves in salt. And salt was still a currency in use in the early 1960s.

Bekele Endeshaw, director general of the Ministry of Commerce and Industry under Haile Selassie, confirmed the use of amoles (salt bars) in the province of Tigre and forwarded, for illustrative purposes a small bar cut from an original amole measuring 19.7 inches in length.

Even in the United States, salt played its currency role. In 1788 the Onondaga Indians of central New York state ceded most of their lands for a peck of salt apiece, some yards of calico, and an individual annuity of $4. Like most In-

Main Street, Salt City, Michigan. *(Photo courtesy International Salt Co.)*

dian treaties, this was amended in 1792. When the Onondagas, as part of the Six Nations, signed a new treaty, they were to share an annual annuity of $4,500. This was to be paid in perpetuity, to be spent in "purchasing clothing, domestic animals, implements of husbandry, and other utensils suited to their circumstances, and in compensating useful atrificers, who shall reside with or near them, and be employed for their benefit."

No lesson in inflationary trends need be cited to realize that by 1950, when a new treaty was formulated, the sum total benefiting each Indian had been reduced to only a few cents each. For those tribes choosing not to be signatories to the revised treaty, the federal government must still purchase cloth valued at the prorated share designated in the original annuity. Possibly believing that the government was not worth its salt in living up to the treaty, salt was dropped as part of the annual payment.

America's Fort Knox of salt, which underlies the city of Detroit, is part of the Michigan Basin, one of the world's great salt deposits. The basin is a mere sector of the great Eastern Salt Basin which underlies Ontario, Ohio, West Virginia, Pennsylvania and New York, and totals more than 70,000 square miles in size. Reserves are enough to supply the entire world's needs far into the conceivable future.

The existence of these salt beds was not discovered until 1895. By 1906, a group of city businessmen had organized the Detroit Salt and Manufacturing Company. They attempted to dig the mine by hand. Accidents and bankruptcy put an end to that endeavor.

In 1910 a newly reorganized Detroit Salt Company had sunk a shaft to the 1,060 foot level and mining got underway. Mining under Detroit forsakes the conventional timbering, wood or metal supports to protect from collapse. The system used is called room and pillar. Rooms, 50 to 60 feet wide, with ceilings 23 to 25 feet in height, are excavated. At regular intervals huge pillars of salt, 60 to 80 feet thick, are left. They are the sole means of support for the roof and tremendous overburden separating the mine from the cellars and streets of Detroit.

Today, more than 40 miles of subterranean highways link the city under the city. Highway equipment includes full-sized diesel trucks, road graders, and electric tractor-trailers. Motorized equipment with gasoline engines must be converted to diesel.

Every bit of automotive equipment on the streets below had been disassembled and lowered, piece by piece, down one of two shafts serving Salt City and reassembled in an underground machine shop. A mine office was built of salt blocks and, at one time, a bank operated underground—for the benefit of employees who were unable to climb to the city above and be back on time during their breaks in the underground metropolis.

Today, plastic has taken away the need of cashing paychecks, so the bank is closed. While no viable substitute has been found for the need for salt on the table at dinner or on the highways in winter, only its name remains to remind us of its monetary days.

SO WHAT'S A PLUGGED NICKEL?

To the odds-makers at the 1980 Kentucky Derby, Plugged Nickle (note the misspelling) was a 3-to-1 prerace favorite. To coin collectors, not normally inclined to wager, it was just a hunch, worth a $2 bet. Although Plugged Nickle led going into the quarter mile, he jammed in the slot and finished out of the money, pardon the pun. And to think that "Plugged Nickle came out of Toll Booth, sired by Key to the Mint." Honest.

But, what is a real plugged nickel? The term is more elusive than one would imagine. It is not listed in the *Dictionary of Numismatic Terms*, not even in the *Oxford Dictionary on the Origin of Words*. A line in the *American Thesaurus of Slang* simply defines plugged nickel as meaning something worthless or insignificant. But plugged nickels have a place in numismatic history and if you lived and played in the 1930s you may well remember seeing one.

Prior to World War II many clubs, restaurants, bars, cigar stores, candy shops—places where men and boys congregated—had vending machines of a gaming nature. Pinball machines, for example. Players vied for scores and high scores were rewarded in free games, or so the authorities were told. Instead of automatically registering the "free" games won, the machines paid off in tokens. Theoretically the tokens went back into the slots for more games, but more often than not, they were exchanged for gum, mints, cigarettes, or even cash.

In order to comply with section 491(b) of title 18 of the United States Code, a law which prohibited the distribution of any tokens, slugs or discs similar in size and shape to any lawful coin of the United States, manufacturers produced tokens with large holes in the center. This made the token lighter in weight and supposedly different in shape from the five-cent piece they were substituting for. But, a simple lead plug, surreptiously added later, brought the token up to a weight sufficient to trip the coin mechanism of juke boxes, vending machines and pay phones, enough to violate the law and relegate the holed token—the plugged nickel of yesteryear—to the junk box of today's coin dealer and the nostalgic recall of growing up in the 1930s.

This "plugged nickel" was issued by an amusement game vendor.

IN OTHER WORLDS

GOODBYE, COLUMBUS—COIN SAYS IT WASN'T SO!

Of all the old contiguous states only one fails to observe Columbus Day. Minnesota feels that the honors belong to an earlier adventurer—Leif Ericsson. Perhaps the Gopher State is the only one in step with history and the others are missing the proper cadence. Minnesotans like to think so.

The positive identification of a coin found several years ago in an ancient Indian rubbish heap along the Maine coast lends credence to the belief that the wrong person has been honored all along as the first European to discover America. Few historians doubt the possibility of Viking visits to the shores of Newfoundland centuries prior to Columbus' 1492 voyage, but the coin find may mean that the continental United States was also a site of such prior landings.

The coin, found near Blue Hill, Maine, in 1961, by an amateur archaeologist, was eventually given to the Maine State Museum. At first, it was thought to be an English coin of the period between 1134 and 1154. This attribution led to the publication of an article entitled, "Were the English the First to Discover America?"

The story came to the attention of Peter Seaby, a noted numismatologist and proprietor of B. A. Seaby's Ltd., a several generations old rare coin firm in London. Although only an obverse photograph of the coin complemented the original article, Seaby knew immediately that the coin was not of English origin.

Suspecting that it might be Norse, Seaby compared it to the specimens in the British Museum. He determined that the coin was an issue struck for Olaf II Kyrre, king of Norway from 1066 to 1093. It is understandable that the first attribution was to England. Early Norwegian coins were often copies of English issues.

Identified as a silver penny, the dime-sized coin had been struck on a low-grade silver planchet, typical of the issues of the period. Olaf Kyrre's father, King Harald, had reduced the silver content of his coinage, using the seigniorage to help underwrite his expensive military campaigns.

The issuance of coins of similar low-quality continued throughout the reign of his sons, Magnus and Olaf. It appears, on close scrutiny, that the coin found suffered more from chemical erosion and breakage than from circulation wear. Thus, by conjectural dating—allowing that the coin may have seen some circulation—a terminal date for its

The Blue Hill, Maine coin find.

loss along the Maine coast has been set between AD 1100 and 1200.

Is the find proof positive that the Vikings did indeed precede Columbus sailing under the Spanish flag?

No. A small portion of the coin is missing, giving rise to the belief that it may have been holed and used as ornamental jewelry. Contemporary Norse coins, found in Greenland, all have holes pierced in them. Some have been discovered with traces of woolen thread, further indication that they were indeed worn as jewelry.

It is conceivable that this coin was once traded by a Viking adventurer to an Indian, more probably a Skraeling (Eskimo) of Viking lore, for pelts or food. If the coin had been retraded, it could have ended up on the Maine coast centuries later, giving misleading evidence of a Viking landing in New England. But, at the same time, the coin's find in the Indian dumps of Blue Hill lends credence to the possibility that Minnesotans may be correct, after all—that even though Columbus tried harder, he was only No. 2!

WHEN THE SHADOW OF NEW COINS SHUT OUT THE SUN!

Even though the sun may shine on April 15th, it is for many a dark and gloomy day. It's the time for Uncle Sam to take his due—it's income tax day!

Once, in a different place and in a different period, taxes really meant dark and gloomy days. All because the king wanted new coins.

If one is to travel the roads and byways of England today, he or she is likely to see old homes, built before the middle of the last century, with few windows; and even older homes where the windows have been bricked in. All are mute testimony to a king's infamous "window tax," a tax first imposed on the citizenry during the reign of William III (1689-1702) for the sole purpose of underwriting the costs of a new coinage for England.

Prior to William's reign, the coins of England were crude, hammered pieces, neither perfectly round nor of equal weight. Common practice of the time, despite severe penalties, led to the clipping of the edges of the coins for scraps of precious silver or gold. The penalty, if one was caught, was

Shillings of William III ushered in the era of milled edge coins designed to discourage the practice of clipping.

death—hanging for men, burning for women. And many a clipper faced the executioner. If one was found with only the parings or filings from old coins, the penalty called for branding on the cheek with a red hot iron. One could escape punishment for the first offense by turning in two others guilty of the same crime. Needless to say, the fear of the branding iron caused many an innocent person to be accused of clipping.

King William had an idea—why not make round coins, from machined blanks of equal weight, and with reeded or milled edges, to discourage clipping? But, the king realized that two types of coins could not circulate side by side, the people would hoard the good, full-weight pieces and spend only the others. His plan called for the hammered coins to be surrendered and exchanged for the new coins. When the government announced that the old coins would be redeemed, face value for face value, an even greater rush to clip and pare the old resulted. The treasury would be hard pressed to exchange full value for part value. A need to underwrite the cost of the transition was evident.

Several taxes were considered, but one seemed much easier than the others to enforce. It was a window tax. An assessor need only walk around the outside of a house to determine the amount of tax due. There was no "hiding of assets." When the tax was announced in 1695, there was a rush to close up windows.

The tax returned approximately $7 million—just about the amount needed to cover the cost of the new coinage. Taxes, however, as unpopular as they are, are harder to drop once they have been introduced than they are to initiate in the first place. Although the window tax achieved its avowed purpose within a few years time, it continued to be enforced for more than 150 years. The new milled coins were successful in their purpose and the real reason for the window tax was soon forgotten, keeping the poorer people of Britain in the dark for more than a century and a half.

COINS TELL THE SAD TALE OF THE LITTLE PRINCESS OF BALTIMORE!

Take all the elements of a fairy tale: a beautiful young girl, a handsome prince from a land across the sea. Set the scene at a gala ball given by a head of state, and you have the story of a dream come true. Almost. The young girl marries her handsome prince. He soon reigns over a little kingdom, but the story does not have the usual ending. They do not live happily ever after, let alone together.

The princess-soon-to-be is Elizabeth Patterson, niece of American Revolutionary War hero Sam Smith. The prince is Jerome Bonaparte, youngest brother of Napoleon. The ball is set at

Elizabeth Patterson Bonaparte.

Baltimore, the host is President Thomas Jefferson, and the year is pre-Waterloo—1803.

Legend relates that Betsy, as she prefers to be called, captures her prince's attention by maneuvering to catch his golden sleeve button in the frilled lace of her blouse. Such is the tale of young love. But, while Baltimore society calls it, "the catch-of-the-year," it is a union not to receive the approval of the great Napoleon. He has higher ambitions for his youngest brother.

Napoleon plans the lives of his family as he does his military campaigns. Little is left to chance. From the Bonaparte siblings emerge the kings of Naples, Spain and Holland; the princesses of Piombino and Lucca, and Guastalla; the grand duchess of Tuscany; and, for Jerome, the crown of Westphalia.

For Jerome's queen, Napoleon has no plans for a merchant's daughter, let alone a girl from a land without nobility. The emperor selects, instead, Princess Catherine of Wurttemberg.

Wily Sam Smith anticipates Napoleon's reaction to the storybook match. Smith seeks to outsmart the emperor. The marriage of Elizabeth Patterson to Jerome Bonaparte is performed by John Carroll, Catholic Archbishop of Baltimore. Surely Napoleon will not overrule the church, but Sam Smith is wrong. The emperor annuls the marriage, an action not condoned by the pope. Pius VII refuses to recognize Jerome's second marriage to Catherine of Wurttemberg.

An ocean voyage to France is all of Elizabeth's and Jerome's honeymoon. It is all the married life that they are to know. As the ship docks in France, Elizabeth is refused permission to land and is sent to exile in England. There, in 1805, a son—Jerome Napoleon Bonaparte—is born. About the same time, the emperor creates a new country. There was no little kingdom ready to give Jerome, so Napoleon makes one!

Napoleon had seized all Prussia west of the Elbe, along with the states of Hesse-Kassel and Hanover. Half of the territory is annexed to France and with the remainder, Napoleon creates the Kingdom of Westphalia. It is to last until 1813, when the Congress of Vienna returns the lands to their former owners.

For so short a period, 1807-1813, so many coins are issued that collectors now have to devote a significant amount of time and a sizable sum of money to build a complete collection. Coins of both French and German

As far as coins go, it is an innocuous little piece, unimaginative of design, inexpensive of fabric, and short-lived of circulation. Yet, it tells a fanciful fairy tale.

standards are issued. Denominations of 1, 2, 3, 5, 10, and 20 centimes circulate side by side with 1 and 24 Mariengroschens and 1/24, 1/12, 1/6, 2/3, 1, 5, and 10 thalers. Some carry Jerome's portrait, others his name only, and a several bear his royal monogram. The monetary system is as chaotic as his short rule.

While Jerome's jilting of his young princess from Baltimore cannot be admired, the French government later tries to make amends. Elizabeth is allowed to call herself, "Madame" Bonaparte, and receives a small government pension. She remains true to her heart and never remarries. But, her snaring of his golden sleeve button on the frilly lace of her blouse, and briefly the heart of the young prince, gives Europe a new country, albeit a very short-lived one, collectors of world coins a series to pursue, and Baltimoreans the tale of a young princess to call their own.

A TOKEN REMEMBRANCE OF A GREAT FAMINE!

Words and scenes from Ethiopia reach out from the pages of our newspapers and magazines, and from the screens of our television sets daily. Few are unaware that a great famine on the African continent claimed more than 300,000 lives and many more thousands will die before long overdue rains end the drought. But what few people realize is that this tragedy, as bad as it is, pales in comparison to those experienced in India during the last two hundred years.

A third of the population, more than 10 million people, perished during the Great Famine in Bengal in 1769-70. Twenty years later, the Skull Famine, so-called because too many died to be buried, hit the province of Madras. By the 1860s, Indian famines were almost an annual occurrence. In 1866 more than one million perished in Bengal and Orissa; in 1869, a 1.5 million died in Rajputana; and again in 1876-78, famine claimed five million Indians in Bombay, Madras and Mysore.

The building of the Indian railways helped alleviate part of the problem by providing a means to transport food from one area to another.

Unlike the present, when the generosity of Western governments and international aid agencies play a major role in famine relief, India's British adminis-

To insure that monies paid for employment during the Indian famines were used exclusively on food, the British administrators devised a special token coinage issue.

trators were opposed to gratuitous relief. Britain believed that public work projects were the proper answer. These endeavors would bring money into the area through employment, they claimed, and when there was money to spend, food supplies would follow through commercial channels. During the famine of 1899-1901, the British government had more than 4.5 million Indians at work on public projects.

Although the system was not without critics, it appeared to work. India was to go for more than 40 years before another major famine struck. This time it was during World War II. In 1943, in Bengal, more than 1.5 million perished from hunger. Officially, the blame was placed on local authorities for failing to notify the government in sufficient time for relief projects to get underway.

To insure that the monies paid for public service employment during the periods of famine were spent on food and not on other goods, the British devised a special token coinage. These particular coins were unlike the regular issues in circulation and could be redeemed only for food. It is apparent that most tokens were so redeemed for they are extremely rare today. The few that are in collections serve as reminders that there are other answers to a major problem confronting the African continent today.

HE COINED A NEW WAY TO ADVERTISE!

He gave life to the countless tales of the ambitious salesman marrying the boss' daughter, and then taking over the company. Fortunately for the father, this son-in-law was a young man with new, ingenious ideas about advertising. Chances are that had Thomas J. Barratt not wooed and married Mary Pears, her father's company would not have survived and the hobby world today would have been deprived of the many intriguing collectibles made to promote Pears soap.

In 1789 Andrew Pears completed his hairdresser's apprenticeship in the Cornish village where he was born, Mevagissy. Pears was not long in realizing that being the village hairdresser offered little promise. He then moved on to London to establish himself in the fashionable Soho. Pears stocked his salon with cosmetics of his own manufacture. After years of experimentation,

To help ease an acute shortage of small coin, a British soap manufacturer imported 250,000 French 10-centime pieces and placed them into circulation—with his company's name.

Andrew Pears perfected a transparent soap, mild, delicately perfumed with the scent of flowers from an English garden.

Introduced in 1807, Pears soap became so immensely popular that he abandoned his hairdressing trade to concentrate on making soap. By 1835, Andrew Pears brought his grandson, Francis, into the firm, taught the younger Pears all he knew about the business, and then retired three years later.

Businesswise, Francis Pears was as conservative as his grandfather. Production of soap concentrated only on quality, never quantity. Competitors, both fair and foul, hurt business. Thomas Barratt, when he entered the firm in 1862, alarmed his new father-in-law with an outlandish proposal to promote business—he wanted to advertise! All Francis Pears could envision was bankruptcy. Francis' son, Andrew, named after his great-grandfather, shared the family's lack of imagination. Barratt's every suggestion met with negative response, his ideas viewed as radical and extravagant.

Then Francis Pears, fearing bankruptcy, not only quit the company, but took most of the cash with him. Barratt and young Andrew Pears were left with only an unpaid loan of $23,000.

In its first 80 years of business the Pears company's advertising budget grand totaled less than $2,500. Barratt now had a free hand and the annual promotional budget soared to almost three-quarters of a million dollars. It was at a time when advertising was still in its infancy in England. Barratt sought testimonials, first from the medical profession, then from a popular actress of the day. Said Lillie Langtry "Since using Pears soap, I have discarded all others." When the satirical magazine *Punch* parodied the testimonial, Barratt used that, too. Punch had featured a cartoon showing an unwashed tramp arduously penning his testimonial, "Two years ago I used your soap, since then I have used no other!" It became an advertising classic.

Barratt's imagination knew no bounds. He finagled the post office into accepting his ads for Pears soap. His messages appeared on the gummed side of British postage stamps in 1881 and again in 1887. But it was Barratt's biggest promotional coup that had the British Parliament up in arms. He had managed to place the Pears name on thousands of coins then in circulation.

During the mid-1880s England was experiencing another of its periodic shortages of small coin. British expediency dictated since French 10-centime pieces were of similar size, value, and metallic content to the English penny, that they be accepted in change at par. Barratt imported a quarter of a million of these French copper pieces and had the name PEARS stamped on each. He then released the coins into circulation through a host of distributors. They, in turn, sold the coins to London bus conductors at 14 to the shilling. While existing law prohibited the defacement of British currency, no mention had been made about foreign coins. Staid English lawmakers were so upset about being outsmarted by a soap maker that they soon enacted legislation making all foreign coins illegal to tender. The Pears advertisements were withdrawn from circulation and melted down. The coins that escaped the mint's crucibles are today cherished additions to the collections of fortunate numismatists. A few examples can be found in the archives of A & F Pears, Limited, now a subsidiary of multinational Unilever. An undetermined number remain in coin dealer junk boxes, unrecognized and waiting to be claimed by collectors who realize what they are—examples of the promotional genius of the man who has become known as "The Father of Modern Advertising,"—Thomas J. Barratt.

MARCUS GARVEY

Rogue or reformer? It depends on the shade of your glasses. To American authorities, Marcus Mosiah Garvey was a fraud, an embezzler, an income-tax cheat, and an ex-convict; to a British observer attending one of his lectures at Albert Hall, he was "crazy as a loon!" But, to fellow Jamaicans, Marcus Garvey was a visionary, a national hero whose portrait appears on coins of the country—tribute to the man they call, "the father of the concept of 'black power.'"

Marcus Garvey was born in Jamaica in 1887, then part of the British West Indies. By virtue of birth he was a British citizen and availed himself of the opportunity to study in England. When war began in Europe in 1914, Garvey retreated to the United States and brought with him a change in name, from Marcus Mosiah to Marcus Aurelius. It was more fitting for the empire that he had in mind for himself.

Taking court in Harlem, Garvey set himself up as "Emperor of the Kingdom of Africa." He also conferred on himself such august titles as Admiral of the Black Star Line, Commander of the Nobles of the Sublime Order of the Nile, Knight of the Distinguished Order of Ethiopia, and, as founder of the United Negro Improvement Association, he elected himself "president general." He was equally generous with titles for his friends and followers. For a time, Harlem was populated with princes and princesses, barons, knights, viscounts, earls, and dukes.

Garvey dressed to match his self-acquired nobility. His favorite uniform of the day was that of an admiral, complete with golden epaulets, campaign ribbons, and medals of non-existent honors. On his head he placed a plumed commodore's hat, for his imaginary nation did, indeed, have a fleet. To underwrite the cost of the African kingdom's navy, Garvey sold stock in his Black Star Steamship Line at $5 per share. It was these certificates that brought Garvey to reign in the Atlanta Penitentiary. The purpose of his fleet was to provide economical transportation for the "return to Africa" of his loyal followers, but the fleet, instead, provided comic relief for newspaper readers across the United States.

Garvey's ships ranged from the *General George W. Goethals,* a single screw steamship launched in 1911 at Bremen as the *Grunewald* and interned during the First World War; a Hudson River excursion boat; the late Col. Henry Huddleston Rogers' pleasure yacht, *Kanawha;* to a small coastal freighter, *The Yarmouth.* When not transporting Garvey's followers to Africa to settle his new empire, the fleet was to earn income for his other enterprises. The first consignment for *The Yarmouth* called for the removal of a $3 million cargo of whiskey from Brooklyn to Havana on the eve of Prohibition in the

Marcus Mosiah Garvey is pictured on the obverse of this coin from Jamaica.

U.S. As the ship left port the crew tended more for refreshments from the ship's cargo hold than from the crew mess. Instead of Havana, they put in at Norfolk and both ship and cargo were seized under the new prohibition laws. The port of Norfolk proved a continuing jinx for the Garvey fleet. On the *Kanawha's* first voyage into that port the skipper miscalculated speed and distance and rammed a pier, his boiler exploded, and the *Kanawha,* too, became a total loss. The excursion boat was too unseaworthy to risk leaving its Hudson River berth, but the *General Goethals,* now renamed the *Booker T. Washington,* did earn revenue for Garvey. Three thousand followers paid 50 cents a head to tour the ship that was to take them to Garvey's new African kingdom. Marcus Garvey's following was large enough to attract world attention and resulted in an invitation to speak before the League of Nations to expound on his proposals. He asked the League to require Britain to turn over to him all the former German West Africa colonies. These, together, with Sierra Leone, Liberia and Ethiopia, would eventually be incorporated into a United States of Africa. He failed to mention his aspirations for a "kingdom" to the league. While the world body listened, America's IRS investigated. Through an earlier grand jury investigation, Garvey had been convicted of using the mails to defraud investors in his Black Star Line. Now, in August 1924, another grand jury found Garvey guilty of perjury in falsifying his income tax returns, resulting in a five-year prison term to be served in the Atlanta Penitentiary.

On his release in 1927, Garvey was deported to Jamaica, not an all unpleasant experience, since millions of dollars raised for his yet-to-be-realized empire had been banked there. But the dream of one's own kingdom remained strong. Since Garvey could no longer save American blacks, he turned, in a heavily publicized tour, to rescue those of Ethiopia. Only a handful of enthusiasts showed in place of an anticipated crowd of 10,000 at London's Albert Hall. Still, Garvey went on stage in a futile attempt to raise funds to rescue the country from the Italians. Instead of applause, he was greeted by a demand to return the price of admission and the cry of "You're as crazy as a loon!"

Dejected, the man who would be king, slipped into obscurity. He died in London on June 10, 1940, but the legend of Marcus Garvey was far from dead. His writings and teachings became the bible for many young nationalists in the emerging nations of Africa following World War II.

In 1964 Garvey's remains were brought back to Jamaica and reinterred with full honors in the National Heroes Park. In 1980 a bust of Garvey was unveiled at the Hall of Heroes of the Organization of American States. Ironically, while Garvey may have dreamed of coins with his portrait on them, they were for his "Kingdom of Africa."

Rogue or reformer, Marcus Mosiah Garvey certainly never envisioned the posthumous recognition of placing his portrait on the coins of the land of his birth, nor that on the centennial of his birth he would be regarded as a national hero in the country he called home for so few years.

CANADA'S MISPLACED BRONCO BUCK!

Canada boasts that it is the home of the rodeo. Why, even a bucking bronco was the central theme of a silver dollar issued in 1975 to mark the 100th anniversary of the founding of Calgary. One of that city's major claims to fame is that it is the home of the famed Calgary Stampede, the world's fair of rodeo.

If any country was to issue a rodeo dollar, it should have been the United States! Within driving minutes of the U.S. Mint in Denver is the Colorado prairie town of Deer Trail. The world's first rodeo—with contestants, prizes and rules—was held there on the Fourth of July in 1869, six years before the first rider was thrown at Calgary.

The reverse design of the Canadian dollar could have remained the same. Only the wording and date needed to be changed. The skyline on the left-hand side could pass for that of Denver and the rigs on the right could be those of the Peoria Oilfield, six miles west of Deer Trail. These rodeo towns have marked similarities, except where population is concerned. More people can congregate on a Calgary street corner than populate the entire Deer Trail community.

The world's first rodeo had its beginnings as a contest between cowhands of the Hashknife, Mill Iron, and Camp Stool ranches. The conditions of the event called for "horses to be ridden with a slick saddle, which means that the saddle must be free from the roll usually tied across the horse, that the stirrups must not be tied under the horse, and that the rider must not wear spurs."

The horses selected for the contest were considered impossible to break—outlaws. The prize offered included the title—"Champion Bronco Buster of the Plains," and a new suit of clothes. While the United States can claim the first rodeo, the championship title went to an Englishman, Emilnie Gardenshire, a ranchhand on the Mill Iron.

Deer Trail failed to host another rodeo for several years. Nonetheless, in 1969, a centennial plaque was unveiled. Although the Denver metropolitan population exceeds 1.5 million, less than 2,000 people attended the ceremonial observance of the centennial of the rodeo.

How different things might have been had the United States made the Bronco Buck, rather than the Royal Canadian Mint. Americans would have been made more aware of the history of one of their own insitutions—the rodeo!

The Royal Canadian Mint issue is one of an annual series of commemorative dollars designed to relate their history. It may have been their coin, but it was our story.

ANGELS OF A LESSER GOD!

Three centuries have passed since the birth of Emanuel Swedenborg. He was an unusual man, one of the most dis-

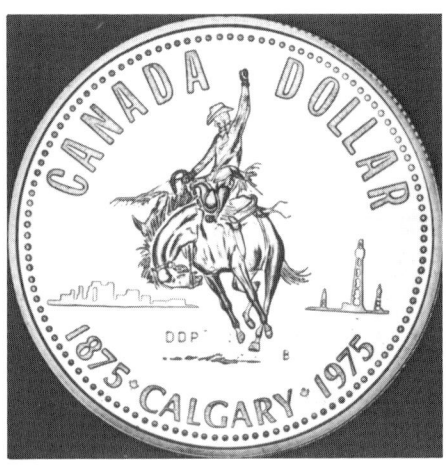

Canada's 1975 commemorative silver dollar marked the centennial of the city of Calgary, home of the famed stampede.

tinguished men of science of the 18th century, and he was the founder of the Church of New Jerusalem. His scientific endeavors dealt with engineering and mining; his theological pursuits were less orthodox. Swedenborg's anniversary was one not overlooked, particularly in Sweden where his followers were many. There were some postage issues, but regretably not a commemorative coin.

Had a coin been struck, one side should have carried the design of an angel, for Swedenborg believed in angels. He thought that through Divine intercession he had been permitted to meet and converse with these inhabitants of the invisible world. "Since angels are men," preached Swedenborg, "and live together in society like men on earth, they have garments, houses and other things familiar to those which exist on earth, but of course, infinitely more beautiful and perfect.

"The garments of the angels correspond to their intelligence. The garments of some glitter as with flame, and those of others resplendent as with light; others are of various colors, and some white and opaque.

"The angels of the inmost heaven are naked, because they are in innocence and nakedness corresponds to innocence. It is because garments represent states of wisdom that they are so much spoken of in the Word, in relation to the Church and good men."

Today, angels refer not only to celestial inhabitants, but are spoken of in relation to the more earthly objects—like money. Modern angels are of a lesser god—but nonetheless have their genesis in Divine belief.

When Edward IV of England was king, some 200 years before Emanuel Swedenborg's proselytizing, angels of a different sort performed miracles for a lesser god, or so it was believed. Had the fates ordained for Swedenborg to meet King Edward on one of the former's transmundane journeys, the monarch may have related the origin of his angels by way of this introduction:

"I am Edward IV, son of Richard, Duke of York, and by the grace of God, King of England. I was born in France on the 28th day of April 1442. As a boy, I was called the Earl of March and was raised at Ludlow. After the friends of my father were defeated in 1459, I retreated with my uncle, the Earl of Salisbury, and my cousin, the Earl of Warwick, to Calais. The following summer, we returned and defeated those Lancastrians at Northampton. We were welcomed in London and my fa-

The angel today is the official five-pound coin of the Isle of Man.

ther was given the crown.

"I was in Wales, where I had returned, when I heard of my father's defeat and death at Wakefield. Quickly I gathered an army and trounced the Earls of Pembroke and Wiltshire at Mortimer's Cross on the 2nd of February 1461. I marched on London and was acclaimed by the citizens in an assembly at Clerkenwell. Not quite 19 years of age, I was declared king. Though the battles were not over, I found time to court Elizabeth, widow of Sir John Grey of Groby and daughter of the Lord Rivers, Richard Woodville. We were married on Michaelmas 1464, much to the dismay of my cousin, Warwick. He had visions of a union with a French princess. 'In the interest of foreign policy,' Warwick said. But Elizabeth had many sisters and brothers. They were to be bethrothed to the foreigners. For my new father-in-law, I had special plans. He was to be my treasurer.

"Briefly, God closed his eyes on me and I had to seek exile in Holland in 1470. But, on the 14th day of March 1471, I returned with but a meager force and set about defeating the Lancastrians, once and for all. The people of London welcomed me back and returned my crown.

"My father-in-law, now the Earl Rivers, served me well as treasurer. While it took money to protect what God had ordained, I was able to support my position without heavy taxation. To increase the supply of bullion to the mint, the treasurer suggested that the weight of the penny be reduced to 12 grains, and the value of the noble raised to eight shillings, four pence. Then, in 1465, a new coin, the Rose Noble of 120 grains weight and a value of 10 shillings, was introduced. Soon, my subjects complained that the older noble was missed for standard professional fees were six shillings, eight pence, so I ordered a new coin to take its place. Royal mints were opened at Canterbury and York, and temporarily at Bristol, Coventry and Norwich, to help with the recoinage.

"Since my choice of Elizabeth had proven fortuitous and we had been married on the Feast of St. Michael the Archangel, I requested that the new coin carry his image slaying the dragon, as I did the Lancastrians, on one side. On the other, I asked that a ship be shown, for twice now, I have been brought back to England. And on the coin, I wanted the words, PER CRUCEM TUAM SALVA NOS CHRISTE REDEMPTOR ('By the cross save us O Christ, Our Redeemer'). My subjects called the coin an angel.

"Not all the troubles during my time were political. Many suffered from the dread disease scrofula. My subjects called it 'the king's evil.' They meant no disrespect calling it so, but prayed that a cure could be effected by my touch. After all, did not Saint Mark write in his first chapter, 'And there came a leper to him beseeching him, and kneeling down to him, and saying to him, If thou wilt, thou canst make me clean. And, Jesus, moved with compassion, put forth his hand and touched him.'

"Do I not rule by Divine Right? Then I, too, can cure. My gold angel is my touch-piece. To those poor souls with the king's evil I have given my coin and they have pierced it, and hung it around their necks by a white ribbon.

"My legacy to my country are those that I have touched."

The practice of touching continued for many years. When the angel, as a coin ceased to be struck after 1634, special medals, bearing the time honored rendition of St. Michael slaying the dragon, were made. The practice of touching was repudiated by William III, in 1689, calling it a "silly superstition."

Numismatic angels were reintroduced in 1984, some say to fight a different evil—apartheid. While it is doubtful that a single angel was purchased in protest of South Africa's racial policies, or at the expense of a krugerrand, the angel has captured the imagination of many and has become a popular bullion piece in its own right. The Isle of

Man entered the bullion gold market in competition with South African krugerrand, which at the time was the prime source of readily available and locally traded gold investment coins.

Today's angels still bear the scene of Michael slaying the dragon, but the portrait of the ruling monarch, Queen Elizabeth II, similar in appearance to coins of Great Britain, shows on the other side.

The Isle of Man retained a special status when it came under the British crown in 1765, including the right to its own coinage. The current gold angels are an exercise of that privilege and are available in several weights or denominations. If you are a bullion investor, interested in convenient-sized, multiple weights, angels are available in five and ten-ounce versions. The most popular size, though, is the one ounce. However, for those interested in angels as gifts, charms or as tokens of love and concern, they are available in denominations of 1/2, 1/4, 1/10 and 1/20 angel. The latter was not authorized until 1986, and measures midway in size between the small and large U.S. gold dollar. All angel denominations are struck in 22-karat (.9167 fine) gold, and each contains the precise amount of fine gold specified on the coin (1 troy ounce or its multiples or fractions thereof), plus copper as a hardener.

While Swedenborg may never have approved this latter-day use of angels in the service of a lesser god, he probably would have taken a specimen or two back with him the next time he visited more heavenly angels.

THE LAST WAMPUM MILL IN AMERICA!

They were not counterfeiters. "Bless you, no," responded Robert excitedly. He was speaking for himself and his brothers James, John, David and Abraham. "They was glad enough to get it."

For many years the Campbell family had monopolized the wampum market. By the late 1880s, the brothers were the last of four generations to operate the wampum mill. The demise of their industry, they claimed, came not from abuse or overproduction. It died for the lack of proper shells to coin the money of the fur trade.

The pastoral setting of America's last wampum mill has long since given way to the urbanization of the New Jersey countryside. The mill had been powered by the swift flow of Pascack Brook as it dropped into the Hackensack a few miles above Englewood. The Hackensack Valley, too, long ago relinquished its title as the "wampum-making capital." But, for a period of more than 120 years, more Caucasian-made, real shell wampum originated from here than from the combined labors of all American Indians. In fact, the Hackensack Valley produced most of the trade beads bartered in the fur trade from Colonial times to post-Civil War years.

In his later years, Robert Campbell told the story of his family's enterprise in an interview with Charles Ledyard Norton for publication in the March 1888 issue of *The American Magazine.* Norton, an early-day Charles Kurault, accidentally stumbled onto the remnants of the wampum operation during a stroll through the New Jersey valley. A padlocked mill and a pile of conch shell fragments piqued Norton's curiosity. Following a footpath from the mill to a nearby home, the writer sought the mill's tenants. It was here that Norton found the retired "master of the mint."

In his home Campbell had a sample collection of the mill's products. "They were neither many nor varied," reported Norton. "Strings of beads, white and purplish black; 'moons,' loose and in sets of five; and 'hairpipe' as the firm called them—namely, bits of shell that looked like clay pipestems, but thicker in the middle than on the ends."

In answer to the reporter's question

about the origins of the business, Campbell related that his grandparents and great-grandparents had worked at wampum-making. "It must be three or four generations since we Campbells have been making wampum right here on the Pascack," he said.

Oral history recalls that after the first Campbell settled here, he began trading with the Indians. He found wampum very handy for small change, but it was in short supply. The elder Campbell studied the wampum carefully, then designed and built much of the equipment necessary to turn seashells into currency. At first this was done for his own private supply, but soon the making of wampum became a commercial endeavor. John Jacob Astor, prominent fur trader, was reported to be one of the first to place large quantity orders.

Campbell's trade beads began circulating at the trading posts along the Missouri River, and then as far away as the mouth of the Columbia on the Pacific Coast. "That was along before the last war with England (1812), and the first shipments were made through his (Astor's) agents," Campbell explained. Afterward, several firms in New York and Philadelphia and St. Louis took hold. The best time was from about 1835 until 1850, but business began to be uncertain by 1866.

"Why, during the flush times," he bragged unabashedly, "we used to turn out a million a year of black beads. We used to have slooploads of clams brought here from Rockaway to Teaneck and Snedden's Landing. The neighbors would take most of the meat and leave us the shells. A million of beads and 900 set of moons! Them was times when the Indian trade amounted to something."

Campbell took Norton to see the interior of the old mill. Here he saw the row of grindstones, the lathes that had replaced the original bow drills, and the crude cutting tools. The interviewer noticed the fragments of shells scattered about and marveled at the scope

The last wampum mill in America operated in New Jersey until late in the 19th century. For more than 120 years, more Caucasian-made, real shell wampum originated from here than from the combined labors of all American Indians.

of the operation.

"We had our trade secrets," winked the old man. While he refused to divulge how they drilled hairpipe, Campbell told of a method to remove the pink color from hairpipe. "The Indians won't have any pink on their hairpipe," Campbell explained, "though they want it on their moons—more the better."

Norton asked why the Indians would accept white man-made wampum when they could make it themselves. To Campbell, the answer was elementary. He gave this lengthy response, "Indians had all the time they wanted and no tools to speak of, and they would grind away for a month on a little piece of shell, and finally turned out a good bit of work, but it was a slow way to coin money, though the money was good enough when it was coined; so great grandfather went to work and he found he could beat the native methods away out of sight. Any level-headed Indian was glad to give a beaver skin or two, that only cost him a day's hunting, which he liked in exchange for a few beads, which would have cost him six weeks' work that he hated."

By the start of the 19th century, wampum-making had become one of the principal industries in the area. The best beads were made from the shells of common, round clams, called "quahogs" in New England. As time passed, the fickle tastes of seafood lovers changed, and by late mid-century diners had developed a fondness for tender littlenecks, whose shells were worthless for the money trade.

Indians demanded beads that were partially black, and this desired color could only be found in the joints of older clams. However, there was no longer a demand for such food. "Everybody wants the young-ust clams they can get and these are called, 'little necks,' no matter how big they be," stated the old wampum-maker. "Anyhow, we can't get enough 'old' clamshells now to pay for the working. They've all died out, and the young-uns aren't allowed to grow up."

Such was the price of progress. When Indians finally accepted the inevitable machine-made counterfeits, the last wampum mill in America closed down.

ON TRAVEL AND OTHER ADVENTURES

COINS—PASSPORTS TO ADVENTURE!

Several years ago the American Numismatic Association chose the slogan, "Coins—Passports to Adventure!" as the theme for National Coin Week. I doubt that a truer statement exists, for the hobby has provided many with passports to adventure. I recall an early incident, all due to a chance remark about a coin.

Chuck Hillinger, the roving reporter for the *Los Angeles Times*, was traveling through Colorado in search of stories. In Colorado Springs it was the site of ANA Headquarters, as it then appeared, that caught his eye and the tomb-like stone marker that carried our name. What he saw piqued his curiosity. "What justified a building so big for coin collectors?" thought Hillinger. He sensed a story and stopped by for a visit.

"What is the American Numismatic Association all about?" the reporter asked. The response, given many times before, was automatic, void of emotion—"The American Numismatic Association is a federally chartered, non-profit educational organization, founded to promote coin collecting as a means of recording history," I then postscripted the remark with, "There are periods of history where the only recorded evidence of a person or of a civilization is found in the coinage, not through written text. And there are instances where coins seems to contradict accepted theory."

I seemed to have forgotten that I was talking to a professional reporter, one who would not accept mere statements as fact, one who might challenge what was said. And Hillinger did. He asked me to cite at least one instance where a coin differed from the accepted. I paused, then remembered a particular slide presentation from the ANA's audio-visual library—"Famous Women on Coins." I had borrowed it a few weeks earlier to present a program to a local group.

"Picture Cleopatra," I whispered. His Cheshire grin betrayed a mental picture of a voluptuous Elizabeth Taylor. I immediately shattered that image of beauty with the unthinking, chance remark, "Hell, Cleopatra was as homely as a toad."

Hillinger went on with his interview asking questions about the hobby, the Association and its members. I soon forgot about his visit. Then, on Sunday, October 3, 1971, a story headlined, "Coins Prove Cleopatra Was As Homely As A Toad," broke in more than four hundred newspapers nationwide. "Was Cleopatra really one of the great beauties of all time as popular belief would have it?" asked the *Los Angeles Times* reporter. "Not so," he credited me with saying. "Coins struck during her reign in Egypt, 50 to 30 BC, portray her as having 'forbidding features.' " The story was picked up by *Time* magazine, wire services, overseas news (a newspaper in The Netherlands ran a picture of a toad and Elizabeth Taylor), even the *National Enquirer* called for an interview. I went on to say that a small bronze coin, issued between 50 and 30 BC, dispelled the vision of beauty for millions. Contemporary biographers recorded that Cleopatra's beauty was in her personality and was not physical. The last Greek ruler of Egypt, Cleopatra probably attracted the likes of Julius Caesar and Marc Antony by the wealth of her lands.

The most unusual response to the story came not from the press, but from Goodman-Todson Productions. Would I appear on "To Tell The Truth?" My instructions were to fly to New York, courtesy of Goodman-Todson, stay at the Park Sheraton Hotel, and at 1:15 p.m. on Tuesday, November 2, 1971, be at NBC studio 6-A. I was to bring a number of coins with me, including the Cleopatra piece. Contestants were provided $70 in expense money to cover limousine, bus and taxi fares, meals, beverages, telephone and incidentals for the three-day period that we were expected to be in New York City. Needless to say, the point in time was 1971.

After a quick briefing, I met my two imposters, one a dancer with the New York City Ballet, the other a free-lance publicist. We did our homework well, for the dancer received three votes from the panel as being the real Ed Rochette, and the publicist got the remaining one. We stumped them!

I have always felt guilty for letting my hobby down. I used my share of the prize money to buy a breakfront for our dining room and not a coin for my collection. But, I think of Cleopatra every time we have company. I think of her and the coin that provided the passport to an unusual adventure.

DIVING FOR TREASURE AND A STORY!

Southampton, Bermuda—The boat is not the *Calypso*; the captain not Jacques Cousteau, but we are heading out for a dive—some for the adventure, I in search of a story. The 30-foot open cruiser *Gombey* is piloted by Robert Limes, a master diver from England. We are still some 20 minutes short of our destination off Bermuda's south coast where we will drop anchor. All of us except our guide, will make our first scuba dive.

Earlier in the week I had been intrigued with the posters in our lobby: ''. . .less than a half-mile off the hotel lies the *Marie Celestia*, a Confederate blockade runner sunk in 1864 while enroute to Savannah, Ga., with a cargo of rifles. Or, you can dive on the British steamer, *Minnie Bresslauer*, wrecked in 1873 while bound for New York.'' Bermuda's treacherous reefs have claimed many ships, including none too few from the Spanish treasure fleets. Pieces-of-eight, I thought, Spanish treasure, Confederate gold, English coin, all waiting to be discovered!

The water had been as smooth as glass when I signed on for this adventure a few days ago, but now the seas are rough. This morning we had skimmed through the rudimentaries of scuba diving in the hotel pool. Fully suited in wet gear, weighted by 26 pounds of lead around my waist, a single tank of compressed air strapped to my back and cumbersome rubber fins on my feet, I am ready for my metamorphosis to underwater man.

English gentlemanship guaranteed that I would not be first off the ladder and into the water. Courtesy called for the two ladies in our group to go first. I am third on the ladder and drop into 30 feet of clear blue, Western Atlantic water. Descending slowly, equalizing

Bermudian coins feature the ''natural'' treasures of the islands.

pressure every few feet, I am soon on the bottom. Ringed by the Atlantic Ocean's northernmost living coral, Bermudian waters are alive with colorful sea creatures—from playful little sergeant majors to stately queen angelfish.

For more than an hour we follow our guide through living coral reefs, into small caves and along sandy bottoms, past schools of brightly-colored fish. But, there are no pieces of eight, no Spanish treasure, Confederate gold or English coin. My recovered "treasure" is limited to one piece of a broken bottle worn medallion smooth, and a few Bermudian five-cent pieces acquired beforehand.

The Bermudian five-cent pieces are appropriate souvenirs. They depict the very fish that gazed into my mask when I first invaded their waters. Bermudian coins feature the island's natural treasures—a wild hog on the one-cent piece, an angelfish on the five, Bermuda lilies on the ten, and a soaring longtail on the 25-cent coin. The designs are part of the charm of the islands and the sale of the coins to tourists and to collectors provides an important source of revenue for the colony.

WHERE FIRST THIS ONION FLOURISHED AND ITS COIN WAS SPENT!

Hamilton, Bermuda. When they talk about their onions, Bermudians want to cry! Not that they really enjoyed raising them—the islanders never have had their roots deep into their soil. Their lament is that once Bermuda onions were theirs alone to boast, to raise, and to export. Today, counterfeits have taken their place in the fruit and produce sections of mainland supermarkets. The island natives have only a reminder of their epicurean past, a coin that is as popular with them as the growers who stole their onions.

Bermudians are seafaring folk. They'll tell you so, and have been since the first days of colonization begun eight years before their country cousins set foot on Plymouth Rock. The seas, privateering, blockade running, rum running, all proved more exciting and far more profitable for Bermudians. Farming was relegated to the necessities of the family's kitchen table and to those too old or too feeble to pursue a sealife. During the U.S. Civil War, Bermuda enjoyed a short-lived prosperity that disappeared with Appomattox. The end of war marked the end of blockade

No larger than a U.S. quarter, this nickel-brass coin has the equivalent value of $5 in U.S. funds.

running, but the taste for the good life remained.

During the closing decades of the last century, someone on the island discovered the New York produce market and a new industry evolved. The specialized production of celery, potatoes, and tomatoes developed, but growing onions became paramount. So famous did the Bermuda onion become that the island was soon called "The Onion Patch!" The island economy centered around the preparation of garden produce for the New York market. Economic life soon evolved around the schedules of the twice monthly sailings of the cargo steamers.

Most onions are grown by sowing seed directly in the field, the *Encyclopedia Britannica* tells us, but Bermuda onions are grown from transplants. A devious Texan absconded with a supply of onion bulbs and developed a substrain that is now marketed as "Bermuda onions." He made an honest man of himself by renaming the Texas growing area for the abducted plants after the islands. The counterfeits, Bermudians say, are not as sweet or firm as the genuine, nor can they be eaten "like an apple." But the damage is done.

Vegetable gardening today is limited to island consumption. To remind Bermudians of their glorious Onion Patch past, the Bermuda Monetary Authority has seen fit to depict the edible relative to the lily on the reverse of its new five-dollar coin.

While Americans experimented with the Susan B. Anthony dollar and England with nickel pound coins, Bermuda, a few years ago, introduced two new, large denomination coins—$1 and $5 pieces, struck in gold colored nickel-brass. The $1 coin, depicting the island's rare Cahow bird in flight, is destined to replace the paper dollar now in circulation. But the $5 coin is fast becoming a major export through tourists' pockets rather than serving as a medium of exchange. The first issue of 90,000 coins immediately disappeared from circulation and specimens could seldom be purchased for less than double face value.

Revenge, it seems, can be as sweet as a Bermuda onion. Genuine, of course!

PUTTING YOUR FATE IN THE HANDS OF THE KITCHEN HELP IN THE NAME OF THE HOBBY

Montego Bay, Jamaica. It is akin to eating fugu, that exotic delicacy known to kill diners within minutes of swallowing, but this is Jamaica, not Japan. The Caribbean version of poison-on-the-menu is a breadfruit called ackee. While the first is one of Japan's most expensive gourmet delights—up to $200 a plate—ackee is for common folk. It is the national dish of Jamaica. One is a fish that poisons, the other is a poison for fishing. In either case, however, to sup on is to put your fate in the hands of the help in the kitchen.

With fugu, which is raw puffer or balloon fish, the poison is called tetrodotoxin, 275 times more potent than cyanide. Death comes within a matter of minutes after biting into an improperly cleaned fish. On the other hand, ackee's poison—hypoglycin—is seldom fatal. A prematurely harvested and improperly cooked fruit can cause what was once known as "vomitting sickness." Pulverized ackee is used as fish bait. Dropped into the water, the fish are stunned and float to the surface for easy picking. Ackee, boiled and cooked together with codfish and seasoning, is considered one of Jamaica's great delicacies.

Ackee is the "special" of the morning menu and the breakfast I order. Why would one play the gastronomical version of Russian roulette? For the sake of numismatic study, of course. Ackee features both in the monied doggerel of the past and is portrayed on the coinage of the present.

Quattie is the most frequently mentioned denomination in Jamaican folksong and lore. It was a coin brought in by the British in 1834 to provide slaves, on the eve of their emancipation, with small change. The name quattie is a corruption from cuarto (quarter) real, and had a face value of one and one half pence (1½d). At one time Spanish reales were the most common coins of all of the Caribbean and the common denominator for much of the commerce. On Jamaica, one real coins circulated in lieu of and at the value of a sixpence.

The rythmic ditty—Carry me ackee/go a Linstead Market, not a quattie wut sell—is from the folksong of the same name—"Linstead Market;" typical of the songs of the day. Ackee is the food; Linstead, a small inland town in St. Catherine, remains the site of a popular weekly market where people still buy food and farmers bring their produce down from the nearby hills; where the quattie was once the coin of exchange.

Folk music tells of other old values in the same quaint pidgin: two quatties is a "fippance" (3d); three quatties, a "bit" (4½d); eight quatties, equal to a shilling (12d), and is the "mac" in verbal shorthand. Old values are combined to produce the likes of "mac-o-fippance" (one shilling, threepence), or 10 quatties. A "bit-an-fippance" (7½p) is five quatties. Then, there is the half quattie, three farthings to the old gentry, a gill to others. The gill, in song, is also a liquid measure, a quarter of a pint for the thirsty.

The first truly Jamaican coinage was not introduced until 1869 when pennies and halfpennies were struck by the British Royal Mint. Current coinage reflects the independence gained from England in 1962. The country remains a member of the British Commonwealth and occasional commemoratives reflect the link, although the Queen's portrait no longer appears on the coinage. Decimalization in 1969 brought an end to the pence-shillings system of old England and terminated many of the colorful nicknames bestowed by the public on the different denominations. But, recall of Linstead Market, the quattie and the ackee can be found on the lowly one-cent piece. For, on the other side of the coin from the coat-of-arms of Jamaica that appears on the obverse, is an ackee in full bloom. Like the quatties of the past, the one cent of the present buys little. It takes 60 Jamaican cents to equal an American dime.

With the exception of most commemorative coins, which are produced by the British Royal Mint for sale to collectors, the only coins for general circulation to bear a portrait are the 50-cent pieces. They carry the bust of Marcus Garvey, a national hero. All other values in circulation show the Jamaican coat-of-arms leaving the reverses to rep-

An ackee can be seen on the reverse of this Jamaican coin.

resent the indigenous of the island nation: the Doctor Bird on the 25-cent piece, the Blue Mahoe on the 20-cent coin, Lignum Vitae on the 10-cent, a crocodile on the 5-cent, and the featured ackee on the lowly cent.

For this particular numismatically related breakfast, the fruit has been properly prepared. It has not been harvested until the pods opened naturally. The aril, that little appendage protecting the seed cover, has been carefully cleaned and the cooking water discarded. There are two varieties of ackee. One is called "butter," for its soft yellow aril; the other "cheese," which is cream colored. Mine is the former. It looks more breakfasty, not too unlike scrambled eggs with chopped ham, except the eggs are ackee, the ham codfish. An honest appraisal by American taste buds would not describe it as "delicious,"—just "o.k." The enjoyment comes from the numismatic lesson, leaving one to wonder why Blighia Sapida, botannicalese for ackee, named for the same Captain Bligh of mutiny on the *Bounty* fame, who introduced it to Jamaica from West Africa, is so popular a dish.

Next time I will settle for the coins, not the story, and order, "two over easy, a side of bacon, and an order of toast, lightly buttered. Please." I would rather take my chances with cholesterol.

TANGIER, CITY OF INTRIGUE—PAST!

Hotel Continental, Tangier, Morocco: A lot of good movies came out of Morocco. "Casablanca" was the best and this 1940s classic is as popular today as it was when it was released. There was the "Road to Morocco," that Bing Crosby, Bob Hope, Dorothy Lamour funster acclaimed the best of their "Road" series. Then, better forgotten, was "Tangier," a cliche-ridden spy film starring a memory-dimmed cast—Maria Montez, Robert Paige, Preston Foster and Sabu. It failed to match the standard of its contemporaries. But today, it is this thriller, with its cloak and dagger intrigue, that captures our imaginations.

Tangier is no longer an international city in the true sense. Morocco, the first country to recognize the United States, signed a pact of friendship with Thomas Jefferson in 1786 and this is recognized as the longest standing treaty in American history. While Morocco was willing to extend the hand of friendship to the new nation, the sultan was not so anxious to let American ambassadors spread Christian influence at the royal court in the country's capital at Meknes. The sultan decreed that foreigners stay in Tangier. Enough ambassadors and foreign personnel populated Tangier for the sultan to grant the foreign representatives the right to settle disputes among their own nationals. In 1912, when France and Spain divided the Moroccan territory and established their respective "protectorates," Tangier was recognized for its "special character." In 1923 the Statute of Tangier agreed to the governing of this city and its surrounding territory by a council consisting of six Moroccan Moslems, six Moroccan Jews, and representatives from Belgium, England, France, Italy, the Netherlands, Spain and Portugal. When Morocco gained its independence in 1956 it was given control of Tangier by agreement with the European nations concerned and the international status of the city ceased.

Other than the names of streets and neighborhoods, there is little to indicate that Tangier was once the hotbed of international intrigue. The foreign community, once numbering more than 60,000, has dwindled to less than 1,000. A handful are Americans.

The movie "Tangier" was staged at the Hotel Continental. It was here that Maria Montez, playing the role of Rita, a Spanish dancer looking for the person who killed her brother, visited. The plot included a has-been journalist looking for one more "big story" to launch his comeback, a search for a large diamond, and the murders surrounding it. Since the time of action is World War II, the culprit had to be a Nazi agent. His death, in an elevator crash, is the most exciting part of the movie. All attempt at seriousness, however, is lost and mystery is for naught when Sabu sings the Moroccan version of "She'll Be Comin' Round the Mountain." Said a contemporary reviewer, "Set in Tangier. It should have stayed there."

But the web of intrigue still spins at the Hotel Continental, albeit with little affect on the international political scene, but with some impact on the numismatic world. The Continental is located in the heart of the medina. The courtyard still offers an unforgettable panoramic view of the harbor, the old town of Tangiers and the Straits of Gibraltar. Gone are the warships of the Allied and Axis powers, the sole ship at dock is a Saudi royal yacht tending a visiting princess. The hotel, at 36 rue Dar Baroud, is in the heart of the "protected craftsman zone." Rugs, caftans, brass lamps, and copper utensils are made here and offered to tourists. In the hotel, off the lobby area, is the Bazar Tarik and there are coins displayed for sale. But, like the handcrafted souvenirs, the coins appear to be of local manufacture, including common date Morgan and Peace silver dollars.

Not all the coins are counterfeit. The Mohammedan era dated bronze falus and silver dirhams are plentiful. "Old," I am told. I had heard this same comment earlier on the road through Morocco. There is a plentiful supply, too, of undated French Protectorate 50 centimes and one-franc nickel pieces. "Silver," says the clerk.

Our guide, Azam, who has been in our company for a week now and had acted as interpreter during my visit to the headquarters of the Bank of Morocco in Rabat, says something in Arabic to the clerk. Then, the person showing me the coins smiles apologetically, shrugs his shoulders, picks up the coins, and places them back in the showcase. "Not for sale," he says, "only for display." But some had price tags. A cast bronze one falus, barely VG and dated 1254, is tabbed for 100 dirhams—$12 (US). It lists in the 1988 Krause *Standard Catalog of World Coins* for one dollar. Of course, one is expected to haggle. It is the custom.

Mixed among the coins are a number of American silver dollars. These, too, after Azam gives the word, are not for sale. But, I was allowed to examine them closely. They are all well made, centrifugally cast copies. The molds have been fashioned so that the two sides are sweated together. One includes the rim area so that no cast marks appear on the edges. The process is not unlike the manufacture of two-headed or two-tailed coins for sale in novelty shops in the U.S. No attempt is made to make the silver dollars appear Uncirculated. The coins look to be in VF to EF, and possible AU conditions.

I ask my friend, "What are you asking for these."

"120 dirhams ($15 US)." Then he hesitates, "But, they are not for sale!" It would have served little purpose to respond "I'm glad, for the genuine in our country sell for almost half that price in the same condition." The guide at Bazar Tarik is very proud of the native handcrafting. But, I do wish that I had been able to buy at least one, for no other reason than to illustrate this article.

Tangier can stake a claim to numismatic fame. For it was here, long before the ballyhoo days of private mints and private issues, that early bullion pieces were offered. They were called most appropriately Hercules after the mythological character linked with an ancient legend to Tangier. It is here that Hercules supposedly stood, straddling the Straits of Gibraltar, one foot in Europe, the other on the soil of North Africa.

The coin Hercules contains one troy ounce of gold and was "manufactured specially and exclusively for the First Banking Corporation at the Royal Mint Refinery by Messrs. N. M. Rothschild and Sons, London." The promotional jargon of 1953 is not too unsimilar to the sales spiels of the present. Mint names remain sounding officious; corporate names, governmental.

The Hercules weighs 1.091 ounces and contains exactly one fine ounce Troy of gold, 31.103 grs., assaying at 916.7. The obverse design includes the name of the corporation and encircles a reproduction of the famed statue of Hercules on display at the British Museum. The reverse bears the weight in fine ounce troy and in grams, the assay and the stamp of Messrs. N. M. Rothschild and Sons, Royal Mint Refinery. Undated, produced beginning in 1953, and distributed in Tangier, specimens of this bullion piece defied current discovery. The Hercules are like the spy thrillers of the past era. Gone, but not forgotten, but there are many imitators.

COINS FOR "THE ROCK!"

When we ferried from the Spanish port city of Algeciras, through the Straits of Gibraltar, to the coast of North Africa, we passed west of the British Crown Colony of Gibraltar. Our view of "The Rock" was very unlike the one seen in advertisements promoting the solidity of the prominent insurance firm that uses the Rock of Gibraltar as its corporate logo. In fact, the view we saw and most residents see, is not quite as spectacular as the advertisements suggest. Fortunately for those purists who insist that everything depicted be as seen, Gibraltar's first circulating coinage in more than a century omits all mention of the Rock per se.

Shortly after our visit, the circulating series of nine coins, seven of which follow the weights, alloys and specifications of the English counterparts, was introduced. The traditional Maklouf bust of Queen Elizabeth II appears on all obverses while various pictorial motifs have been selected for the other side of the coins.

Flora or fauna was picked for three of the coins: a Barbary partridge for the penny, a Barbary ape for the five pence, and Gibraltar Candyturf in floral motif for the 50 pence. Important landmarks are also used: the lighthouse at Europa Point on the two pence and one of the colony's most popular tourist attractions, the Moorish Castle, is shown on the 10 pence. The Patroness of Gibraltar, Our Lady of Europa, taken from a polychromed wood carving dis-

Issued too late to bring home as a souvenir, the Gibraltar pound introduced the first new series of circulating coins in more than a century.

played in the Shrine of Our Lady at Europa Point, is to be seen on the 20-pence piece.

The first of the series minted was the one pound, which features the coat of arms of Gibraltar, a shield bearing a triple-towered castle from the base of which hangs a key. This symbolizes the colony as the Key to Europe and its strategic importance for the past 300 years, particularly during the last two world wars. During World War II, British engineers tunneled deep into the Rock to construct a maze of fortifications alluded to on the two-pound coin which shows a cannon in one of the casements. There is now more roadway inside the Rock than outside.

The lofty promontories on either side of the straits—the Rock on the European side, Mount Abyla on the African coast—were known in ancient times as the Pillars of Hercules. For this reason the hero of Greek mythology, Hercules, and his pillars are depicted on the five-pound coin.

While in recent years Gibraltar has had a number of commemorative coins issued for collectors, this series, produced for the colony by the Pobjoy Mint, is the first for general circulation since the coins of Queen Victoria in the last century. Unfortunately, the coins were not among our souvenirs of the trip to Spain and Morocco. They had yet to be issued. We settled on a Spanish piece-of-eight, one that showed the Pillars of Hercules on the reverse.

TREASURE AT DEVIL'S HEAD

After decades of business trips to Denver the 68 mile stretch of Interstate 25, connecting the Front Range cities, becomes tedious. Alternate routes between Colorado Springs and the state's capital city are sought out, if only for a change in scenery.

Taking U.S. 24 northwest to Woodland Park, and Colorado 67 to Sedalia north, doubles the driving time. But, if you have the extra hour to spare, the rewards are worth the mileage. You pass through the Pike National Forest and, on a well-paved little-traveled road, you drive over "The Top of the World." Near Deckers, after you have crossed the South Platte River, you can see an unusual formation silhouetted against the mountain sky. It is called, "Devil's Head."

I expect to explore Devil's Head this summer, for somewhere near the base is hidden a cache of 6,000 United States $10 gold pieces. Not one dated later than 1872!

There is an old story told among the forest rangers of one of their own meeting an old prospector camped near Devil's Head. From the appearance of both the old man and the campsite, it was apparent to the ranger that the visitor had been there for several weeks. The ranger befriended the old man, inviting him to an occasional meal at the ranger station.

This good Samaritan experience happened many years ago, during the summer of 1923. It was some time before the usually closed-mouth old prospector felt comfortable enough to tell the ranger, Roy Dupre, the follow-

There may be 6,000 $10 gold eagles buried somewhere near Devil's Head.

ing story.

General Palmer's Denver and Rio Grande Railroad followed the Plum Creek flats through Sedalia, south to Larkspur, Palmer Lake and through Colorado Springs. The railroad provided the setting for more than one shoot-em-up-real-wild-west train robbery. In the early 1870s, not too far east of Devil's Head, one gang held up the train and made off with an estimated $60,000 in $10 gold pieces. The bandits knew the area well and headed for Devil's Head. But, unfortunately for them, the posses in pursuit knew the area equally as well. The loot was hastily buried and the spot noted by marking a nearby tree. Stories differ as to survivors of the subsequent gunfight, but the episode had been forgotten long before the old prospector appeared on the scene a half century later.

The ranger and the prospector parted company for the last time when Dupre informed the old man that a forest fire had cleared the area many years earlier and that the trees he had been inspecting for some telltale sign had grown after the train robbery. Dupre told fellow rangers that the old man had simply left.

It is not hard to get excited about the Devil's Head treasure. Six thousand gold eagles, probably all Uncirculated, or, at least, in AU condition. Few from 1866 through 1872 are even priced in Uncirculated condition in the current issue of *Coin Prices*. Those struck before the motto, In God We Trust, was added to the reverse in 1866, average from four to five thousand dollars each in Uncirculated. The 1863 lists for $9,000. To carry wishful thinking a step or two further, multiply 6,000 coins times an average of $4,000 per coin. You have a conservative total of $24 million! The prospect is worth a weekend or two of time and the rental of a metal detector.

The area is not new to prospectors, though few have searched for the train robbers' loot. In 1883, W. B. Smith discovered a rich deposit of topaz in the side of Devil's Head. Rock hounds know the area and have prospected it well. I have been told that some of the topaz mined grades among the finest ever found in the U.S. But mineral hunters are searching for a mother lode. They may have come ever so close to the gold cache, but missed it since that is not what they were looking for.

If I am unsuccessful in my search for the lost gold of Devil's Head, perhaps the reward of a few topaz gem stones might be offsetting. But, then, if I find neither, I will have another tale of adventure to recall and that is reward enough.

WEST POINT—AMERICA'S SECRET MINT

To most, the mere mention of the name West Point conjures visions of smartly dressed cadets on parade. It has been the site of the United States Military Academy since 1802. To the historically minded, however, West Point's past is very much a part of America's founding story. During the Revolutionary War General George Washington called this rocky crag jutting into the Hudson River, "the most important post in America." West Point then guarded the vital water route from Canada and was fortified to deny access to the British forces and guarantee free passage to the colonists. West Point, during the Revolutionary War, was also the headquarters for a man who was to make his name synonymous with treason, at least to American ears. It was there that General Benedict Arnold conspired to surrender the fort and sell its defense secrets to the British. Had Arnold succeeded, there would have been no need to establish a American military academy a few decades later, and the rest of the world might still refer to Americans as "colonials."

On location at the West Point campus, by the west side of Trophy Point, are several links of the Great Chain that stretched across the Hudson during the Revolution. The chain, which weighed 150 tons and was over 600 yards long, was floated on log booms and secured from Constitution Island, due north across the river, to the West Point shore directly beneath Trophy Point. This barrier, under the guns of Fort Clinton, effectively sealed the river to British traffic.

Ironically, the engineer who designed the chain and forged the links, Capt. Thomas Machin, turned to forging coin of Great Britain after independence. Along with copies of coins of Connecticut, Vermont, New Jersey and New York, Machin produced copper halfpence copies of the coins of George II and George III. Although Great Britain suspended coinage of coppers in 1775, Machin continued to date a vast majority of his issues through 1788.

This is not the story of a clandestine mint, however, but one of a latter-day facility. Most of the general public does not realize that West Point is now the site of a subsidiary mint of the United States. The U.S. Treasury does not designate the facility as a branch mint, recognizing it only as an adjunct to the Philadelphia Mint, some 141 miles to the south. This way, no mintmark need distinguish its products from those of the parent mint and thus create a collectible among general circulation coins. (One-cent pieces have been produced here since 1974 and these cannot be distinguished from cents produced at Philadelphia). However, with such numismatic issues as the Olympic and Statue of Liberty gold coins, the addition of a "W" stimulates sales and appears on the these collector products solely for promotional purposes.

The mint at West Point is unlike other coining facilities. The operations are conducted within the United States Bullion Depository and the plant is not open to public inspection. Therefore, when the Treasury has a special event, like the first strike ceremonies, the invited guests do not go inside to see the presses in operation—a press is moved outside the plant, to a storage and shipping room, to meet the public.

Nine months after the passage of Public Law 99-105 on December 17, 1985, a bill providing for the U. S. Treasury to mint and issue gold bullion coins in four weights and denominations, numismatic and general media were invited to witness Secretary of the

Few passersby traveling the road to West Point realize that behind the barbed wire and chain link fence of the U.S. Bullion Depository is another of America's minting facilities.

Treasury James A. Baker, III press an electronic button activating the drop hammer on an HME coining press to strike the first $50 gold eagle bullion coin. Millions of bullion coins have been produced since that date, all at the mint that few know about.

Had the fates of history chosen to have written American history differently, West Point today might still be called Fort Arnold, a name originally bestowed on the fortifications in honor of a hero at the Battle of Saratoga. But Benedict Arnold's later plans gave his name to mean treason instead. Fort Arnold became Fort Clinton and the property gave way to a well-known military academy and a not so well-recognized minting facility of the United States.

BEWARE THE COINS OF CHINATOWN!

Except for an enlistment in the military, there is no greater budget tour of the Orient than a trip to San Francisco. In a 16 block area, bounded by Bay Street to the north, California to the south, Sansome to the east, and Van Ness to the west, is a microcosm of the Far East, complete with sounds, smells, and scenery. This is the fabled Chinatown of San Francisco.

The first Chinese arrived here in 1849, spurred by the gold rush of that year. They came to work the mines in the hills to the east, but some stayed to remain in their gateway city to the land of promise. The Chinese gave it a name meaning The Great City of the Golden Hill; non-celestials called it Little China, then abbreviated it to Chinatown!

The main street of Chinatown is Grant Avenue. Once called Dupont Street, the merchant thoroughfare was renamed following the earthquake in 1906 for Ulysses S. Grant. If you are fortunate enough to be here on the Chinese Lunar New Year, it is on this street that the Golden Dragon slithers past the tiny shops of acupuncturists and herbalists, fish markets and groceries, bakeries and restaurants.

There is treasure and trivia to be found in Chinatown. Some stores are literally jam packed with oriental jade, handwoven silks, cloisonne bowls, and teakwood furniture. Most are genuine, but there are some stores pandering to the passing tourists and seldom selling to the Chinese residents. Much of what is offered in these bazaars and curio shops is worthless gimcrackery.

The quest for numismatic curiosities is bound to lead you into some of the stores along Grant Avenue. How can a collector resist a bowlful of loose Chinese coins, strategically placed in store windows to catch the eyes of passers-by, and enticingly marked, "Antique Coins/49 cents," or, an attractively packaged three-century type set of Chinese cash, for only $4.95?

Modern packaging of coin sets has reached the Orient, at least, the orient of the West Coast of the United States. Plastic walleted sets of 10 Chinese cash, purported to date from the Shun-chi reign (1644-1661), to the Shuen-tung (1909-1911), are described in Chinese and quaint English transliteration as, "Chinese Old Coins."

Cash is the Chinese coin of copper alloy with the large, square hole in the middle. Sometimes they are seen strung together in multiples of 50 or 100. On the surface of the coin are four Chinese characters, the two at the side reading Current Money, the ones at the top and bottom identifying the emperor's reign. This particular coin design format was standard from the time of the T'ang Dynasty (7th century AD) through the turn of this century.

Each of the modern day coin packets bears a little gold sticker with an imprint in black ink reading, "Made In Hong Kong." This statement must apply to the coins, as well as the packaging, for there is not a genuine coin among the sets. The coins are all carefully patined to look old, but they are only cast imitations of recent manufacture. For the collector, there are also the odd shaped examples of knife and hoe money. These, too, are of equally dubious pedigree.

One should not become too disenchanted with the numismatic promises of Chinatown. You need only lift your eyes from the shop windows and look up to the intricate rooflines of the area. Take almost any alley off the main thoroughfare and walk the streets made narrower by the markets that overflow onto the sidewalks with vegetables, that unless you are a gourmet, you have never seen nor sensed before. If your stomach cannot savor hot, spicy Chinese sausage, black-bean filled dumplings, or golden-glazed pressed duck, there is always the standard cop-out, a pair of golden arches on Grant Avenue where you can order a Big Mac, fries and a Coke, from a menu printed in Chinese. But, that is being about as phony as the coins you can buy in the stores nearby.

How treasures are displayed in one Chinatown store.

ON PRESIDENTS AND HOPEFULS

WHAT THIS COUNTRY NEEDS IS A GOOD FIVE-CENT NICKEL!

Woodrow Wilson was in the White House at the time. His vice president, Thomas Marshall, was admirably performing one of the few official tasks assigned to the man a heart beat away from the presidency—presiding over a Senate debate. On that particular day, the topic, ever timely, was what was good for the country. Marshall then made the history books with one memorable quote. "What this country needs is a good five-cent cigar."

Like most politicians, Marshall had a staff of secretaries and a writer or two. The fault may not have been his, but the quotation the vice president has been credited with was not his to give. It came from the newspaper columns of Frank McKinney Hubbard.

Hubbard was born in Bellefontaine, Ohio, where his father was the editor and publisher of a weekly newspaper. Young Hubbard grew up with printer's ink in his blood. He worked as a printer's devil in his father's shop, setting and distributing type. In 1891, Hubbard joined the staff of the *Indianapolis News* as staff artist and cub reporter. By 1904 he had his own column featuring a fictional Hoosier named Abe Martin. His homespun philosophy became a hit of the period, sort of an early day Herb Shriner. Eventually the column was syndicated and appeared in more than three hundred newspapers nationwide. One of Abe Martin's country maxims was taken by Vice President Marshall for his Senate speech.

Marshall was not the only name of the day making note of the remark. Franklin Pierce Adams, columnist for the *New York Evening Mail* at the time, picked up on it and reported, "There are plenty of good five-cent cigars in the country. The trouble is they cost a quarter. What this country really needs

Three of Fraser's suggested designs for a new five-cent piece.

is a good five-cent nickel."

James Earl Fraser, an instructor at the Art Student League, may well have been a reader of Adams. Shortly afterward, Fraser prepared a number of suggested designs for a new five-cent piece and submitted them to the Treasury. American coinage was coming into a renaissance of its own. Augustus Saint-Gaudens, at the instigation of Theodore Roosevelt, had designed handsome new $10 and $20 gold pieces, and Victor D. Brenner produced a Lincoln cent to mark the 100th anniversary of the birth of the Civil War president. But other than these three coins, all remaining denominations in circulation featured the "monotonous head of Liberty." It was on nickels, dimes, quarters, halves and silver dollars.

Fraser's design of an Indian head on one side and an American bison on the other was accepted and introduced into circulation in 1913. But, Fraser had submitted other five-cent designs, including another Liberty head, thankfully rejected, and an interesting Lincoln study. The latter was rejected on the basis that Lincoln already appeared on the one-cent piece.

Thanks to Frank McKinney Hubbard America had a good laugh, Thomas Marshall made it into the books of quotations, and from 1913 to 1938, the country enjoyed a good five-cent nickel.

THE GENERAL THE ARMY WANTED TO FORGET!

The telephone message from the Pentagon was as cold as it was short. "There is no record of a general named Holdridge," the caller bluntly advised. Then, as an afterthought, added, "Perhaps he was with the Marines."

Not only had an inquiry directed to the Army's chief of media relations brought a negative response, but a follow up, addressed to the records administration at the National Archives, brought a similar answer. "No record."

Brigadier General Herbert Charles Holdridge, United States Military Academy Class of 1917, was an officer the Army wanted to forget. He had distinguished himself early in his career, but his days of fading away had been a disappointment to himself, to his colleagues, and to the Army. Perhaps his eccentricities could have been excused for having heard one cannon shot too many, his actions attributed to a classic case of shell shock.

Holdridge aspired to be President of the United States, an ambition not too uncommon of retired Army generals. However, much to the embarrassment of the Army, Holdridge's campaign tactics for high office gave way to the bizarre when rational means failed. While supporters of the usual type of candidate distribute campaign buttons and promotional literature, Holdridge's helpers busied themselves putting red fingernail polish on quarters to warn of an imagined theocratic dictatorship threatening America.

It was in 1952 that Holdridge first sought the nation's highest office. He hit the electioneering trail coincident with the presidential campaign of his World War II commanding officer, Dwight Eisenhower. While the supreme commander sought and secured the Republican nomination, Holdridge campaigned for the Democratic nod with all the strategem of a military expedition. His primary tactic was diversionary. He helped found "The American Rally," a group seeking to take control of the Democratic party through the presidential primaries.

Organized in Detroit in February 1952, the rally gave Holdridge the "provisional nomination" for the nation's highest office. Interviewed by the press, Holdridge was asked to explain why his nomination was called provisional. He replied that the nomination was temporary until his followers were able to "capture the Democratic Party and the nomination, in Chicago, in July."

Victory at Chicago went to a nonmilitary man instead, Adlai Stevenson,

Brigadier General Herbert C. Holdridge, USMA 1917.

but Holdridge was not about to concede defeat. He stayed in the fray, switching tactics and party. He now chose to be the running mate of 74-year-old Dr. Enoch A. Holtwick. Together, they carried the banner of the Prohibition Party. The wily general reasoned that Holtwick might not survive the four-year term and the office of president would be his by default. Holdridge's conventional wisdom dictated that he not accept the number two spot offered to him on the Vegetarian ticket. That running mate was much younger.

By the time of the 1960 presidential campaign, when Richard Nixon faced John F. Kennedy, Holdridge had tired of the American Rallyists, the Prohibitionists, and the Vegetarians. He grasped a new banner to wave and new crusade to lead. The retired general helped launch a new political party, The Minute Men of the Constitution. The Minute Men named Holdridge their standard bearer for 1960. This was enough for the Army to want to lose his records and wish that he had never marched the parade grounds at West Point.

After the polls closed in November 1960, Holdridge refused to accept the fact that the American public had elected John F. Kennedy 35th President of the United States. The old campaigner saw, instead, a conspiracy engineered in concert by the Federal Reserve System, the Vatican, and NATO. To Holdridge, the latter was a mere front for the Holy Roman Empire reincarnated.

The 67-year-old retired Army officer believed that the election of Kennedy called for drastic and immediate action. He was ready for the challenge. If the United States Army abrogated its responsibility in upholding and defending the Constitution, he would take charge. Holdridge dispatched an ultimatum to J. Edgar Hoover at the Federal Bureau of Investigation headquarters in Washington. He ordered the immediate arrest of the President-elect, charging that the former senator from Massachusetts conspired with Pope John XXIII to establish a theocratic dictatorship in America.

On officious looking stationery of the Constitutional Provisional Government of the United States, Holdridge pronounced the federal government defunct. He stopped short of naming himself to his cherished goal of the presidency. He modestly accepted the title chief magistrate.

Attempts to have the old warrior declared incompetent failed, as did his imagined assassins dispatched by the CIA, the FBI, the Post Office Department, and the Vatican. During the election campaign, the press gave the general an occasional sidebar for history's sake. Meanwhile, Holdridge's supporters left a more visible reminder on the numismatic scene. They flooded commerce with 1960-dated Washington quarters, first painting them with red fingernail polish to show a papal cap and gown on the head and shoulders of the first president. It was their not-too-subtle attempt to warn the voting public of the dire consequences should a Catholic president be elected. Thousands of the coins were removed from circulation by the Treasury Department, cleansed, and then recirculated. Some found their way into the hands of political item collectors and numismatists. Their message, however, was respectfully ignored.

A "Catholic" quarter altered by Holdridge's followers.

THE UNUSUAL SIDES OF THE KENNEDY HALF DOLLAR!

When the American Atheists, at their national convention held a few years ago in Denver, Colorado, voted to disband, albeit temporarily, they brought respite to their organized campaign to remove the words, "In God We Trust," from the coins coins and currency of the United States.

American Atheists was founded in 1963 by then Madalyn Murray O'Hair soon after her Supreme Court victory in a case setting limits on Bible study and the banning of prayer in the nation's public schools. After she secured a court ruling in her favor, Mrs. O'Hair turned to a campaign to try to have the national motto removed from the money of the country, pleading that the motto violated the constitutional concept of separation of church and state. Mrs. O'Hair would have been chagrined to learn that while she campaigned to have the motto removed, there were others who believed that God himself was appearing on a current coin of the United States.

There are throughout the country more than 2,000 people who think of John F. Kennedy as a god, believing that he gave his life for his people in an effort to warn of the evil that surrounds them. They look to Los Angeles as their Vatican, the John F. Kennedy Memorial Temple as their Saint Peter's, and the Reverend Farley McGivern as their temporal leader. They are called "Kennedy Worshippers," and are recognized as an organized faith in the *Encyclopedia of American Religions*.

Soon after the death of John F. Kennedy in Dallas, Texas, on November 22, 1963, people started attributing miraculous cures to the spiritual intercession of the late president. Author Glenn Meadows published the paper "107 Miracles Have Been Credited to JFK," and Lyle Gordon, in 1972, authored a religious treatise "Thousands of Americans Worship the Spirit of President Kennedy." There were other articles of similar vein, including Andrew Gordon's, "The Psychic Powers of JFK," and Krista Lee's "Spirit of JFK Tells What Really Happened in Dallas."

Americans are not the only ones attributing psychic powers to President

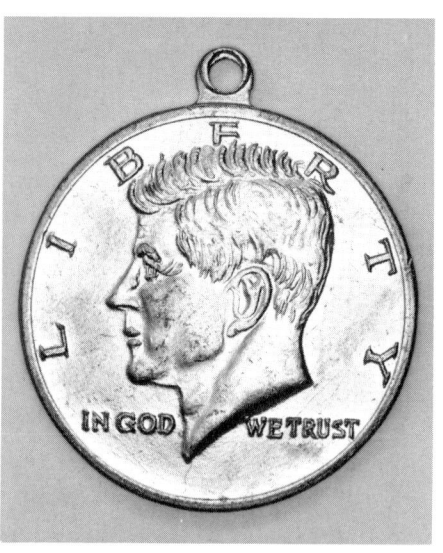 

In Japan, the image of John F. Kennedy served as a reward for safe driving.

Kennedy or the Kennedy half dollar. In my collection of John F. Kennedy memorabilia, and listed in *Medallic Portraits of John F. Kennedy*, is a half dollar sized, nickel-silver medal produced in Osaka, Japan, on behalf of a traffic safety program. The granting of drivers' licenses in Japan has been attributed as a diabolical means of population control. Others call it domestic hari-kari. Nevertheless, traffic safety in Japan has been the subject of official concern for many years. In 1965 an award medal was produced and presented in recognition for successfully driving a specified number of accident-free miles. On one side of the medal is a symbolic dove, the other side is an exact copy of the Kennedy half dollar without date. If one succumbed to statistics in his or her effort to achieve the required safe mileage, a smaller version, 28 millimeters in size, was also available. It is listed as K-64-8 and K-64-8a in *Medallic Portraits*.

The island nation of Japan is not the only foreign country to find disciples of the mystique of John F. Kennedy. In the Latin world of South America, Argentina in particular, miniatures of the Kennedy half dollar were stamped and sold. The mini-coins have loops and are often found attached to rosaries, along with other small medals of religious nature. While the devout of Argentina fail to see Kennedy as a god incarnate, many certainly believe he is heaven-bound and can intercede on their behalf.

As the 25th anniversary of the assassination approached there were more stories about the late president and there was an increase in interest in Kennedy half dollars as well as a revival in the search for Kennedy memorabilia. There are a few today who see more than a coin of the realm in the face of the current half dollar, much to the consternation of the likes of Madalyn Murray O'Hair.

THE CANDIDATE FROM LAKE NEBAGAMON

Back in 1964, when memory seems to recall a more leisurely pace, presidential elections averaged no more than 14 months in campaign. Today, the forthcoming quadrennial exercise to select the next head of state seems to begin even before the last vote is counted in the previous election.

While the majority of the public concern themselves with two major candidates, there are other contenders. In 1964, I reported, "In each presidential election year, a number of individualistic, non-conformist, one-man parties appear bearing strange ideas and stranger platforms. These fringe parties scarcely disturb the political patterns of the major parties, their votes number in the hundreds against the hundred million cast." These words are from a yearlong series published under the heading, "Politicana Americana." A different column appeared in each of the 26 issues of *Numismatic News* published that year.

Emil Matalik.

Not only were numismatically related political items of the major candidates presented,—Romney, Rockefeller, Lodge, Margaret Chase Smith, Scranton, Nixon and Goldwater, for the Republicans; Johnson for the Democrats;—but we covered Munn-Shaw for the Prohibition Party; DeBerry and Shaw for Socialist Workers; Bishops Tomlinson and Rogers for the Theocrats; white supremacists Kasper and Stone for States Rights; Haas and Blommen for the Socialist Labor Party; and Dixiecrat George Wallace. Also noted were the campaigns of D.X.B. Schwartz on behalf of the National Tax Payers' Party; Marvin Kittman as a Lincoln Republican; and the Christian Constitutional Party support of Barry Goldwater. Dero Cook chose no labels, he was simply a "write-in candidate," and Minnesota's lesser-known son, Dr. Walter Judd, issued campaign material, too. But, the most bizarre candidacy of all was that of Emil Matalik, from Wisconsin!

At the time, in 1964, Matalik was a 34-year-old bachelor-farmer from Lake Nebagamon. He was the author of a utopian plan designed to cope with the problem of world over-population. Matalik launched his United Nations Party presidential campaign by trying to deed his 160-acre farm to the world body of the same name. The only response Matalik received resulted in the UN challenging his right to use their name. He then dropped the plural and the United Nation Party was born.

Matalik's long range plans called for all land donated to his party to be subdivided into 2½ acre parcels. In turn, these plots would be distributed on a world seniority basis to all inhabitants of the planet Earth. Each family would be provided one bicycle, a house, living essentials, and a two-way television set (for educational purposes). The land would revert back to the party upon the tenant's death, for redistribution. Matalik recognized that not everyone would appreciate this lifestyle, so he planned to erect an escape proof fence around the property—removable only after occupants showed a desire to "do right."

In a telephone interview, Matalik attributed all the world's problems to overpopulation. His platform called for drastic measures to meet an equally drastic situation. "Even severe droughts can be attributed to overpopulation," said Matalik. "The average person has about 100 pounds of water in his body. With some three billion persons on earth, there are about 300 billion pounds of water walking around the earth that could go to fill reservoirs, streams and lakes, and, in turn, irrigate crops and relieve food shortages."

Matalik's views on money were equally drastic. One campaign platform called for the permanent stationing of UN troops in the Congo and South Vietnam. Soldiers were to be provided room and board, and all recreational needs. But, they were not to be paid! "Money corrupts," said Matalik profoundly, basing his observation on his nine years in the Air Force.

Candidate Emil Matalik invited me to visit him at Lake Nebagamon. It was the opportunity for an exclusive interview with a presidential hopeful. But then I recalled his plan to curb overpopulation. Each family would be limited to two children and the edict enforced by compulsory castration.

I declined the invitation. I have three sons.

THE PERFECT GIFT FOR THE PRESIDENT

First Lady Nancy Reagan gave the president a special gift for his 75th birthday, which—according to the president's math—was really "the 36th anniversary of his 39th birthday!"

Had Ronald Reagan insisted on the use of Jack Bennyesque dating, the First Lady would have been hard pressed to give the president the special gift she had planned, since U.S. gold coins were not minted in the year 1950. But, for the real date of the president's birth (1911) Mrs. Reagan was able to buy him a $20 gold double eagle designed by Saint-Gaudens.

The coin was apropos, since the piece, the most beautiful of all American coins, would never have been made had it not been for the persistence of another president, Theodore Roosevelt—and his concern for the design of American coins.

Augustus Saint-Gaudens was already recognized as a great American sculptor when chance brought him to the dinner table to sit next to President Roosevelt. Their after-dinner conversation centered around their mutual admiration of ancient Greek coins. Roosevelt offered Saint-Gaudens a proposition—if the famed sculptor would design a new series of U.S. coins, the president would order the Mint to produce them for circulation. A handshake concluded the deal.

The Mint staff, protective and jealous of their positions, used every conceivable argument to dissuade T.R. from using the Saint-Gaudens' designs. But, in a showdown with the president known for speaking softly and carrying a big stick, the Mint employees finally backed down.

Roosevelt had intended for Saint-Gaudens to redesign all U.S. coins, from the cent to the $20 gold pieces but time was not on the artist's side. While the Mint was procrastinating, Saint-Gaudens was dying of cancer. Only his $10 and $20 gold designs were completed.

The Saint-Gaudens double eagles were issued from 1907 to 1933, until another Roosevelt, Franklin D., took America off the gold standard and brought an end to gold coin production. Both terminal issues of this design are extremely rare. A number of varieties are known for the first year, 1907. Some are extremely high relief patterns that required modification by the Mint before coins for general circulation could be made. Some bear Roman numeral dates and none have the motto "In God We Trust." Roosevelt did not believe in using God's name on money. On the other end of the issue, the gold moratorium prevented the almost one half million coins minted in 1933 from being legally released.

The Saint-Gaudens $20 double eagle was a meaningful gift for a president who liked to quote Theodore Roosevelt.

Although Mrs. Reagan's press secretary did not release information on the condition of the coin she purchased, or whether it was a 1911 Philadelphia, Denver or San Francisco Mint issue, the

The birth-year double eagle of the president.

values at the time were: $525 for VF, $610 for AU-50 and $730 for MS-60. An MS-65 would have cost her $2,100, but it is doubtful that she would have bought a Proof. $35,000 was a lot of money, even for the President of the United States!

HART'S NAME SHORT CHANGED!

A fact unnoticed by almost all but the very astute coin buff is that there is a certain numismatic ring to the original, full surname of presidential candidate Gary Hart.

Hartpence. Hart—pence. Pence is, after all, plural for English penny, and the name, Hart, has in the past been used as a corruptive term for half. Did we, by chance, have a halfpenny hopeful?

According to Mark Antony Lower, in his *English Surnames, An Essay on Family Nomenclature, Historical, Etymological, and Humorous*, published in London in 1875, such is not the case.

Lower's essay notes that Englishmen turned to every imaginable description of locality as a prime source of surname nomenclature. "Hart," according to Lower's study, is another name for "stag," of the quadruped variety! The excised half of the Hart family name, "pence," Lower pointed out—shattering any hope of numismatic correlation—meant "banner" or "sign." The presidential candidate's ancestors may once have lived "by the banner (pence) of the hart (stag)," and so developed their family name.

Collectors should not despair, however, for all is not lost numismatically for the candidacy of one Democratic party hopeful. There is an old English token that some political wags might deem appropriate. Featured on the obverse is a stag (hart), surrounded by the banner (pence) carrying the motto "Freedom with Innocence!"

Bearing a date of 1796, this particular English token was issued by The Buck Society, a late 18th-century fraternal organization not unlike the Elks, Moose, and similar organizations that developed in the United States during the last century. The Buck Society token was a pocket piece that was circulated in England as currency due to an extreme shortage of copper currency. Tradesmen, shopkeepers and manufacturers commissioned the striking of private trade tokens to accommodate customers and pay employees. For society members an assessment of one shil-

A "Hart-pence." Freedom With Innocence!

ling twopence for each lodge visit often resulted in Bucks substituting their tokens as penny pieces in meeting their fraternal obligations.

The origin of the family name Hartpence is neither numismatological nor humorous, but its meaning may help explain the former Colorado senator's subliminal desire to pursue the call of the doe.

PRESIDENTIAL CANDIDATE PROMISED COIN DESIGN CHANGE... AND MORE!

They are ready to strike up the band. The parade is about to begin. Although the count is well short of 76 trombones, the uniforms of the Shriner's El Jebel Marching Band match any from Robert Preston's "Music Man."

I find myself seated on the back of a flag bedecked 1959 Chevrolet Impala convertible, the lead, and only, car in a summer Sunday parade through the streets of downtown Denver, Colorado. There are three of us sitting upon the back of the leather upholstered seat. To one side is Paul Sternick, the out-going president of the Colorado Society of Association Executives. I am on the right by virtue of being the incoming president, and between us, is a real-live, honest-to-goodness, fingers-crossed candidate for the office of President of the United States.

Notwithstanding the fact that he has been a perennial White House hopeful ever since Richard Nixon defeated him in the quest for the Republican nomination in 1968, Pat Paulsen continues to remind the public with an "Aren't you sorry now" reminder.

The police escort motorcycle siren competes with the sounds of the marching band to warn traffic that the one-car, one band parade, is fast approaching. The miniscule cavalcade proceeds from the downtown Hyatt Regency Hotel to Denver's Corrigan Hall, followed by several hundred Association executives representing the 17 Western states and four Canadian provinces, in ragged formation.

Ostensibly, the parade is to culminate in the opening of the 17th Western Conference of Association Executives, but few in the parade can resist shouting to startled onlookers "Vote for Paulsen," including our political star of the day.

The parade offers the opportunity to interview a presidential hopeful and to question him on new coinage designs. Paulsen promises to end the controversy on whose portrait will appear on the coinage of the United States. If elected, Paulsen will put his own portrait on all coins, from the cent through the "large" silver dollar. His answer leaves little doubt about the possibility of another Susan B. Anthony mini-dollar. He assures us that he has a better chance of getting elected than the Treasury has of resurrecting the small dollar under a Paulsen administration.

Candidate Paulsen curries numismatic favor with the promise "if elected" he will name this reporter-at-large his Secretary of the Treasury. Politely objecting, I protest that I would rather be his director of the Mint. "No chance," says Paulsen, "I want someone who knows nothing about coins. After all, we have a tradition to uphold." He also rejects the idea that some might construe this to be negative campaigning.

The seal of the almost President of the United States

Press coverage of Paulsen's campaign has been scant. The only ink candidate Paulsen will receive from his Denver visit may be this column. His campaign has become "old shoe" for the established political press corps. This 1988 election year effort marks Paulsen's sixth quest for the nation's highest office and he has yet to garner a single vote.

Politicana collectors will be disappointed, too. Collectibles from this campaign are scarce. The former Smothers Brothers Comedy Hour regular is running an austere crusade, he is conducting a one-button campaign. While he flashes a red, white and blue Paulsen for President button on his lapel, he is reluctant to let it go. Undated, he plans to use the button again in four years should the American electorate fail to recognize that here is a man who knows how to cut spending to the core; and collectors don't realize they have a better chance to change the existing designs of coins with a President Pat Paulsen in the White House than with a President George Bush or a President Michael Dukakis.

QUAYLE EPISODE RECALLS CIVIL WAR DRAFT MONEY

The fact that Republican vice presidential candidate Dan Quayle's Vietnam draft brouhaha missed by a few days the 125th anniversary of New York's infamous draft riots may have escaped the attention of the pundits, but collectors can recall what reporters of the time called "a rich man's war and a poor man's fight."

The Civil War boded ill for the Union in early days of the year of 1863. The anticipated few months needed to put down the rebellion of the Southern states had now stretched into almost two years. Union troops were not renewing their 24-month tours of duty, casualties exceeded new enlistments. Congress tried to solve the dilemma with The Enrollment Act, the nation's first draft lottery, to meet the military's need for men in uniform. Legislators, however, refused to keep the law simple. Men did not have to flee to Canada, or burn their draft cards to avoid military service. All they had do was to hire a substitute or pay a $300 "Commutation Fee." The latter has provided collectors with a series of unusual pseudo-currency called Commuta-

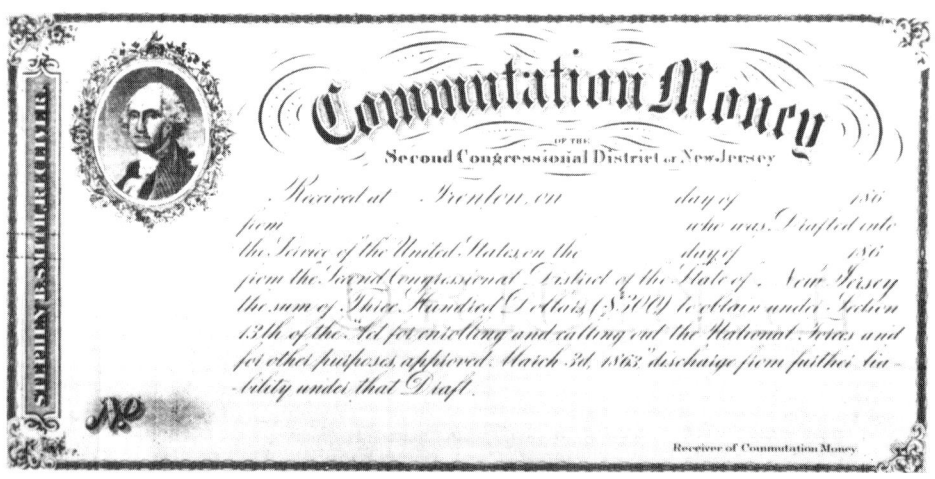

Commutation Money was introduced during the Civil War as a receipt of proof of payment of the sum of $300 to avoid military service.

tion Money to look for.

The loopholes provided by Congress led to the familiar charges that the sons of the rich did not have to fight. With $500 the average annual income for the workingman, the congressionally-mandated fee was beyond the reach of most, as was the price of hiring a substitute. Records of the day give credence to the complaints of the poor. Of the 250,000 men called, a full third avoided active military service by paying the commutation fee and even more bought a substitute to fight in their place. The unfairness of the draft law hit New York City, with its teeming immigrant population, the hardest. Within hours of the first draft calls in early July 1863, mobs took to violence to express their displeasure. Before peace returned to the city a week later, thousands of troops had been called from the front, property damage amounted to millions of dollars, and casualties were counted in the hundreds. Treasury Secretary Salmon P. Chase was to note caustically that, although the Commutation Fee raised more than $12 million in gold coin for the government, it "was not the purpose for which the act was passed."

Commutation money was in fact a receipt, proof of payment that the fee had been paid. The word "Money" appearing on the face of the bill, along with a vignette of George Washington, has made the notes numismatically-related collectibles.

Collectors should be indebted to Senator Dan Quayle, for these notes are a bit of Americana that may have gone unnoticed had it not been for the events of the recent Republican National Convention.

A FEW WORDS WITH MILLARD FILLMORE!

January 7 afforded an opportunity to interview the 13th president of the United States. On this day, national attention focuses on Colorado Springs—not as the headquarters' city of the American Numismatic Association—but as the home of an organization the honors mediocrity in American life. The Society for the Preservation and Enrichment of the Memory of Millard Fillmore, Last of the Whigs, meets annually on this date to observe the former president's birthday.

Every year Fillmore fans, better known as Fillmorons, meet with the former head of state at the Hall of Presidents, a wax museum in Colorado Springs. The meeting is followed by a banquet in Fillmore's honor and the presentation of an annual Medal of Mediocrity. This year's honors went to the Coca-Cola Company for "classic indecisiveness for changing its product more often than Fillmore changed political parties."

Millard Fillmore was never elected president. He had been Zachary Taylor's running mate and assumed the chair in the Oval Office on Taylor's death in 1850. Fillmore's stay at the White House ended in 1853 after he failed to receive his own party's nomination for the presidency. He tried again in 1856 while carrying the standard of the Know Nothing Party. His luck was without change.

When Fillmore found that Franklin Pierce's wife was unable to ride in the inaugural parade, the immediate past president suggested to his successor that his wife Abigail represent the new First Lady. Unfortunately it rained. Mrs. Fillmore caught cold and died. Fillmore's son was so unimpressed with his father's presidential papers that he ordered them burned following the president's death in 1874.

While Fillmore's term was not exactly an outstanding one, history records a major achievement—the introduction of the bathtub to the White House. Ironically, Fillmore cannot even accept credit, it belongs to his successor, Franklin Pierce. The source of the intentional misinformation is attributed to the great story teller, H. L. Mencken. In 1917, a Mencken column appearing in the *New*

York Evening Mail gave an apocryphal history of the bathtub. Tongue-in-cheek, the story related how the intrepid Fillmore took the first presidential bath. Mencken capped his yarn by reporting that the medical profession opposed the new invention as dangerous to health and that laws were passed in Massachusetts, Pennsylvania, and Virginia against using it. Subsequent retractions by Mencken were to no avail in removing this "fact" from history books.

Millard Fillmore appears destined to be remembered for doing nothing. Yet, serious numismatists know that this assessment is incorrect. January 7th afforded the opportunity to interview the past president and recall his contributions to the hobby.

Q - Mr. President, it was reported that during your Administration silver coins disappeared from circulation. It was said that their intrinsic value exceeded their face value. Was anything done to correct this situation?

A - I am glad that you asked that question. Several ideas were discussed. The most innovative, if I must say so, was the consideration given to annulated gold half dollars and dollars.

Q - Annulated dollars?

A - Perforated money, my good man. You know, like a ring. You use a large blank, punch a hole through the center and you have a fair-sized coin with little metal. The gold dollar of the time was too small, much too small. Why, we could make it the size of a dime and use no more metal than before. The half dollar could be the size of a half dime.

Q - It sounded like a good idea, Mr. President. Why didn't the Mint go ahead with it?

A - The standard excuse. Mechanical problems. We could not get the damnable things out of the press. Just made a mess of things.

Q - Were any other solutions to the silver problem considered, Mr. President?

A - We thought of increasing the size of the gold dollar by adding a little silver.

Q - What happened?

A - The little beggars turned silver, and when we tried copper, they turned brown. Democrats would have had a field day, you know.

Q - Anyone think of reducing the precious metal content in the silver coins to make them worth less than face as bullion?

A - Hurrumph, hurrumph. Well, Congress did just that,—after I left office.

Q - Mr. President, at the time there were complaints from the public about the size and weight of the one-cent piece. Citizens avoided them as much as possible. Would you care to comment?

A - Good question. Very reasonable of you to ask. The large cent was too heavy, wore holes in pockets, you know. We made some billon cents: 10% silver, the rest copper. Not bad, except that the Mint thought they could be counterfeited too easily. Tried other metals, too.

Q - Mr. President, what do you think coin collectors should best remember your Administration for?

A - Why, for a unique accomplishment. It was during my term that we introduced cheaper postal rates. Three cents for a letter and your collectors have a silver three-cent piece as testi-

The author discusses coins with Millard Fillmore.

mony to that unusual accomplishment. How many presidents do you know who reduced the cost of anything?

Now, let me ask you a question my good man. This Medal of Mediocrity that is presented annually, does it have my portrait on it?

Yes, Mr. President. It is from the United States Mint's Presidential series.

ON THE STATE OF THE HOBBY

IS THIS ANY WAY TO BUY COINS?

The caller on the other end of the line opened with a classic understatement. "I understand you are interested in coins!"

"Yes," I answered, half expecting to hear from a reader about a recent column. But the caller was neither complimentary nor seeking additional information. In fact, he was downright ego deflating.

"Did you know that there is a big celebration soon to take place and are you ready to cash in on it," he asked?

For a minute it sounded like I was receiving a belated congratulatory call on my retirement, but that happened three years ago. I suspected the celebration he was referring to had already occurred, after I left ANA, and I've already earned my pension benefits. He was too late.

Before I had a chance to explain, the caller continued. "In 1993, the world will celebrate the 500th anniversary of the Discovery of America by Christopher Columbus."

Was it "1493 when Columbus sailed the deep blue sea," or was it "1492 when he sailed the ocean blue?" Oh, well, what's one year in 500?

"It's going to be an even bigger celebration than was held in Chicago in 1893. That year there was a Columbian Exposition and the government issued two silver half dollar 50-cent pieces, one dated 1892 and the other 1893. They sold them to the public for a dollar each, but the exposition was a bust and so was the coin. Four million were made, 2½ million were melted leaving 1½ million. The government tried selling them again and could not, so the coins were put in circulation. Only 5% remain in Mint State."

So, his figures are a little askew. Surely, no one would waste the price of a call to sell coins that retail for but a few dollars. Sunday supplements carry advertisements offering "very fine" specimens of Columbian half dollars for $19 each and I think these are overpriced.

"A few years ago these coins were $190 each," my caller continued. "Only a few months ago the 1892 was selling for $2,500 in MS-65. On November 11, the Grey Sheet price was $2,575. The 1893 listed for $3,300 just a few months ago, on November 11 the price was $3,400."

I take it back, the cost of this pitch is worth the price of the call. Though I could not hear any pipes banging, I had, through the magic of telecommunications, a direct line to what many

The highly "touted" Columbian Exposition half dollar.

call, "a boiler room."

"Until last week we were out of these," the pitchman continued, "but we just bought an estate that had 20 sets. I am the senior salesman here, so I get the better material. The Japanese, Koreans and Chinese are trying to corner the market on Columbian half dollars. Foreign money is coming in to buy."

Poetic justice. We buy their Isuzus, Hyundais, and Daihatsus, and they buy our Columbian half dollars!

"Congress has passed a bill for two more coins in 1993, so these (Columbians) will be hot items."

Even Burnett Anderson missed this story.

"I am holding two for you. You can put it on your credit card. Only $5,800 for the pair. At the current rate of increase, in five years your investment will be worth $72,000. I usually tell my clients to hold on to their coins for three to five years, but these are so hot that if you choose to sell them back in just two years YOU CAN EXPECT IN EXCESS OF $20,000!"

So that's why its called a boiler room. Hot coins!

"Your best investment is to start with commemorative coins. I'll be your eyes and ears to the market. I am only a phone call away. Just call me anytime, even if you only want to talk or need some information about coins."

His offer has advantages. I could be typing a column at home and not need to go to the ANA library for background information. I could just call Joe and get the real scoop. Anytime. Instead of an outright and enthusiastic, "yes," I played coy. I did not want him to think I was naive, so I told my new found telephone pal, "Before I invest thousands of dollars with you, I want to know a little more about your company."

"Well, we've been in business 24½ years. We are registered with the American Numismatic Association—the ANA. They license dealers selling investment coins. They have about 1,500 dealers registered. Let me give you our license number."

Faith in my caller was fast disappearing. The "license" number sounded very much like a membership number. A new one at that. Unless things have happened since the last Board meeting, the Association neither licenses dealers to sell investment coins nor has a corporate membership. Belonging is on an individual basis. "In whose name is the company," I ask?

A boy genius! Not unusual for the coin hobby, but if this company has been in business for 24½ years under the same management, the owner was only 9½ years old when he launched his enterprise. His tenure with ANA, though, has not been as lengthy. Records show that the principal became a member last month, in November 1988.

"I don't want to pressure you, but I am holding these coins just for you. It is your last chance to make $70,000 in the next five years."

It's hedging time. It will take a lot of columns to make 70 grand. "How do I know these coins are graded properly? Who grades your coins?"

"PCGS, NGC, ING, NCI—there are a lot of grading services."

My pride is hurt. No ANA? "You don't use ANACS," I said with feigned surprise.

"Sometimes. But we rather use others. Whenever we buy coins, we send them in for upgrades!"

A Freudian slip?

The caller is persistent. Our phone-palship resumes the following day. I tell him ANACS was suggested by ANA.

"Why would they push ANACS? I don't know why ANA would pick one company over another. There is no difference in any grading."

The Christmas respite gives my phone-friend a chance to research the answer. He calls back again.

"The only reason ANA pushes their own grading is, that even though they are a regulatory agency, they have their own coin division. They're selling their own coins."

Again, I've learned something new,

something not anyone on the Board of Governors or for that matter at ANA Headquarters knows. For those just tuning in to the phone conversations, and for the caller from an East Coast firm having a fiduciary sounding name, the ANA is a federally chartered, non-profit educational organization. ANA promotes the educational aspects of the hobby. It cannot, and does not, buy or sell coins, nor can ANA act as a regulatory agency for investment numismatics.

Sorry, Joe. You really have a nice telephone personality, but, at the cost of losing a 1,200% increase on my money, I am going to forego the chance to own two more Columbian Exposition half dollars.

ELIMINATING THE PENNY WILL NOT MAKE CENTS!

Should the members of the National Association of Convenience Stores have their way, a new word may soon find its way into American jargon. Tired of counting pennies in their tills, of running to banks for rolls whenever they give out more cents than they receive in change, and having to reroll the coins whenever bank deposits are to be made, association members believe that they have found a practical answer and have coined it rounding.

NACS estimates that an extra two seconds is added to every cash transaction involving pennies in change. Eliminate the cent, association representatives say, and 5.5 million hours at a cost of $22 million will be saved annually.

Will the savings be passed on to the consumer? Some state legislators are already coveting the projected savings as a windfall tax. Alan S. Binder, a Princeton University economics professor and advisor to the unsuccessful presidential candidacy of Michael Dukakis, writes, "My suggestion is to round it up to the next nickel and throw the extra pennies into a state or local sales tax kitty."

Pricing, according to other advocates of the elimination of the penny, would continue to be in dollars and cents. Should the bill for a cash purchase end with the need for one or two cents in change, the total would be "rounded-down" to the nearest nickel. Example: If a candy bar costs 30 cents and there is two cents in sales tax to be added, the consumer will pay only 30 cents.

Unloved and unwanted, the convenience store lobby is spearheading a movement to discontinue the one-cent piece. They find the coin "inconvenient."

However, should there one more cent in tax, the cost would be "rounded-up," from 33 to 35 cents. Since there would be an equal mathematical chance of prices ending with the need for one or two cents in change as there would be with for three or four, consumer expense would balance out. Paying to the cent by check or credit card would continue, rounding would apply only to cash transactions.

The United States Mint currently produces an average of nine billion cents per year. True, many are not returned to circulation after they have been received in change. The cents often end up in piggy banks, Mason jars, or bureau drawers. Eventually the coins are rolled and carted to the bank or grocery store, a minor windfall to help underwrite an evening on the town. However, what advocates for the elimination of the cent fail to consider is the profit to the government in making money.

Today's Lincoln cent is 98% zinc, 2% copper. It costs the U.S. Mint six-tenths of one cent to make one cent. The end result is a net profit to the government of $31 million annually, and this figure takes into consideration the costs of handling, shipping and accounting. Additionally, the metal used is American mined and refined with a net appreciation of thousands of manhours of productive labor.

Before Congress votes to eliminate the cent, they need to consider asking, "Is it worth two seconds time per cash transaction to save jobs in the mining industry and to make money on the manufacture of coins for circulation, or is doing less to make more a primary objective?"

THE INDUSTRY WITH FRIENDS IN HIGH PLACES!

Just as the rulers of the ancient empires learned not to turn their backs on fellow countrymen, the guardians of the Greek and Roman temples found that they could not trust their faithful. All too often worshippers were suspected of being all too generous at the holy water fonts and far too stingy with their drachmae and denarii. To keep the blessed wells from running dry without proper recompense, the vending machine industry was born.

The origins of the first vending machine trace back almost 2,000 years, to the last half of the first century. The inventor was a genius of the Leonardo da Vinci caliber and known as Hero, or Heron of Alexandria. The first coin-operated machine dispensed holy water in the ancient temples.

Hero designed an urn to contain the holy water. A short dispenser pipe, not unlike a spigot, led out from the bottom. Considering the time, the mechanics of operation inside the urn

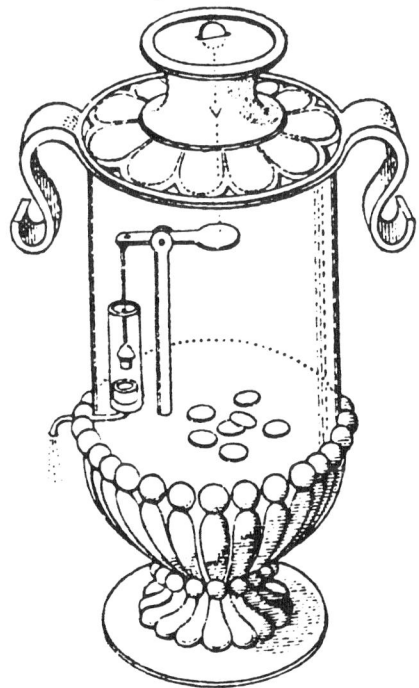

Though practical applications have changed since the first vending machine dispensed holy water, the concept remains with us today.

reflected Hero's genius. A small plug, attached to one end of a balance bar, sealed the other end of the pipe. When a coin was dropped through the slot in the top of the urn, it fell on the other end of the balance bar, its weight causing the plug to lift and water to flow. As the coin slid off the bar, the flow of the water and the weight of the plug sealed the top of the pipe once again. The actual amount of water dispensed could be measured and rationed.

Practical as it was, some today might find the first coin operated dispenser unsanitary. Coins collected rested in the water at the bottom of the urn. The principal of operation employed, nonetheless, remains virtually unchanged to this day.

Hero's genius is reflected in the number of his inventions. He is credited with the design of one of the earliest calculating devices—the odometer. His mileage meter measured distance traveled. And to Hero go the honors for the creation of a screw press to extract juice from grapes and oil from olives.

It was a design, however, other than one to save water and make money, that endeared Hero to the priests of the temples. The inventor applied his genius to devise temple doors that closed by themselves at the beginning of services and opened as the worship ended, as if by the will of the gods, mystifying worshippers. His secret was an air chamber heated by the symbolic fire at the altar. As the warm air rose in the chamber it forced water through a pipe causing the doors to close. Then, as the fires died down toward the end of the ceremony the cooling air retracted and the doors reopened.

Descriptions of many of Hero's inventions survive in an Arabic translation of one his books. The title has a familiar ring to it—*Pneumatica!*

Today, manufacturers and operating companies associated with the vending machine industry remain as well organized as they did with the priests in ancient society. Joined by food service management firms, office coffee machine operators, suppliers of products and services such as food, candy, beverages, cigarettes and packaging, the vending machine industry maintains a powerful lobby in the nation's capital.

The strength of the industry's legislative influence can be easily measured. This was the industry that dictated the size and shape of the ill-destined Susan B. Anthony mini-dollar to the Treasury Department. When the coin proved to be a disaster, failing to circulate due to its similarity to the 25-cent piece, few pointed accusatory fingers at the vending machine industry. They just let the Treasury take full responsibility and sole blame.

Collectors, too, experienced the power of the vending machine lobby in the early 1960s. When a severe coin shortage manifested itself throughout the country, the industry lobby was able to shift the blame for not projecting an increased demand for coins for circulation from themselves to the shoulders of coin collectors. Their efforts lead the government to consider such punitive measures as removing mintmarks from coins, not changing dates on an annual basis, mixing circulated and Uncirculated coins in bags shipped out, and the cessation of production of Proof sets.

But then, when an industry has been around for almost 2,000 years, you would expect it to have friends in high places.

MOTTOES ON MONEY MAY FACE NEW CHALLENGES!

Far fetched as it seems today, the country may, in the not too distant future, face a new attack from a unexpected quarter on the wording of the mottoes appearing on our currency.

For some time, Madalyn Murray O'Hair's American Atheists have actively campaigned to remove the motto, "In God We Trust," from coin and currency. Following the voting results in recent elections, Mrs O'Hair's group may find an unlikely ally in having mottoes challenged.

The new front will not base its attack on the premise that expressing a belief in God violates the symbolic separation of church and state, but on the appearance of a second language on our money.

Recently, legislators in 31 states debated the merits of mandating English as the language of government. Three states, Arizona, Colorado and Florida, put the fate of such controversial legislation in the hands of their voters and asked that the language initiatives be voted up or down. The majority cast their ballots in favor of legislating English as their sole and "official" language.

Prior to Election Tuesday 1988, fourteen states had added "official" English laws to their state constitutions. Nebraska was the first to pass such legislation, in 1920. Illinois followed suit three years later. Then, for almost six decades, the idea of mandating an offical language lay dormant. Not until 1981 did a third state, Virginia, rule on "official" English and initiate a new surge of interest. Proposed regulations run counter to the federally enacted Voting Rights Act of 1965 and the Bilingual Education legislation of 1967. The former requires that bilingual voting materials be provided in certain areas to insure that citizens are not denied voting privileges for the reason they cannot read English. The latter applies to schooling.

Proponents of English only point to Canada as an example of where bilingualism has divided the country. Even currency bills must be printed in both French and English. Advocates say that without everyone sharing a common language, the nation stands in peril of becoming as divided as Canada, or even Belgium, where a separate coinage serves the French and Flemish speaking population.

Opponents of the legislation note that the authors of the U.S. Constitution rejected the idea of declaring English the official language for fear that such action would be used to restrict language, cultural, and religious liberties.

The movement receives national impetus from U.S. English, a non-profit organization formed in 1983 to promote the language as the sole and official word of the American government. The finance arm of the organization, The U.S. English Legislative Task Force, has contributed substantial funds to support attempts in a number of states to make English singular and official. In Colorado, to secure sufficient signatures to insure the initiative a place on the November ballot, the task force pumped hundreds of thousands of dollars into the state effort, going so far as to pay recruiters from 75-cents to $1.25 per signature obtained on petitions requesting amendement consideration. With the avowed goal of prohibiting the use of a second language by the federal government, it is not unlikely to believe that Latin, as well as Spanish, will be an eventual target.

Precedent for change was inadvertently set by the Treasury Department a few years ago when the design of the Treasury seal, as it appeared on the currency, was modified. The most pronounced change was the removal of a second language, Latin, from the legend in the letter ring of the Treasury seal, as it appeared on the obverse of circulating paper money. THESAUR. AMER. SEPTENT. SIGIL. is the abbreviation of Thesauri Americae Septentrionalis Sigillum, meaning "The Seal of the Treasury of North America." The present legend reads, "The Department of the Treasury."

The dollar bill incorporates Latin legends in the design of the Great Seal of the United States appearing on the reverse. The obverse of the Great Seal carries the Latin motto, "Annuit Coeptis" above with "Novus Ordo Seclorum" below, commonly accepted to mean, "The new series of ages is favorable to our undertakings." E Pluribus Unum was originally considered for the Great Seal. Meaning "Out of many, one," it is now mandated that the motto appear on all legal tender coins of the U.S.

Several leading proponents of the English only initiative in Colorado have been interviewed. Without exception, they were surprised to learn that American currency can be considered bilingual. Still, none offered the suggestion that coins and currency be made exempt from the proposed legislation. In this era of zealots, it will not be surprising to find someday a demand that American money be printed in "English only."

IN THE NEW HOBBY, GRADING IS A WAY OF LIFE!

An interpreter greets us at the door as we enter the bourse area of the 13th Midwinter Convention of the American Numismatic Association at Buffalo, New York. Translation service is the latest benefit of membership, offered to enable collectors to understand the language of the new grading system established by the Board of Governors.

Officers of ANA feel that the language of the hobby is disintegrating into regional dialects. The staid East Coast constituency turned to suffix signs shortly after the Board acquiesced to single number gradation for mint states several years ago. Advertisements from eastern dealers in the numismatic press supplement their descriptions with plus signs: e.g. 62+; or slightly better, 62++.

West Coast competitors show a preference for prefix symbolism, arguing that their descriptions are better market oriented. While an East Coast dealer may describe a silver dollar as MS-62++, his Pacific area counterpart calls it a -63. One dealer, speaking on condition of anonymity, acknowledged that while there is no difference between a 62++ and a -63, the latter description offers better marketability to the collector world.

The ANA executive directorship announced that, after careful deliberation and study, the grading of Mint State conditions will be expanded to five decimal points.

A tangential benefit of new grades is one of theft deterence. With a potential of one million possible grades for obverse descriptions alone, every coin could, theoretically, be unique. Stolen coins could easily be traced by grade alone.

Focus on grading has shifted from the center of the coin toward the edge. ANACS recognizes that there is more surface area to examine away from the middle than there is in the center. Graders are now concentrating their attention outwardly. ANACS is meeting the new challenge with the addition of a competent denticle technician to the staff. As demand increases for re-examination and regrading, two denticle assistants may be hired.

While the new grading standards appear to be greeted with dealer enthusiasm, the welcome is not unanimous. The American Civil Liberties Union has announced that it will file a class action suit on behalf of ancient coin dealers. The ACLU will charge ANACS with discrimination based on the service's refusal to grade coins because of age.

The United States Mint, cognizant of collector demand for accurate grading, is considering the placement of the grade directly on the coin when striking. The Federated Association of Professional Grading Services, representing the one hundred and eight grading services in the U.S., is asking collectors to write to their congressmen to protest this possible incursion against free enterprise.

Collectors submitting coins for the new grading will receive a Deep-in-Depth Grading Analysis to help eliminate any possible confusion over the reasons for their exclusive grades. In order to arrive at the finite grade of a particular coin, every specimen will be examined twice—once in the morning while the grader's eyes are still fresh, and once again in the late afternoon.

An average of the two grades will be placed on the certificate.

When asked to comment on the new grading, the president of the Association, succinctly noted, "We will be remembered for this period of creative subjectivity!"

TO HAVE AND TO HOLD—FOREVER!

To the average person, the word cache conjures an image in agreement with the dictionary—a hiding place, a secure place, something hidden. The serious numismatist sees cache as a copper coin, issued by France from 1720 to 1837 for its possessions in Pondichery and Karikal on the Coromandel Coast. But, now, comes the American Numismatic Association to give us a new meaning for the word. Cache is the name given by the ANA for its newly designed, hermetically sealed coin holders.

For several years now, high-grade, high-value investment coins, particularly silver dollars, have been encapsulated in plastic slabs. Ease of marketing, storage and security have made the hard plastic holders a popular alternative to vinyl wallets and paper envelopes, particularly for dealers specializing in investment coins.

A scandal in 1988 with counterfeit slabs and the question of the possibility of coins of lesser grade being substituted within the slabs, led the ANA to commit $125,000 and almost a year of research to develop a safe, substitution-proof holder. The recently unveiled ANA Cache is the result.

The new holders represent a cooperative venture between the Professional Numismatists Guild and the American Numismatic Association. A copy-proof, 3-dimensional hologram, displaying the logos of both organizations, is sealed within the holder.

The need to encapsulate precious specimens became apparent as one point grading variations often devel-

An ANACS "slab" of early 1989.

oped into value differentials of several thousands of dollars per coin. One example is the 1928 Hawaii commemorative half dollar. At the time I am writing, an average Uncirculated specimen (MS-60) lists for $990; an MS-63 catalogs at $1,400; but one a grade point better and advertised as MS-64 lists at $2,500, and an MS-65 tops $6,200.

The value differential between single grade points in Uncirculated coins emphasizes the need for impartial grading. Coins sealed by the Association within the caches are independently graded by at least four graders, then re-examined by a qualified specialist who is a member of the Professional Numismatists Guild.

The new encapsulation is an option offered in addition to the regular authentication and grading services pioneered by the ANA and widely imitated throughout the industry. The cost of either option is the same—$23 per coin.

THE SPRING RITE OF WHIMSY!

It was right there, in a recent issue of *Advertising Age*. Lenore Skenazy's weekly column was looking into the future, forecasting Madison Avenue's "next" trend.

How fortunate the hobby would be if we could foretell the next collector craze. Editors, copywriters, and columnists could do their research far ahead of time and then call their output "timely." And think of the dealers—what they wouldn't give to know what you will want to buy next?

There was a time when a few tried to set the trends for many. Years ago, when the hobby danced to the tunes played by the Treasury Department's Office of Domestic Gold and Silver Operations (ODGSO), few modern world gold coins were legally collectible. Gold bullion pieces and medals of the same fabric were subject to confiscation and fines and other penalties were assessed against collector-owners. It was at this same time that noncirculating legal tender coins (NCLT) were making their debut. A trend was in its embryonic stage.

The island nation of Tonga was just beginning to emerge from British protectorship when a visiting coin dealer induced Queen Salote Tupou III to issue her own "coinage." The year was 1962, a full eight years short of independence, but Tonga released 1/4, 1/2 and one koula collector coins, in both gold and platinum. Dr. Leland Howard, director of ODGSO, ruled against legal ownership of the gold coins by American citizens. However the imaginative adviser to the queen was not about to let a "golden" opportunity to slip through his hands. Tonga was induced to reproduce its new gold coinage on the postage stamps of the country. Embossed circular metallic foil adhesives were introduced. Sales were disappointing at first, but then, with a little encouragement, a trend developed.

Full page advertisements began to appear in both the philatelic and numismatic press. There was one noticeable difference, however. Each week the price for the coin stamps in the numismatic press increased progressively, but the cost remained constant in the philatelic papers. Before long, the price in the coin papers was exactly double the cost asked of stamp collectors.

The hobby has progressed considerably since those days of blatant trend setting. But there are still occasions when price increases are neither merited nor reflect greater demand. The intent is to get the purchaser to buy under the premise, "Look at that, it keeps climbing in value every week. I had better buy before it increases any further."

Wonder for a moment how great it would be for coin readers should just one *Numismatic News* columnist be blessed with the foresight to recognize the next hobby trend far enough in advance for us to take advantage of the forecasts.

In case Ms. Skenazy's hints at the yet-to-come could be applied to the hobby, let us delve fancifully into her latest forecast. Recognizing that these early spring months help generate a $125 million dollar market for manufacturers and dispensers of cold and allergy medicines, Skenazy's latest forecasted trends focused on problems of the nose. She called her prognostications "Sinus of the Times."

Should her predicted trends hold true for our hobby, collectors could expect to see sometime this spring:

* a Cheyenne-based commercial television blitz for a face-value only, limited edition series on the coins of Pollenesia.

* purveyors of one-ounce silver rounds to abandon the current series of cartoon characters and nose ahead with a series on Pinocchio, look-alike Richard Nixon, Jimmy Durante, or possibly a solo piece depicting Sneezy, one of the Seven Dwarfs.

* a New York dealer to offer a late release Korean Olympic coin featuring the spring rite of "Ha-Chu." Sales would be restricted to those who have previously purchased all four complete series of Korean Olympic coins. This restriction will insure the new issue's ultimate rarity.

* the newly organized Belgian Mint USA will advertise the first North American release of Phlemish coins.

* as part of the economic sinus of the times, the U.S. Mint to reduce the thickness of the cupro-nickel plating on 1989 quarters. Unable to withstand the rigors of circulation, Washington's proboscis may show signs of wear first and earn for the circulated quarters the sobriquet, "Old Brown Nose!"

* a year late, the British Royal Mint to issue a commemorative coin marking the 400th anniversary of the Great Nasal Victory over the invincible Spanish Flu.

* the Warsaw Mint's new series of eight coins will be marketed under the trade name "Poland-eight." Proceeds from the sale to go to Overseas Allergy Relief.

* and, finally, a current Georgia-based ANA governor to change his mind and announce for re-election. With all this emphasis on allergies and allergy cures, he would be foolish not to take advantage of the well-publicized nostrums for "Hey Fivaz!"

THE NUMISMATIC AGE OF THE COMPUTER HAS ARRIVED!

A few years ago, collectors found themselves rearranging their bookshelves. The *Guide Book of United States Coins, The Standard Catalog of Modern World Coins,* and sundry other references were being moved to make room for the likes of *An Introduction to Personal Computers* and *Programming and Applications of Your PC.*

Collectors added new words to their hobby vocabulary. No longer was it sufficient to know that "MS" stood for Mint State or that "Good" meant the poorest collectible grade. They now had to grapple with bauds, hard or floppy disks, drives, and the inevitable response, "Invalid Command." The age of the numismatic computer network had arrived.

The introduction in 1983 of the Complete Electronic Numismatic Trading Systems provided the ideal acronym—CENTS, but hobbyists were far from ready for "Coin Talk," at least not to a machine. While professional coin dealers soon recognized the benefits of instantaneous response to customer want-lists and up-to-the-minute price changes, the collector at home failed to appreciate the marvel of buying, selling and trading via telephone modems. The CENTS network died prematurely.

Now collectors are faced with a reality thought impossible just a few years ago—computer-designed coins. Reality made its debut earlier this year when the Netherlands Commission for Special Coin Issues unveiled a computer designed, legal tender, sterling silver commemorative 50-guilder coin.

Marking 300 years since Prince William III of Orange and his consort, Mary Stuart, crossed the channel to become King and Queen of England, the coin is only the fourth Dutch guilder piece in history. However, the coin's uniqueness comes from its design. One side relies on the established coinage art tradition. It features one of the most famous double portraits in numismatic history, the conjoined busts of William and Mary, sculptured as they appeared on the 5-guinea gold coin of 1691.

Design for the other side of the coin, however, turns to the wizardry of the computer age. The portrait of reigning Queen Beatrice of the Netherlands was created by laser-generated graphics programmed to a portrait by Vincent Wentzel. The unique application of modern technology introduces the computer to the art of coinage.

CHERRYPICKERS' TOP 25

Cherrypicking is the art of separating numismatic wheat from common coin chaff. It is the art of finding rare coins among common date offerings. Cherrypicking is putting fun back into the hobby. It is the buying of a coin valued at hundreds of dollars for only a few and it is being done now!

For the past several years, Bill Fivaz has been an instructor at the American Numismatic Association's summer seminars in Colorado Springs. He teaches counterfeit detection and coin grading, but it is his after-class, evening sessions that prove to be the most popular among students. One session is on cherrypicking and few collectors fail to be interested in finding bargains.

Fivaz's objects of search are primarily overdates, repunched mintmarks, and doubled dies not listed in the standard catalogs, but are the quest of specialists in the field of mint error collecting. Many dealers are unaware of, or do not have the time to separate, these rarities from their regular stock. Thus a common date coin that may be priced at catalog for less than a dollar may, in reality, have a repunched date and be worth several hundreds of dollars.

The 55-year old Fivaz has been a col-

The conjoined busts of William and Mary, copied from a 1691 gold piece, left, contrasts sharply with the laser generated portrait of Queen Beatrix on the right.

lector since 1950 and all during these years he has shared his knowledge with collectors. In addition to his cherrypicking talks, Fivaz has produced dozens of slide programs that he makes available to coin clubs on a no-charge basis. For these efforts he has been recognized as a Numismatic Ambassador by the publishers of *Numismatic News* and *Coins* magazine and has twice received the American Numismatic Association's Medal of Merit. Fivaz is also a former member of the ANA's Board of Governors. In business life Fivaz is a regional sales manager for Nestle Foods, out of its Atlanta, Georgia, office.

Fivaz has compiled a list that he has entitled, "Cherrypickers' Top 25." The list includes most denominations, with five-cent pieces predominating. All are coins ordinarily offered at standard catalog prices—coins that could bring hundreds, even thousands of dollars each. Almost all are coins that Fivaz has found himself. For example, a 1916-dated Buffalo nickel lists for 60 cents in good condition, yet one in the same grade offered with a doubled-die obverse lists for $800! The same coin can be purchased in Uncirculated condition for $40, but if your trained eye can find the doubled die on the Mint State piece, your coin could be worth $4,700 in the same condition.

It is all worth the investment of a few dollars for an eight-power magnifying glass and a few moments time to review Fivaz' list.

CHERRYPICKERS' TOP 25

This is the list compiled by Bill Fivaz, an instructor at the American Numismatic Association's annual summer seminars at Colorado College.

1. 1888/7 Indian 1c
   Overdate—very rare
2. 1894 Indian 1c
   Repunched date
3. 1944-D/S Lincoln 1c
   Overmintmark
4. 1867 2c
   Doubled obverse die
5. 1883/2 Shield 5c
   Overdate
6. 1916/1916 Buffalo 5c
   Doubled obverse die

By carefully observing the reverse of this Philadelphia five-cent piece, one can see the doubled outline caused by an imperfect die. Instead of a few dollars value, this coin is worth several hundreds of dollars!

7. 1935-P Buffalo 5c
   Doubled reverse die
8. 1936-D Buffalo 5c
   3½ leg (very rare)
9. 1939-P Jefferson 5c
   Doubled rev. die (6 steps)
10. 1939 Proof Jefferson 5c
    Var. 2 (sharp steps).
11. 1940 Proof Jefferson 5c
    Var. 1 (wavy steps).
12. 1942-D/Horiz.D Jefferson 5c
    Repunched mintmark
13. 1943-P Jefferson 5c
    Doubled obv. die
14. 1943/2-P Jefferson 5c
    Overdate
15. 1945-P Jefferson 5c
    Doubled reverse die
16. 1949-D/S Jefferson 5c
    Overmintmark
17. 1854/3 Seated Liberty 25c
    Overdate
18. 1934-P Washington 25c
    Doubled obverse die
19. 1942-D Washington 25c
    Doubled obv. die (v. rare)
20. 1942-D Washington 25c
    Doubled reverse die
21. 1943-S Washington 25c
    Doubled obverse die
22. 1950-S/D Washington 25c
    Overmintmark
23. 1950-D/S Washington 25c
    Overmintmark
24. 1901-P Morgan dollar
    Doubled reverse die
25. 1862 $1 gold
    Doubled obverse die

REFLECTIONS

GOING STRAIGHT TO THE SOURCE OFTEN CONTRADICTED THE COIN BOOKS

There are many of us in the hobby today who turn to "remember when," as our mark of maturity—rather than the more obvious growing paunch and thinning hair. Recall of the times when we could find Barber quarters and halves, Liberty Head nickels, even an occasional Indian Head cent in circulation, I believe, is a knee-jerk response to an inner wish that we had the foresight to save all that we had once considered "too common."

While we may bemoan the fact that we could have all been millionaires, there is one loss we tend to overlook. In the days when collecting moved at a slower pace, when we took time to cultivate friendships and share a hobby, letter writing was an enjoyable by-product of numismatics. We all had our pen pals, one or two fellow collectors to whom we related our hobby experiences and shared information gleaned through study.

I cannot recall how I first "met" John Tetso, but it was through him that I developed the not-yet-satisfied urge to visit the Canadian Arctic. And, it is to John that I owe the true story of the Hudson's Bay tokens.

John Tetso was a Slavy Indian trapper and once had been the elected chief of his band. Getting mail to and from John was no easy task. He summered at Willow River Camp, 110 miles north of Fort Simpson, in Canada's Northwest Territories. This distance from civilization was to cost John his life when he contracted pneumonia in camp and died within a few days. At the time there was no quick means of securing medical help or obtaining medical supplies. John Tetso was 43 years old when he passed away on September 20, 1964.

Our letters back and forth, however infrequent, dealt a great deal on life in Canada's far north. Having acquired a set of Hudson's Bay tokens, I was curious to find out more about them and, despite what we read in coin books, the word "token" is a misnomer. They were really counters.

According to John Tetso, a fur trader by profession, the Hudson's Bay tokens were never used as a form of currency. They had no monetary value. The tokens were used simply as a means for the trapper to keep check on his purchases. Not all trading posts used them. Some used polished white sticks, others even used thimbles. Trading with an Inuit or Indian with furs would start with an evaluation of the pelts and an agreement on the price to be paid. Then, the trading tokens, or whatever was used to indicate the value, were placed on the counter. As the native selected items he wanted or needed, the "factor" or trading post manager, would withdraw tokens to show how much each item cost and to give an indication on the balance of credit left. The trading post never had more than a few sets of these tokens on hand!

The Hudson's Bay Company substantiated John Tetso's description of the use of these tokens. Officially, they were referred to as "Arctic Tokens" in the archives of the company. Their listing in the records of the "Bay" is prefaced with the following notation, "As the beaver was the standard of trade in the fur trade of the 19th century, so was the white fox in the Canadian Arctic of the 20th century."

Following the end of World War II, the company realized that modern transportation would open up the Arctic to more people and believed that the Inuit should become familiar with the decimal monetary system of Canada.

Aluminum tokens issued were a square one, with the numeral "1" on it representing one Arctic white fox, and circular tokens in denominations of 100, 50, 25, 10 and 5—for "cents." "These tokens," noted a company manual, "were used on the counter when the furs were evaluated. First, the furs were figured in 'white fox' value, using square tokens. Then they were figured at the current rate of white fox skins in dollars using circular tokens. But with an expanding educational system, tokens have been replaced by the regular cash system of the country."

Not only was the misconception of the use of these tokens corrected by John Tetso, but another fallacy reported in some coin books on the earlier Hudson's Bay tokens was also brought to light.

Beaver was the chief commodity received in trade for goods at the trading posts in the earlier days. Needing a standard by which all other furs and commodities could be rated for trading, a brass token, called "One Made-Beaver," was selected as the unit of currency in the fur trade. It was equal in value to the skin of an adult male beaver in prime condition. Three other tokens completed the series—1/2, 1/4, and 1/8 Made Beaver.

These tokens were designed by George McTavish of Albany Fort in 1854 and sent to London to be struck. It was the designer's intent that the M B—Made-Beaver—be joined as in the monogram H B for Hudson's Bay. The die cutter misinterpreted the monogram as the letters "N B" joined by mistake. So "N B" went on the tokens and many collectors and authors have incorrectly translated the initials to mean "New Beaver," a term not used by the company.

The initials "E M," which also appear on the tokens, stand for East Main, the district on the East Mainland of Hudson Bay.

One Canadian coin guide book notes that the Indians preferred to trust the company accounts rather than take the tokens which were easily lost and for this reason the tokens never circulated in large quantities. "Not so," wrote John Tetso, "the tokens were never intended for use in circulation or in place of coin of the realm. The tokens were used merely as counters and the only things that they substituted for were porcupine quills, ivory discs, musket balls or anything else in use at a particular trading post."

I may not have made a fortune in gleaning coins from circulation, but I certainly amassed a wealth of information from the pen pal practice of the past, especially from friends like John Tetso.

GROWING UP NUMISMATIC!

United's Flight 167, Boeing 727 service from New York LaGuardia to Denver Stapleton, is delayed due to weather. No new departure time has been posted and there is time to kill. Lots of time. I have already read the newspapers and the terminal bookstore seems as likely a place as any to find more meaningful reading. The hobby section of the bookstore offers little numismatically—a choice between *A Guide Book of United States Coins* by R.S. Yeoman (37th Revised Edition), or the *"Official" 1984 Blackbook Price Guide of United States Coins* (Twenty-second Edition), "16,700 Up-Dated Prices for U.S. Coinage, 1616 to Date." Thanks, but no thanks.

Browsing other aisles my eyes catch a glimpse of an intriguing title—*Growing Up Catholic—An Infinitely Funny Guide for the Faithful, the Fallen, and Everyone In-Between.* Since I consider myself one of the latter, I buy the book.

From the index on, the book hits home. The authors and I share a common upbringing—parochial school. "Every Catholic, whether devout, practicing, grudgingly observant, lapsed or excommunicated, shares with millions of other Catholics the indelible marks of his or her upbringing." I still find hot dogs tastier on Fridays, than on any other day of the week.

The book keeps me mesmerized. I am reliving the fun years of growing up. I cannot stop reading, even though the flight has now been announced and boarding is now underway. I read it through the line and to my seat. Flight 167 is crowded, every seat in non-smoking is taken. Thankfully, mine is a window seat, but the man next to me flexes his wings. His right elbow becomes an adjunct to my tie. I keep on reading until I find a particularly funny passage and laugh out loud. My seat partner stares, an explanation is in order—"I grew up Catholic!"

The man stretches for the stewardess' call button and demands to be moved. He'll even take "smoking." He must have been one of those Congregationalists the nuns always warned me about. It is more relaxing to spread out and the book is to stay in my traveling briefcase for all future trips.

Catholicism helped develop the collector instinct. One starts with holy pictures, then graduates to medals—religious medals. As youngsters we vied with one another to get the most different, the most unusual, or the most unheard of saints: St. Bibinia, Martyr; St. Ansgar of Scandinavia; St. Ambrose, patron of marble workers; even St. Eligius, guardian of coin collectors. The "best of show" went to the one with the most medals attached to his rosary. It was a natural evolution to graduate from medals to coins. Perhaps, in this rationale, lies the reason that Francis Cardinal Spellman and Terrence Cardinal Cooke were such numismatists of note. They had early starts.

Being raised in parochial school—Sacred Heart Academy in Fairhaven, Massachusetts—for the most part, left indelible marks. One has to do with papal infallibility. Church teachings are "immutable, designed to last forever," no matter how many times they are changed. A few saints come, a lot of saints go. St. Christopher, whose medals were a must for early collectors, has been demoted to a question mark. No longer can a thousand angels crowd on the head of a pin, but with inhibitions being what they are, I am uncomfortable questioning the divine word.

Being raised numismatic, my eyes tend to catch innocuous little statements that portend to be of collector interest. There was one such item, on page 96, a filler from the *Catholic Almanac*—"Seven papal stamps and six papal coins were issued in 1982!"

Far be it for me to question the "bible" of my church's apostolic knowledge, but if this reference is correct, then the authority for the hobby, *The Standard Catalog of Modern World Coins* is not! The authorities at Krause Publications list not six but seven coins for 1982: (1) a 10 lire aluminum coin commemorating the Creation of Woman; (2) a 20 lire aluminum-bronze piece honoring marriage; (3) a 50 lire stainless steel coin depicting maternity; (4) a 100 lire, also stainless steel, featuring the family; (5) a 200 lire aluminum-bronze issue with a labor motif; (6) a 500 lire, stainless steel aluminum-bronze bimetallic coin showing education; and (7) a silver 1000 lire issue with the papal arms on the reverse. All seven coins share a common obverse—the head of Pope John Paul II.

I have written the editors of the *Almanac* asking which "bible" is correct. At press time there has been no answer.

ALL FOR THE SAKE OF A STORY

For the sake of a story, I sold my soul to the devil—Mephistopheles to be precise. At least, that is the way it seemed after four weeks of steady rehearsal culminating with the opening night performance of Gounod's "Faust" at Colorado Springs' Pikes Peak Center. To secure a fresh approach for a column, I became a supernumerary, an extra, in the cast of the Colorado Opera Festival's production of one of the world's favorite operas. Readers concerned with the future of the performing arts in America can rest at ease, all my parts were non-verbal!

Faust is the story of an aged philosopher who sells his soul to the devil in exchange for youth and possession of the fair Marguerite. Drinking a magic potion, Dr. Faust's youth returns and Marguerite, bewitched by a spell wrought by Mephistopheles, succumbs to Faust's advances. She bears Faust's child and, in shame, kills it. Half-crazed, awaiting execution, Marguerite languishes in prison. Faust, guilt ridden, seeks to save her, but Marguerite recognizes now that it was the devil who guided Faust and she renounces her love for him. She dies as a chorus of angels proclaim her salvation and welcome her to heaven.

Not as author Charles Gounod intended when he set the German poet Goethe's tragedy to music in 1858, numismatic undertones were added to several scenes. After all, I was acting only to share these experiences with fellow coin collectors. Act One opened in the gloomy, 16th-century study of Dr. Faust. As the curtain rose, Faust looked up from a book before him and voiced his despair and weariness. The book was a thick tome, hinting of secret formulae for such scientific experiments as the transmutation of base metal into gold. The book used—Krause Publications *Standard Catalog of World Coins*, 1983 edition! Quipped director

Depictions of the devil, turning base metal into gold coin and making flowers wilt, scenes often seen on magic coins and tokens, come from the story of Faust.

Patrick Bakman, "If they can get those prices for small copper coins, they have discovered the secret of turning base metal in gold!"

In Act Two, the scene shifted to the square in a German village. A kermis, or fair, was underway and a group of students and soldiers struck up a rousing tune in praise of drinking. At stage center, in a striking baritone voice, Valentin, a soldier and brother of Marguerite, mused about a medallion given to him by his sister to protect him in battle. "O holy medal," he sang. Holy or not, it was a souvenir medal from the American Numismatic Association's 88th anniversary convention in St. Louis.

Later in the same act, Mephistopheles appeared and asked if he might join in song with the students. Invited to join, he sang the Song of the Golden Calf. With scorn he told how all men worship gold and then threw out gold coins for the villagers to scramble for. The prop man was delighted with the box of gold anodized Mardi Gras doubloons supplied by the ANA for the scene. Regretably, several of the cast took the devil's offer quite literally and a number of opera singers now have the nucleus of a collection of golden doubloons.

Frivolity aside, the opera "Faust" did have genuine impact on numismatics, at least in the collecting of magician's tokens and medals. Mephistopheles, as he is depicted on many of these pieces, owes his appearance to Goethe's "Faust." The plumed hat, the cape and dress, are all borrowed from this story. The name Mephistopheles is the best known personification of the devil when he relates to the world of magic.

Though I played three parts, a burgher in a village scene, a monk at Valentin's wake, and the captain of the guard ordering the execution of Marguerite, I have not applied for membership in Actors' Equity. I feel that my operatic career, like that of ANA management, has come to an end.

THE STRAWBERRY MONEY OF MISSOURI!

I note the beginning of summer, not by any calendar or juxtaposition of the moon with Earth, but by the arrival of fresh, luscious, red ripe strawberries at the supermarket! Topping a fresh-from-the-oven shortcake with juicy berries or having strawberries straight—with rich cream and powdered sugar—is excuse enough to stretch my imagination and make coin collecting a bowl of berries.

A mental vision of a dish of strawberries conjures memories of an oilcloth-draped table, a bulge-necked bottle of milk with cream at the top, and a wafer thin, cottonwood veneer box filled with berries. Incidentally, these too are collectibles today, but the rest is sheer memory from the past. Now strawberries are packaged in plastic and, often as not, sold by the pound as by the quart. Even the sweet taste seems to have diminished over the years, but recollections provide an opportunity to research the past and relate to the strawberry money of Missouri.

Once, promoters were hard pressed to sell the marginal land of the southwestern Missouri Ozarks. This rocky soil was not productive enough to sustain commercial agriculture on a large scale, but small lots of 40 to 80 acres each could attract independent-minded farmers desiring to be "on their own."

What cash crop could earn enough money to sustain the farmer and still turn profit enough to pay for the land? Strawberries were suggested and strawberries were promoted. Associations were formed to market and publicize the crop. Refrigerated trains made it possible for the berries to be offered in Kansas City and St. Louis within a day or two of picking. An outlet for the crop was created as were jobs for pickers, planters, weeders, sorters, and boxers. The labor pool was provided by families—mother, father and older children all worked. First locals and later itinerants by the hundreds worked the Ozark berry patches. They were called "gaumers," from the juice of the berries that "gaumed" their hands and clothes. While the gaumers wanted to be paid as they picked, few farmers had enough cash. Farmers were not paid for their crops until after the berries had been marketed and sold. As a result a token coinage was developed by the farm associations and local banks. Bookkeeping and payroll records were kept at a minimum. From the 1890s to the mid-1920s, a token currency circulated throughout the area. This money was readily accepted by merchants, service people and banks. Each town had its own—Aurora, Carthage, Duenweg, Exeter, Joplin, Mount Vernon, Neosho, Pierce City, Republic, and Sarcoxie.

A Bank of Sarcoxie token good for one tray of local strawberries.

It was in Sarcoxie in 1883 that commerical strawberry growing was first introduced to the region, and at its peak more than 25,000 laborers were employed picking strawberries. The average worker in 1900 could receive as much as $2 per day, earned at a rate of two cents per quart picked! By the end of World War I, the annual yield averaged one half million crates of Missouri-grown berries. With 24 quarts to the crate, the number of tokens in circulation often exceeded the number of U.S. coins in town.

Tokens were made in denominations of one quart, one tray, six quarts and one crate each. The face value was fixed to the market price of the crop. The tokens could be redeemed at local bank on week's end, or used in stores during the week. An observant Secret Service agent, noticing the token transactions, reminded local officials of a U.S. law to the contrary, and brought the use of strawberry money to an end.

ON MEETING INDIANS IN COLORADO!

In 1966, following the close of the American Numismatic Association's 75th anniversary convention in Chicago, I returned to Iola, Wisconsin full of excitement and anticipation on my pending move to Colorado Springs. The ANA's Board of Governors had just hired me to take over the editorship of *The Numismatist*. The well-wishes of the Krause staff were comingled with a great deal of good natured ribbing and pseudo-caution to be wary of Indians in the wild west of Colorado. Little did I realize, at the time, that one of the first collectors I would meet in Colorado was one who claimed Indian parentage, albeit foster.

Lone Eagle, the White Sioux, was known locally for his controversial interpretation of Indian history, his not-too-well accepted version of the Battle of the Little Big Horn and General Custer's death by his own hand being one example. Lone Eagle was also known for his extensive stamp and coin collection, often exhibited piecemeal at local club gatherings. The adopted Indian was given to tall tales and many of his claims were met with skepticism. Doubt faded when he brought an unusual, often expensive specimen to a meeting—be it a stamp or a coin.

Lone Eagle claimed that as the infant son of missionary parents, who died during a smallpox epidemic while ministering to the spritual needs of the Oglala Sioux, he was adopted by Chief Big Elk and his wife Cloud Woman, and raised as their child. He was called "Lone Eagle" after a brave who died in the Battle of the Little Big Horn.

Lone Eagle recalled that tales of the Indian victory were told and retold countless times around the tribal campfires. According to his Indian father, Lone Eagle said, General Custer suffered two wounds, neither fatal. During the final charge Custer was observed seated on the ground, his service revolver pointed to his head. The general fired the shot that ended his own life. Lone Eagle believed that Custer feared

Lone Eagle, the White Sioux.

torture at the hands of his enemies, but Lone Eagle was just as convinced that the Indians would have spared Custer's life out of respect for a brave man.

Lone Eagle's collectible stories carried the same blend of truth and tall talk, making his stories enjoyable to listen to but difficult to believe. Most listeners played doubting Thomas when Lone Eagle first spoke of the rarities that made up his collection. People only believed when they saw. Lone Eagle, whose birth name had been Floyd Shuster Maine, alleged the collection had been compiled by and inherited from a relative who had been a "director of the United States Mint," a slight embellishment. The collection had been assembled by his maternal grandfather, Jacob Shuster, who had been postmaster at Morristown, New Jersey prior to the Civil War. Shuster's collection of coins and stamps was reported to have been among the best of his day.

When I first met Lone Eagle he proudly showed me a few tantalizing samples from his collection—a 1794 Flowing Hair Liberty dollar; a 1796 Draped Bust half (I no longer recall if it was the 15 or 16 star variety). He kept his collection in an old Wells Fargo strong box, stored under his bed on the third floor of an old rooming house at 327 North Weber Street in Colorado Springs.

Lone Eagle served vice presidential terms at both the Colorado Springs Stamp Club and the Colorado Springs Coin Club. He regaled fellow members with tales of collectibles and Indian lore, providing a fine blend of entertainment. Age finally caught up with the White Sioux, he lived out his last days in a California Veterans Hospital. What became of his collection? No one in Colorado Springs knows. If someone is aware, it is a another story, one not yet told.

IOLA: A WORLD CAPITAL!

It is hard to believe that a quarter century has passed since the day the village of Iola awakened to find itself dubbed, "The Coin Collectors' Capital."

Every town needs a feeling of recognition. For this central Wisconsin village, the claim was more than justified. The employment rolls at Numismatic News had edged passed those of the town's major agribusinesses—the milk plant and the pickle station. *Numismatic News* was well on its way to making "Iola" a household word, at least in those households giving shelter to a coin collector.

We had ambitious plans for the "capital." First considered was renaming the streets. Numismatically, of course. There would be a Saint-Gaudens Boulevard, a Barber Avenue, a Liberty Street, even a Penny Alley. There were plenty of names to go around. Iola, after all, is a small village.

Next, we needed a recognizable emblem, a logo, one that would say "This is THE Place!" There were no in-residence artists on the staff in those days, so we relied heavily on clip art. Chosen was a line drawing of the Capitol dome, taken from the nation's capital, from the reverse of the $50 dollar bill! Few, if anyone, ever bothered to point out that had such an edifice been built in Iola, it would have towered over every existing building. Two stories was the maximum height in town, although one or two houses, including mine, had an inverted ice cream cone cupola.

The town fathers did go so far as erecting a billboard along the highway, welcoming neighbors from nearby Scandinavia to the "Coin Collector's Capitol." No amount of argument could persuade the sign painter that not only should "collector" have been made plural, but that "Capitol" should have been spelled with an "a," as it was referring to location, and not with an "o," used in designating a building. All the stationery at Krause Publications was changed to reflect our newfound status. Iola was about to join other world capitals in deserved recognition. The name was now to be ranked with other self-proclaimed national sites. Surely, higher status must be accorded a "Coin Collectors' Capital," than to Texas' Crystal City "Spinach Capital," or to Breaux Bridge, Louisiana's claim of being "The Crawfish Capital," though gourmands might issue a challenge.

A "Coin Collectors' Capital" is no less a legitimate excuse than to honor communities with such innocuous claims as Rayne, Louisiana, "The Frog Capit(o)l of the World" (Calaveras County, California, lays claim to being the "Jumping Frog Capital" thanks to Mark Twain); or Beaver, Oklahoma's malodorous right to being known as "The Cow Chip Capital." Iola's lien on fame stands strong with such as the "Shoe Capital" Lynn, Massachusetts; "Gambling Capital" Las Vegas, Nevada; "Automobile Capital" Detroit, Michigan; even the "Soaring Capital" Elmira, New York; or with places that have lost their former standing, as Reno, Nevada, "Divorce Capital," or the "Movie Capital," Hollywood, California.

Iola's days of wanting to be known as the "Coin Collectors' Capital" are bygone. The highway sign is down. First, it was first replaced with one boasting, "Home of the Midwest's Largest Car Show." But stardom is fickle. That sign has since been replaced with one reading, "Birthplace of Dave Krieg, Quarterback, Seattle Seahawks."

Time marched on, even in Iola. Krause now caters to dozens of unrelated avocational pursuits. Published today is the antique car buffs' *Wall Street Journal—Old Cars Weekly*. Deltiologists subscribe to the Iola produced *Postcard Collector*. If one has an interest in old records, sheet music, jukeboxes, and the like, he turns to Krause's *Goldmine*. The only weekly source of hobby news and values in the world of comic book collectors comes from *The Comic Book Buyer's Guide*, published in Iola, and that interest is complemented by the quarterly *Comics Collector*.

If one deals in sports memorabilia, he turns to the pages of *Sports Collectors Digest* for current information and pricing. The same applies to buffs interested in the movies of yesteryear. For them it is Krause's *Movie Collector's World*.

More than a quarter million employee hours annually are spent enlightening collectors of various other pursuits. Still, interest in coin collecting remains paramount. Now there is *Coins* magazine, *Coin Prices*, *The Bank Note Reporter*, and *World Coin News*, to complement the original *Numismatic News*.

Since there are now other interests to consider, there are some who dispute Iola's claim to remaining "The Coin Collectors' Capital." I disagree with them. But it would be better not to argue and end here—before someone directs me to Lebanon, Pennsylvania, "The Bologna Capital."

THE FIRST COIN SHOW ON ICE!

Several weeks ago, when much of the nation was battling near record snowfalls, the American Numismatic Association held its 9th midwinter convention in Charlotte, North Carolina. No snow fell on the city. The air of the site of the first branch mint of the United States was cleansed instead by a rainfall that must have equaled the city's anticipated annual average.

I may have noticed the precipitation more than others. A great procrastinator, I waited until 30 days from ribbon cutting to book my hotel reservations and arrived to find myself housed just "five minutes" from the convention center. I can still remember when Roger Bannister recorded the first four-minute mile and I was flattered that someone believed I could do the same distance in an extra 60 seconds. Most Charlotte taxi drivers feared for the seaworthiness of their cabs and the only way to the convention center was to wade upstream from the Quality Inn.

The Charlotte meeting brought chilling memories of the first ANA midwinter convention. The show is filed in the memory banks of those who attended as the first coin show on ice! Snow and bitter cold took the place of Charlotte's rain. It was February 15, 1978, and that first midwinter convention was held in Colorado Springs. It was to be an opportunity for collectors to visit their hobby's Home and Headquarters, but the gods of well-intentioned plans willed differently.

For 11 years the Board of Governors had held their interim board meetings in Colorado Springs. Balmy weather, with almost short-sleeve temperatures, lulled everyone into believing that winter never came to Colorado Springs in mid-February. The law of averages was about to shatter that belief. Cold weather, a few inches of snow, could have been coped with, but a set of circumstances guaranteed that the first midwinter convention would always be remembered.

A Lincoln day dinner, scheduled for February 16, precluded the Association from using the International Center at the Broadmoor Hotel. But alternate facilities were available. "Just perfect for your needs," said the hotel sales staff. The Broadmoor World Arena was reserved for the dealer bourse. This is the site for the world figure skating championships and the arena hosts all Colorado College's home hockey games. No one from the hotel volunteered the information that whenever a trade show is held in the arena, the ice remains. It is simply covered by a thin composition board. It was a question that no one from ANA thought to ask, myself included. The hotel did invite us to visit the arena on a nice warm, late November day to see a trade show underway. It was comfortable, well attended and the participants seemed well pleased. ANA would have a good premier for midwinter events. What no one realized was that the arena is solar heated—passively.

A heavy snowfall heralded the opening of the midwinter event. The snow had followed several days of overcast skies and the passage of a cold front brought sub-zero temperatures. There was no way, short of building a bonfire, to warm the world arena. At least that is what the hotel announced. But management failed to recognize the ingenuity of coin dealers chilled to their bones.

Within a mile of the Broadmoor Hotel is Colorado Springs' first shopping mall, Southgate, and within that complex is a Sears store. It was Sears Roebuck then. Its bedding department experienced a phenomenal sales rush—on electric blankets! Most of the 141 dealers with tables bought at least one, more often two, of the plug-in blankets. One was spread out on the floor, rug-like, and the second was to wrap around one's self, Indian-like. Business was great. Many dealers still say it was better than any midwinter convention held since. No one dickered about price. It was simply a teeth chattering—"How-much-is-that-coin?"

Fine-I'll-take-it."

The hotel sales department had offered, as an incentive to use the world arena, to supply free electrical outlets to each bourse table. When their engineers saw the draw on electrical output, they quickly sought, from local building contractors, portable butane-fired space heaters. By the closing day of the convention, the inside temperatures reached the "tolerable" level, but the last word was yet to come.

After the show closed, the pipe and drape removed, the tables and chairs folded and returned to the rental agency, the managers of the ice arena were shocked to see the condition of "their" ice. The heat from the electric blankets had created "cellar holes" on the sites of each of the individual bourse tables.

Nor was the cold bourse the only migraine for the ANA staff. A ribbon-cutting and grand opening of the Stacks' Galleries was scheduled for Saturday afternoon at ANA Headquarters. Despite reconfirmation that the busses were indeed scheduled for the proper time to take convention registrants to the ANA from the Broadmoor, they failed to show. The dispatcher had marked the wrong Saturday on the drivers' schedules. Quipped ANA President Grover C. Criswell, "When are the locusts due?"

IT WASN'T IN THE BOOK!

Few employee manuals adequately describe the responsibilities of an executive director. None has ever listed the proper procedures to follow in payment of rewards for information leading to the arrest of killers. None has ever mentioned—murder!

The particular case in question came to mind while preparing a news release for the American Numismatic Association's new reward decals. Earle D. Sherwood retired to Florida following an active numismatic life in the Northeast. Sherwood had been a past president of the Albany (NY) Numismatic Society and the Mid-Hudson Numismatic Club of Saugerties, NY. He was a founder of the Reading (PA) Coin Club, a prolific writer, and a contributor to many coin publications. Earle Sherwood was 80 years old when he fell victim to robbery and brutal murder on January 20, 1974.

Police investigation showed that the elderly collector had been bound, gagged, and bludgeoned. A small safe had been dragged from his home and loaded into a car. Ironically, Sherwood had disposed of all but a few odd pieces of his collection. Total value of the material taken was less than $1,000. For a while the case remained unsolved.

On the first anniversary of Sherwood's death, the *St. Petersburg Times* ran a full page story headlined, "The Case of the Deadly Coins—We Know Who Killed Him—We Just Can't Prove It." As a sidebar to the story, the *Times* published "Coin Collectors' $5,000 Reward Offer Still Stands." The paper announced that the ANA's offer of $5,000 for information was still outstanding. Someone with knowledge of the case read the story. But it was to be almost another year before anyone realized just how much this anonymous reader knew. On October 25, 1976 James B. Meehan, Deputy Chief New York Police Department, sent the following letter to the ANA:

"I am pleased to inform you that as a direct result of information supplied by a confidential informant, registered to the Intelligence Division, NYPD, the person responsible for the murder of Earle D. Sherwood, has been arrested and convicted.

"On January 10, 1976, Sgt. Thomas Boyle and Detective Harry Tice, assigned to the Intelligence Division, in conjunction with Lt. Donald Anderson, Pasco County Sheriff's Office, New Port Richey, Florida, took into custody John Vivian Schoonmaker for the murder of Mr. Sherwood. On April 13, 1976, Mr. Schoonmaker was extradited to the state of Florida.

"On September 24, 1976, before the

Sixth Judicial Circuit Court, Florida, Mr. Schoonmaker pled guilty to murder in the second degree.

"Please advise us of the procedure the informant must follow in order for the informant to accept his reward. While the confidentiality of the informant's identity is of the utmost concern, it can be arranged to have the informant meet with your representative to make any transaction necessary. The officers involved in the investigation are prepared to verify the facts of the role of the informant in affecting the arrest and conviction."

The reward was not paid for several months. The ANA voted that the money be delivered to New York and that the informant be paid in the presence of the police. But, there was a catch. The informant wanted cash. If payment was tendered by check, his identity would become known. My trip to New York coincided with a major coin show. ANA's bookkeeper supplied me with a cashier's check in the proper amount. All I needed to do when I arrived was to walk into any bank and cash the check, a task more easily contemplated than accomplished. Finally, a visit to Stack's on West 57th, a call to their banker, and I had 50 $100 bills. Reading New York's horror stories in their local papers did little to calm my nerves.

Returning to my hotel room, I awaited a call from Lt. Remo Franceschini, NYPD Intelligence Division. It was not long in coming. His instructions were to meet him in front of the hotel. He would be driving an unmarked car, the informant would accompany him, and we would all "go for a little ride!" I've watched too many movies not to associate the worse with "going for a ride."

I asked the lieutenant why he could not bring the informant in and meet me in the hotel—the bar or the lobby would do. The officer explained that a coin show was underway and the informant would be recognized. "Is it someone I might know," I interrupted. "Yes."

There was nothing in the Board instructions, nor in any job description, requiring that I know the identity of a killer's informant. I informed Lt. Franceschini that I would rather meet him at the police station, that I did not care to know the identity of the informant, and that I would deliver the reward directly to the officer. All that I required was a receipt from the lieutenant that he had received the money. He could pay the informant.

The Intelligence Division of the New York Police Department, I was told, was located on the third floor at 325 Hudson Street. It is an area of town where police need only step out their front door to find suspects. The building looked more like warehouse, an abandoned one at that. As I reached the entrance marked "325" a man stepped out and I stepped in. The door locked behind me.

Since the elevator door was open, I boarded and pressed "3." The doors closed and we went up—2, 3, 4, 5. Thankfully the doors opened. But, I wanted the third floor. Back into the small elevator, pressing "3" again. Down 4, 3, 2, 1, and once again into the lobby but the outside doors were still locked. To hell with the reward, I wanted OUT. Again the elevator repeated its refusal to stop on the third floor. On the fifth I found an exit leading to a stairway that lead to a garage. I cannot recall touching a single stair, my feet reached the street long before my heart. There was a police cruiser at the corner and the officer answered my query with, "Ya, the Intelligence Division's on the third floor. Ya gotta ring the bell 'n somebody'll come down to meetcha. It's a secured buildin' and nobody gets in or out without their knowin' it."

I was not about to tell the officer that this would be my second trip into the building. There was nothing in the manual about that.

A YEN FOR THE SUPERNATURAL!

Coins are sometimes called upon to serve some very unusual purposes. If you have any doubts, pick up a copy of *The Ladies Birthday Almanac*, a patent medicine newsprint published annually since 1890. I found my copy at the Botica Guadalupana, along Produce Row, in the Market Square of old San Antonio. The botica advertises that it is the Alamo city's oldest pharmacy. You can find remedies here never offered at your corner pharmacy, including the free copy of the ladies' almanac.

The booklet holds a wealth of vital information and promising advertisements. The contents range from hints to farmers based on the maxims of ancient astrologers to a story on creative visualism and how to make it work for you. But, it is the numismatically related ads that catch a collector's eye. You can buy a miraculous medal for only $5, if you promise beforehand to testify "after you receive the miracle of thousands of dollars." You must first promise to let the advertiser know as soon as you have the medal in your possession AND you have received your miracle of money, before you are allowed to purchase the medal at such a bargain price! But, the advertiser is not so trusting of you. Your $5 must be sent in advance along with $2 more if you desire RUSH mailing.

The offer that really aroused my numismatic curiosity was listed under a banner warning—DON'T LET A TERRIBLE THING HAPPEN TO YOU! The full-page advertisement promised that "secret knowledge, handed down through history, will be revealed" to help give me a richer life. The items offered included "money drawing" spiritual oils, "triple win" Bingo bags, special incense and—for the numismatist aspiring to find elusive specimens—a "powerful" occult doll.

How could collectors resist—"Money Drawing Doll, D-500-$5.98. Green Doll handmade with coins and herbs inside. We believe that Green has the power of attracting money. Strong directions included." Visions of an 1894-S dime, even an Uncirculated 1916 Liberty Standing quarter, or—better still—an 1856 Flying Eagle cent turning up in the folds of an upholstered antique chair filled my mind. I rushed the $5.95, plus $1.95 for postage to the advertiser—Ann Howard, Dept. LA-5, 200 West Sunrise Highway, Freeport, NY 11520.

Ann Howard was true to her word. By return mail, a little green occult companion arrived. As promised, "strong" money directions were included. Said Ms. Howard, "You now have a Green Doll that was made by hand with special items and herbs inside. We believe this doll is powerful and can help you with any money you may have. We sent you a pin to use with this doll.

"HERE IS WHAT YOU MUST DO:

The magic of this Money Drawing Doll lies in the magic of the coin sewn inside—a Lincoln cent of recent mintage!

Take a $1 bill and first rub it on your doll, then pin this dollar bill to your doll with the pin. It is very important that you clear your mind of everything and think only of the money that you want to come to you. Think of yourself holding large sums of money and being very happy to have this money. Try to get a clear picture of yourself with this money as you hold your green doll.

"When this is done, say these words and pull on the cord that is around your doll—'Dollars and more dollars, I need you today—Make my pockets full I pray.' Say these words 3 times as you pull on the cord—then put the doll away in a safe place.

"You should get the best results when you do this for 9 days in a row. Take the doll out and say the words 3 times, as you pull on the cord. After the 9th day, remove the $1 bill, but do not spend it. Keep it as a lucky $1. Then, either bury the doll outside your home or place it in a bag and discard it. Your thoughts and words, combined with the items in the doll and the color of the doll, we believe, all work together to help you get the money you want and need."

Ms. Howard also promised to pray for me to achieve my wishes. If I desired, she would mention me in her daily prayers for one month for only $4, $10 for three months. She should have prayed for her doll. It underwent surgery to remove a troublesome coin lodged in its bowels. I now know that in the magic world of the occult, the coin of doll power is a Lincoln cent, dated 1967 and not even Uncirculated.

INDEX

Adams, Franklin Pierce, 136
Addison, Joseph, 85, 86
Advertising Age, 160
A & F Pears, Limited, 111
African Ostrich Farm and Feather Co., 67
Alaska Rural Rehabilitation Corp., 38, 39
Allibone, S. Austin, 86
American Accomptant, 91
American Art Association, 77
American Atheists, 140, 156
American Heritage Dictionary, 93
American Israel Numismatic Society, 67
American Journal of Numismatics, 5, 6, 97
American Magazine, The, 117
American Numismatic Association, 5, 7, 26, 27, 40, 51, 52, 58, 70, 71, 74, 76, 83, 85, 90, 94, 96, 97, 98, 122, 147, 152-154, 158-163, 169, 171, 173-176
American Numismatic Society, 97
American Thesaurus of Slang, 101
Anderson, Donald, 175
An Introduction to Personal Computers and Programming and Applications of Your PC, 161
Annunzio, Frank, 29
Anthony, Susan B., 35, 83, 145, 156
Antony, Marc, 122
Antoinette, Marie, 69
Arnold, Gen. Benedict, 131, 133
Arts and Architecture Department, 70
Astor, John Jacob, 118
Austin, Stephen, 66

Baker, James A., III, 133
Bakman, Patrick, 169
Baldwin, Charles, 70
Baldwin, Mrs. Virginia, 71
Bank Note Reporter, The 173
Bank of Canada, 33, 34
Barber, Charles E., 3, 14, 15
Barnum, Phineas T., 40, 80, 84, 85
Barratt, Thomas J., 109, 111
Barraud, Francis, 49
Bartlett, Paul Wayland, 14, 15
B.A. Seaby's Ltd., 104
Beach, Chester, 11
Bellamy, 56
Bennyesque, Jack, 142
Bilious Bessie, 45
Binder, Alan, 154
Binghamton, New York, 5
Binkley, George, 20, 21
Bland, Richard Parks, 5
Bonaparte, Elizabeth Patterson, 106, 107
Bonaparte, Jerome, 106-108
Bonaparte, Napoleon, 106, 107
Borden, Cleo, 76
Bowers and Merena Galleries, 5
Boyer, Henry, 16
Boyle, Thomas, 175
Brenner, Victor David, 3, 137
British-American Mercantile Co., 69
British Royal Mint, 126
Broome County, 5
Bulletin of the American Numismatic and Archaeological Society, 97
Bureau of Engraving and Printing, 23, 26, 27, 29, 34, 35, 82
Bureau of the Mint, 83
Burghardt, Edward, 84
Burke, Billie, 83
Bush, George, 146

Cafarelli, Teresa, 7, 9
Cajouri, Dr. Florian, 90, 91
Calhoun, John C., 32
Calibran, James, 23
Campbell, Governor Carroll, 13
Campbell, Robert, 117-119
Caperon, Paulin, 70
Capitol Building, 9
Capital Preservation Fund, 9
Carr, Eugene, 39
Carroll, John, 107
Caruso, Enrico, 79
Casimer, John, 78
Catherine of Aragon, 95
Catherine, Princess of Wurttemburg, 107
Caunois, 15
Chabas, Paul Emile, 81
Chapman, Henry, 77, 78, 79
Chapman, J.G., 67
Charles I, 87
Charles II of York, 80
Chase, Salmon P., 147
Chief Big Elk, 171
Christian X of Denmark, 43
Civilian Conservation Corps, 39
Civil War, 25, 57, 58
Clark, Gruber & Company, 56, 57, 58
Clark, Austin M., 57, 58
Clark, Milton E., 57, 58
Clarke, C.W.E., 78
Cleaver, Ralph, 71
Cleopatra, 122, 123
Clinton, General, 13
Cloud Woman, 171
Coin Collector's Journal, The, 97
Coin Prices, 131, 173
Coins magazine, 163, 173
Collier's magazine, 45
Columbian Exposition, 14, 43, 152
Columbus, Christopher, 92, 105
Columbus Day, 104
Commission of Fine Arts, 12, 13, 14
Comprehensive Catalog of U.S. Paper Money, The, 22
Comstock, Anthony, 81, 82
Concord National Bank, 12

Congress of the United States, 2, 6, 8, 9, 11, 14, 21, 31, 32, 34, 56, 63, 69, 147, 155
Congressional Record, 23
Cooke, Terrence Cardinal, 168
Coolidge, Calvin, 33
Coughlin, Mrs. T.J., 50
Coughlin, Rev. Charles E., 49, 50
Cousteau, Jacques, 123
Crawford, Thomas, 10
Chronicle, 23
Criswell, Grover C., 175
Cunningham, Mary, 16-18
Custer, General, 171, 172

D'Angers, David, 2
Darwin, Charles, 85
Davidson, A. Wolfe, 13, 14
Davis, Bleven, 71
Davis, Jefferson, 10
Dawes, William, 10
Declaration of Independence, 2, 12
de Francisci, Anthony, 7, 8
de Lafayette, Marquis, 14, 15, 16, 24
Denver Mint, 8
Dept. of Anatomy and Osteology, 23
Dept. of Energy, 30
Detroit Salt and Manufacturing Company, 100
De Vere, Pearl, 45
Diaz, Porfirio, 59, 60
Dictionaries of English Literature, 86
Dictionary of Numismatic Terms, 100
Dictionary of Word and Phrase Origins, 95
Dirty Neck Nell, 45
Division of Analysis and Research of the Federal Reserve Bank, 32
Dodge, Gov. Grenville, 65, 66
Donlon's *Catalog of U.S. Paper Money 1861 to 1923,* 22
Duffield, Frank G., 74, 85
Dukakis, Michael, 146, 154
Duke of York, 80
Dupre, Roy, 130, 131
Durant, Thomas, 66
Durante, Jimmy, 161
Duval, Alexander, 70

Edison, Thomas, 30, 32
Edward IV, 115
Elizabeth II, 129
Endeshaw, Bekele, 99
English Surnames, An Essay of Family Nomenclature, Historical, Etymological, and Humorous, 144
Enrollment Act, The, 146
Eisenhower, Pres. Dwight D., 71, 137
Elder, Thomas, 78
Elk Mountain Pilot, 23
Emergency Banking Act, 63
Emerson, 12
Empire Coin Company, Inc., 5

Empress Eugenie, 70
Encyclopedia Britannica, 125
Encyclopedia of American Religions, 140
Engley, Eugene, 59
Epperson, Frank, 42
Ericsson, Leif, 104

Falwell, Jerry, 49
Federal Emergency Relief Administration, 38
Federal Reserve, 35
Federal Energy Administration, 28, 30
Federated Association of Professional Grading Services, 158
Field & Farm, 20, 21
Filmore, Abigail, 147
Filmore, Millard, 147, 148
Fivaz, Bill, 26, 162, 163
Ford, Henry, 30, 33
Fouts, Jim, 23
Franceschini, Remo, 176
Franklin Mint, 8
Fraser, James Earle, 3, 76, 137
Freer, Charles Lang, 96
French, Daniel Chester, 11, 12
Frye, Joe, 76
Funk, Charles Earle, 97

Gage, General, 10
Garvey, Marcus Mosiah, 112, 113, 126
Gasparro, Frank, 64
Geary, Miss, 16
Gentle Art of Making Enemies, 95
Gerry, Eldridge, 54
Giachetti, Ada, 79
Gilpin, William, 57
Gimlett, Frank, 62, 63, 64
Glyn, Elinor, 81
Godiva, Lady, 46, 47
Goodwin, Mary, 23
Goodwin, William, 23
Gounod, Charles, 169
Grant, Ulysses S., 2, 11, 21, 40, 95, 133
Greenpeace, 33, 34
Greer, Bill, 58
Gregor, Peter, 24
Growing Up Catholic—An Infinitely Funny Guide for the Faithful, the Fallen, and Everyone In-Between, 167
Gruber, Emanuel Henry, 57, 58
Guide Book of United States Coins, 16, 161, 167
Guinness Book of World Records, 67
Guttag, Julius, 78

Harald, King, 104
Harbert, Josiah, 68, 69
Harding, Pres. Warren G., 8
Hard Times Tokens, 54
Harlan Brothers Orchestra, 23
Hart, Gary, 144, 145
Hatch, Lorenzo, 22
Hauteval, Lucien, 56

Heath, Dr. George, 97
Henderson, William C., 40, 72
Henry III, 47
Henry VIII, 86, 95
Herald Democrat, 23
Herald Journal, 96
Hertz, Alfred, 79
Hessler, Gene, 21, 22, 82
Heyliger, Phyl, 45
Heyliger, Vic, 45
Hickman, Capt. Tom, 61
Higley, Dr. Brewster M., 23
Hillinger, Chuck, 122
History of Mathematics, A, 90
Hobart, Virginia, 70
Hobart, Walter Scott, 70
Holdridge, Bng. Gen. Herbert Charles, 137-139
Holtwick, Dr. Enoch A., 139
Hooker, General, 24
Hoover, J. Edgar, 139
Hottinguer, Jean Conrad, 56
Houdon, 2, 14
House Banking and Currency Committee, 32
House Subcommittee on Consumer Affairs and Coinage, 2, 29
Houston, Sam, 66
Howard, Ann, 177, 178
Hubbard, Frank McKinney, 136, 137
Hudson's Bay Company, 166
Hugh of Avranches, 86
Hull, George W., 83-85

Iacocca, Lee, 30
Indianapolis News, 136
International Whaling Commission, 33

Jeckyll, Thomas, 95, 96
Jefferson, President Thomas, 2, 107, 127
Joe Lowe Corporation, 42
Journal and Courier, 96
Journals of Each Provincial Congress, The, 12

Kadin, Paul, 42
Kelley, Dan, 23
Kennedy, John F., 139-141
King of Siam, 43
Kirka, Al, 94
Kirka, Sally, 94
Knight, Charles R., 23
Koenig, Joseph, 43, 44
Krause Publications, 168, 169, 172, 173
Krider, P.L., 15
Kurault, Charles, 117

Ladd, Senator, 32
Ladies Birthday Almanac, The, 177
Lafayette Memorial Commission, 14, 16
Lamar *Daily News*, 23
Lamb, Charles, 86
Laurel Brigade Inn, 24, 25

Lawrie, Lee, 14
Lee, Ann, 84
Lee, Chauncey, 91
Leesburg Town Council, 25
Lemke, William, 50
Leofric, Earl of Mercia, 46
Leslie, Col. Alexander, 10
Leuver, Robert J., 27, 28
Levy, Uriah P., 2
Lewis and Clark Centennial Exposition, 23
Lexington Trust Company, 12
Leyland, Richard, 95, 96
Life of Sir Walter Scott, 86
Limes, Robert, 123
Lincoln Memorial, 27
Lockhart, John Gibson, 86
Lone Eagle, 171, 1712
Longfellow, Henry Wadsworth, 10, 12
Los Angeles Times, 122
Loubet, Emile, 16
Louden County Historical Society, 25
Low, Lyman H., 54, 56
Lower, Mark Antony, 144

Macauley, Lord, 86
MacLaren, Thomas, 70
Machin, Captain Thomas, 132
MacNeil, Hermon A., 3, 4
Mail and Express, 5
Manning, Mrs. Catherine, 23
Marshall, John, 54
Marshall, Thomas, 136, 137
Martin, Abe, 136
Matalik, Emil, 141, 142
Medallic Portraits of John F. Kennedy, 141
Medina, T.F., 91
Meehan, James B., 175
McCabe, Bill, 23
McDonald, Lt. Col. John A., 61
McGivern, Reverand Farley, 140
McKinley, William, 16
McLean, Joyce, 33, 34
McTavish, George, 167
Meishner, Henry, 44
Mencken, H.L., 147, 148
Messrs. N.M. Rothschild and Sons, 128, 129
Mexico City Mint, 59
Miller, Colonel A.B., 58
Mint, 3, 4, 7, 9
Mohrmann, Fred, 84
Monroe, Pres. James, 32
Montez, Maria, 127
Montgomery Journal, 96
Morgan, George, 6, 7
Morganthau, Henry, 63, 74, Treasurer, spelled Morgenthau in second reference
Morris, John, 95
Morris, Robert, 91
Murray, W.H., "Alfafa Bill," Gov., 60, 61
Museum of Fine Arts, 2
Mysterious West, The, 69

Napoleon, 43
Napoleon III, 70
Nast, Thomas, 93
National Archives, 30
National Association of Convenience Stores, 154
National Convention of the Order of Independent Americans, 16
National Defense Act of 1916, 32
National Enquirer, 122
National Honest Money Association, 32
National Museum, 23
Nestle Company, 26
Nestle Foods, 163
New York Evening Mail, 136
New York Times, 3, 5, 7, 32, 78, 82
Nixon, Pres. Richard, 28, 139, 145, 161
Norton, Charles Ledyard, 117, 118
Norton, Frank H., 97
Numismatic Art in America, 7
Numismatic News, 99, 141, 160, 163, 172, 173
Numismatic Scrapbook, The, 97
Numismatist, The, 5, 7, 8, 74, 85, 90, 96, 97, 171

Office of the Inspector General, 29, 30
Official 1984 Blackbook Price Guide of United States Coins, 167
O'Hair, Madalyn Murray, 140, 141, 156, 157
Olaf II Kyrre, 104
O'Malley, Charles F., 74, 76
Orr, Major John M., 25
Over the Trails of Yesterday, 62
Overton, Al C., 72
Owen, William, 49
Oxford Dictionary on the Origin of Words, 101
Oxford English Dictionary, 95

Panama-Pacific Exposition, 8
Paris Exposition, 16
Paris Mint, 15
Patriot's Day, 10, 12
Patterson, Elizabeth, 106, 108
Paulsen, Pat, 145, 146
Pears, Andrew, 109, 111
Pears, Francis, 111
Pears, Mary, 109
Peck, Frank, 41
Peck, Gracie, 41
Peck, James, 40, 41
Pedrick, Major John, 10
Penzes, Mrs., 94
Penzes, Steve, 94
Pepper, Choral, 69
Philadelphia Mint, 6, 14, 132
Philadelphia *Record, The,* 7
Pierce, Pres. Franklin, 147
Pietz, Adam, 42, 43
Pike's Peak National Bank, 40
Pinckney, Charles Coteworth, 54, 56
Pius VII, 107
Pocahontas, 10

Polish State Spirits Industry, The, 76
Pope John XXIII, 139
Popsicle Industries, 42
Popular Science Monthly, 90
Powills, Mike, 94
Pratt, Bela Lyon, 3
Preston, Robert, 145
Professional Numismatists Guild, 159, 160
P.R. Schuman Duster Co., 67, 69
Punch, 111
Purity Distilling Co., 51

Quaker Oats Company, 44
Quayle, Dan, 146, 147

Rawlon, Wright, and Hatch, 66
Raymond, Wayte, 16, 97
Reagan, Nancy, 142, 143
Reagan, Ronald, 142
Reichenbach, Harry, 80, 81
Republican National Convention, 147
Revere, Paul, 10, 12
Revolutionary War, 10, 12, 16, 54, 131
Reynolds, Robert and Company, 47
Roberts, George E., 14, 16
Rochette, Ed, 123
Rochette, Mary Ann, 40
Rockwell, Robert, 23
Rogers, Ginger, 62
Roosevelt, Pres. Franklin Delano, 38, 62, 63
Roosevelt, Pres. Theodore, 17, 79, 137, 143
Royal Canadian Mint, 114
Royal Company of Adventurers, 80
Royal Mint of England, 6
Rulau, Russell, 54, 56

Saint-Gaudens, Augustus, 3, 17, 18, 137, 143
Saint-Gaudens, Homer, 17
Salle, Henry, 84
Salote Tupou III, Queen, 160
Schlag, Felix, 2
Schoonmaker, John Vivian, 175, 176
Schuman, Edward, 67, 68
Schuman, Philip, 69
Schurz, Carl, 93
Schwab, Herman, 44
Scott & Company, 97
Scott, Caroline, 5
Scott Stamp and Coin Co., 97
Seaby, Peter, 104
Sears Roebuck and Co., 44, 174
Selassie, Haile, 99
September Morn, 81, 82
Sharpe, Robert, 47
Sharpe, Thomas, 47, 48
Shekel, The, 67
Sheridan, Gen. Philip Henry, 20-22
Sherman, Gen. William Tecumseh, 21, 22, 24, 40
Sherman Silver Purchase Act of 1890, 59

Sherwood, Earle D., 175
Shuster, Jacob, 172
Simon, William E., 28
64th Infantry Reg., 10
Skenazy, Lenore, 160, 161
Smillie, G.F.C., 23
Smith County *Pioneer*, 23
Smith, Deaf, 67
Smith, Erastus, 66
Smith, Joseph, 84
Smith, Sam, 106, 107
Smith, W.B., 131
Smithsonian, 23, 95
Smothers Brothers, 146
Snyder, George, 5
Social Justice, 50
Society for the Preservation and Enrichment of the Memory of Millard Filmore, 147
Society of the Army of Tennessee, 24
Spar City *Spark*, 23
Spellman, Francis Cardinal, 168
Stack's Galleries, 175, 176
Standard Catalogue of Modern World Coins, 161, 168
Standard Catalog of United States Coins, 16
Standard Catalogue of World Coins, 128, 169
Standard Dictionary, 90
Stanford, Leland, 65, 66
Stearns, Dr. Redford, 83
Sterling, Ross B., 60
Sternick, Paul, 145
Stevenson, Adlai, 137
St. Mihiel, 38
St. Petersburg Times, 175
Street, Julian, 45
St. Therese Martin, 50
Stuart, Mary, 162
Study of Diophantine Analysis in the United States, The, 90
Sunday Republic, 5, 7
Supreme Court, 33
Swartz, Bob, 23
Swedenborg, Emanuel, 114, 117

Talleyrand, 54, 56
Tatham, William, 32
Taylor, Elizabeth, 122
Taylor, Zachary, 147
Tchkotova, Prince, 70
Tennyson, 42
Tetso, John, 166, 167
Thomas, Johnny, 13
Thompson, Robert J., 16
Thorpe, Prescott H., 97
Three Weeks, 81
Tice, Harry, 175
Treasury Dept., 6, 16, 24, 156
Turk, Reverand, 84

United States Industrial Alcohol Co., 51, 52

United States Mint, 42, 43, 64, 65, 66, 97, 98, 113, 143, 155, 158, 172
United States Treasury, 24
Untermyer, Samuel, 32
U.S. Department of Energy, 29, 30
U.S. Essay, Proof, and Specimen Notes, 21, 82
U.S.S. Constitution, 51

Vanderberg, Arthur, 38
Vermuele, Cornelius, 7
Victoria, Queen, 130
Virginia General Assembly, 25
Voting Rights Act of 1965, 157

Waite, Davis H., 59, 60
Wall Street Journal, The, 8, 96, 173
Warman, Cy, 23
Washington City Council, 24
Washington, Gen. George, 29, 54, 131, 147
Washingtonian, The, 25
Weinman, Adolph A., 3
Wenceslaus II, 77
West, Benjamin, 67
West, Mae, 74, 76
West Point, 21, 131, 132
Whichler, Joseph, 11
Whistler, James Abbott McNeil, 95, 96
White, Col. Elijah, 25
White House, the, 63, 71, 95, 136, 145-147
William III, King, 85, 105, 106
William III, Prince, 162
Williams, Anna, 5-7
Williams, Brad, 69
Williams, Mrs. Caroline, 5, 7
William the Conqueror, 86
Willis, Parker
Wilson, President Woodrow, 32, 136
Woolworth, F.W., 44
World Coin News, 173
Wormser, Moritz, 78

Yeoman, R.S., 16, 167

Zerbe, Farran, 7

ABOUT THE AUTHOR

As a professional numismatist, Ed Rochette has spent the last 30 years actively involved in the hobby on a full time basis. Currently, he serves as vice president of the American Numismatic Association and authors a weekly column on coins for the *Los Angeles Times Syndicate* appearing in 40 newspapers nationwide.

Rochette began his hobby career with Krause Publications in 1960, starting as editor of *Numismatic News* before being named executive editor in 1963. His tenure with the ANA began in 1966 as editor of *The Numismatist*, the Association's official journal. In 1972, he was the unanimous choice of the Board for the executive directorship and served as CEO until his retirement in 1986. This is his third book published since he "retired" four years ago!

Recognition as a hobby leader has come in many ways:
* Appointed to the United States Assay Commission by President Lyndon Johnson in 1965.
* Member of three-person panel to select the official U.S. Bicentennial Medal.
* Advisory panel, General Services Administration, for the disposal of surplus silver dollars.
* Chairman, Colorado Centennial-Bicentennial Commission Medals Committee.
* American delegate, Fédération Internationale de la Médaille conferences at Florence, Italy (1983); Stockholm, Sweden (1985); and general chairman, Colorado Springs, (1987).
* Leader, State Department endorsed People-to-People Goodwill Tour of Eastern Europe.
* Recipient, American Numismatic Association's Medal of Merit and Farran Zerbe Award.
* Initiated, developed and supervised the American Numismatic Association's Annual Summer Seminar, now in its 21st year.

As a writer, Ed Rochette's byline has appeared in most hobby publications. He has earned the Numismatic Literary Guild's honors for Best Feature Writer and Best Syndicated Column. His "Coin Roundup" has appeared for the last 20 years in major newspapers including the prestigious *Newsday* and *Chicago Sun-Times*. His book, *Medallic Portraits of John F. Kennedy*, is a standard reference for collectors and earned the coveted Sandra Rae Mishler Gold Medal for original research. His travels to more than 30 countries and tours of nearly 50 government and private mints serves as the source for many of his articles and lectures.